CONCISE COMPANION TO LITERATURE

Concise Companion to Literature

JAMES H. PICKERING
Michigan State University
JEFFREY D. HOEPER
Arkansas State University

MACMILLAN PUBLISHING CO., INC.
New York

Printed in the United States of America

Macmillan Publishing Co., Inc.
866 Third Avenue, New York, New York 10022

Collier Macmillan Canada, Ltd.

Library of Congress Cataloging in Publication Data

Pickering, James H.
Concise companion to literature.

Includes index.
1. Literature. I. Hoeper, Jeffrey D., joint author. II. Title.
PN45.P517 801'.95 80-12196
ISBN 0-02-395400-0

Printing: 1 2 3 4 5 6 7 8 Year: 1 2 3 4 5 6 7

ACKNOWLEDGMENTS

Jonathan Cape Ltd. ERNEST HEMINGWAY, "The Killers," from *The First Forty-nine Stories*. Reprinted by permission of Jonathan Cape Ltd. HENRY REED, "Naming of Parts," from *A Map of Verona*. Reprinted by permission of Jonathan Cape Ltd.

Doubleday & Company, Inc. JOSEPH CONRAD, "The Lagoon," from *Tales of Unrest*. Reprinted by permission of Doubleday & Company, Inc.

Faber and Faber Limited. W. H. AUDEN, "Look, stranger, at this island now," from *The English Auden*. Reprinted by permission of Faber and Faber Limited. THOM GUNN, "Vox Humana," from *The Sense of Movement*. Reprinted by permission of Faber and Faber Limited.

Farrar, Straus & Giroux, Inc. ELIZABETH BISHOP, "The Sandpiper," from *Complete Poems*. Copyright © 1962 by Elizabeth Bishop. Reprinted by permission of Farrar, Straus & Giroux, Inc. FLANNERY O'CONNOR, "Mystery and Manners," from *Writing Short Stories*, selected and edited by Sally and Robert Fitzgerald. Copyright © 1957, 1961, 1963, 1964, 1967, 1969 by the Estate of Mary Flannery O'Connor. Copyright © 1962 by Flannery O'Connor. Copyright © 1961 by Farrar, Straus and Cuddahy (now Farrar, Straus & Giroux, Inc.). Reprinted by permission of Farrar, Straus & Giroux, Inc.

Harcourt Brace Jovanovich, Inc. T. S. ELIOT, "The Love Song of J. Alfred Prufrock," from *Collected Poems 1909–1962*. Copyright © 1963. Reprinted by permission of Harcourt Brace Jovanovich, Inc. MOLIERE, *Tartuffe*, translated by Richard Wilbur. Copyright © 1961, 1962, 1963 by Richard Wilbur. Reprinted by permission of Harcourt Brace Jovanovich, Inc. SOPHOCLES, *Oedipus Rex*, translated by Dudley Fitts and Robert Fitzgerald. Copyright © 1949 by Harcourt Brace Jovanovich; renewed 1977 by Cornelia Fitts and Robert Fitzgerald. Reprinted by permission of Harcourt Brace Jovanovich, Inc.

CARL SANDBURG, "Fog," from *Chicago Poems*. Copyright 1916 by Holt, Rinehart and Winston; copyright 1944 by Carl Sandburg, Reprinted by permission of Harcourt Brace Jovanovich, Inc.

William Heinemann Ltd. D. H. LAWRENCE, "The Rocking-Horse Winner," from *The Complete Short Stories of D. H. Lawrence*. Reprinted by permission of William Heinemann Ltd., Laurence Pollinger Ltd., and the Estate of the late Mrs. Frieda Lawrence Ravagli.

Holt, Rinehart and Winston. STEPHEN VINCENT BENÉT, "The Mountain Whippoorwill," from *Ballads and Poems*. Copyright © 1931 by Stephen Vincent Benét. Copyright © 1959 by Rosemary Carr Benét. Reprinted by permission of Holt, Rinehart and Winston, Publishers. ROBERT FROST, "Design," and "Stopping by Woods on a Snowy Evening" from *The Poetry of Robert Frost*, edited by Edward Connery Lathem. Copyright © 1936 by Robert Frost. Copyright © 1964 by Lesley Frost Ballantine. Copyright © 1969 by Holt, Rinehart and Winston. Reprinted by permission of Holt, Rinehart and Winston, Publishers.

Houghton Mifflin Company. ARCHIBALD MACLEISH, "Ars Poetica," from *New and Collected Poems 1917–1976*. Copyright © 1976. Reprinted by permission of Houghton Mifflin Company.

Liveright Publishing Corporation. E. E. CUMMINGS, "Buffalo Bill's," from *Tulips & Chimneys*, edited by George James Firmage. Copyright © 1973, 1976 by Nancy T. Andrews. Copyright © 1973, 1976 by George James Firmage. Reprinted by permission of Liveright Publishing Corporation.

Macmillan Publishing Co., Inc. RALPH HODGSON, "Eve," from *Collected Poems.* Copyright © 1917 by Macmillan Publishing Co., Inc.; renewed 1945 by Ralph Hodgson. Reprinted by permission of Mrs. Hodgson and Macmillan Publishing Co., Inc. Permission for rights in England reserved by Macmillan Press Ltd., Houndsmills, Basingstoke, Hampshire.

Random House, Inc. W. H. AUDEN, "Look, stranger, at this island now," from *W. H. Auden: Collected Poems,* edited by Edward Mendelson. Copyright © 1977. Reprinted by permission of Random House, Inc. WILLIAM FAULKNER, *The Sound and the Fury.* Copyright © 1929. Reprinted by permission of Random House, Inc.

Charles Scribner's Sons. ERNEST HEMINGWAY, "The Killers," from *Men Without Women.* Copyright © 1927. Reprinted by permission of Charles Scribner's Sons. EDWIN ARLINGTON ROBINSON, "Richard Cory". Reprinted by permission of Charles Scribner's Sons.

Viking Penguin, Inc. D. H. LAWRENCE, "The Rocking-Horse Winner," from *The Complete Short Stories of D. H. Lawrence.* Copyright © 1976. Reprinted by permission of Viking Penguin, Inc.

Withers. JOSEPH CONRAD, "The Lagoon," from *Tales of Unrest.* Reprinted by permission of Withers.

Preface

Concise Companion to Literature is intended as a practical guide for the college student who is approaching the formal study of literature for the first time. As its title suggests, it is designed as a companion volume, to be used in connection with existing anthologies of short stories, poetry, and drama.

Our underlying premises are simply stated. We believe that the close and careful reading of a literary text—the activity we call literary criticism—can be learned by anyone willing to take the time and trouble to do so. We also believe that such an activity, once learned, inevitably increases the understanding, appreciation, satisfaction, and pleasure to be derived from literature.

The three major sections that follow introduce the basic elements that go into the making of a story, a poem, or a play, and discuss the ways in which such elements relate to each other and to the work as a whole. We believe that such an approach is indispensable to anyone beginning literary study because it provides *both* a method of analysis and a critical vocabulary that can be transferred from one text to another. Such an approach will encourage students to sharpen and clarify their own responses to the literature they read and will equip them with a critical language to articulate those responses.

Each section of this book, although inevitably related, is self-contained and can be read and studied independently. A glossary of literary terms has also been provided to acquaint students with the meaning of terms most frequently used in literary criticism. The page number (or numbers) following the terms in the glossary refer the reader to pertinent discussion in the text.

JAMES H. PICKERING
JEFFREY D. HOEPER

East Lansing, Michigan
April, 1980

Contents

II
Poetry 93

III
Drama 219

Introduction: Reading and Studying Literature

The creation of literature is a uniquely human activity, born of man's timeless desire to understand, express, and finally share experiences. Initially the literary impulse is quiet, contemplative, and private—existing only in the human consciousness and imagination. It is the task of the artist to translate this impulse into a concrete artifact—a story, a poem, or a play—so that it can be shared and enjoyed by others. The medium of translation, of course, is language, the written and spoken word. When we speak of literature, however, we have in mind a special kind of language that differs from the ordinary discourse with which we conduct our daily affairs. The term *literature,* as we will use it in this book, refers to language that is deliberately structured in such a way as to have identifiable artistic qualities. It is these qualities that we set out to describe and illustrate in the following pages.

Our impulse to read literature, like an author's original impulse to write, is a universal one, answering to a number of psychological needs that all of us in certain moods and on certain occasions share. Such needs vary greatly from individual to individual because they are the products of our separate tastes, experiences, and educations. They also vary *within* each of us; they shift and alter as we change and grow. Certain books that are "right" for us at one stage of life seem "wrong" or irrelevant later on. *The Wizard of Oz* and *Treasure Island* thrill us as children. When we reread these classics in adulthood and find new pleasure in them, we are likely to find the quality of the experience quite different from the one remembered. Our reading tastes will also vary from one day to the next, depending on our current moods and intellectual and aesthetic needs. More than one professor of English, for example, has been known to teach Shakespeare or Melville by day, only to turn in the evening to the latest spy novel by John le Carré. There is nothing particularly unusual in such a phenomenon, for one may have many purposes in reading. Four of these purposes come at once to mind.

READING FOR VICARIOUS ESCAPE

All of the works already mentioned, here—*The Wizard of Oz, Treasure Island,* the plays of William Shakespeare, and the novels and short stories of Herman Melville—offer exciting narratives that can be read uncritically simply because they allow us to escape the problems and responsibilities of our everyday lives and to participate, however briefly, in a world of experience that differs radically from our own. The college-age student is most likely to think of vicarious reading in terms of the spy or detective story or the science fiction or historical novel—any kind of fiction that is read for the fun of it. But many works of literature, classics as well as paperback pulps, survive precisely because they succeed in temporarily detaching us from time and place and transporting us to some imaginary world that we otherwise would never know. Although some people tend to regard such a motive as adolescent or even anti-intellectual, the fact remains that literature flourishes, in part at least, because of the freedom and escape it affords our imagination.

READING TO LEARN

Literature offers the reader "knowledge" in the form of information. Part of our interest in reading works as different as Jane Austen's *Pride and Prejudice,* Charles Dickens's *Oliver Twist,* Edwin Arlington Robinson's "Tilbury Town" poems, or Anton Chekhov's *The Cherry Orchard* lies in the fact that in the process we gain a good deal of information about rural England at the beginning of the nineteenth century, life in Victorian London, the New England industrial town, and the declining gentry of Czarist Russia—information that at the time is all the more fascinating because it is part of the author's re-created world. Literature read in this way serves as a social document, giving us insight into the laws, customs, institutions, attitudes, and values of the age in which it was written or in which it is set.

When you think about it, there is scarcely a story, a poem, a play we read that doesn't offer us some new piece of information that broadens our knowledge of the world. Not all of this "knowledge" is particularly valuable; and much of it will be forgotten quickly. Some of it may, in fact, turn out to be misleading or even false, and as such must always be checked and verified against other sources. The Indians in James Fenimore Cooper's *Leatherstocking Tales,* for example, do not stand up under scrutiny. But, even such misinformation may have its uses. Cooper's stylized "good" and "bad" Indians, it turns out, do reflect many of the widely shared attitudes toward the "red man" held by Americans in the 1820s, 1830s, and 1840s. Those attitudes, in turn, explain something of the foolish arrogance of Custer's 7th Cavalry when they rode into the valley of the Little Big Horn three decades later.

READING TO CONFRONT EXPERIENCE

One of the most compelling aspects of literature is its relationship to human experience. Reading is an act of engagement and participation. It is also, simultaneously, an act of clarification and discovery. Literature allows us, as perhaps no other medium can, the chance to overcome the limitations of our own subjectivity and those limitations imposed by sex, age, social and economic condition, and the times in which we live. Literary characters offer us immediate access to a wide range of human experiences we otherwise might never know. As readers we observe these characters' private as well as public lives, and become privy to their innermost thoughts, feelings, and motivations. It is the very intimacy of this access that explains why psychologists have traditionally found imaginative literature a rich source for case studies to illustrate theories of personality and behavior.

The relationship between literature and experience, however, is a reciprocal one. Just as literature allows us to participate in the experience of others, so too it has the power to shape and alter our attitudes and expectations. To know why we identify with one character and not another may tell us about the kind of person we are or aspire to be. If we are sensitive and perceptive readers, we have much to learn from these encounters, which can enrich the quality and affect the direction of our lives, though the precise effects of these encounters are impossible to predict and will vary from one reader to the next. One mark of a "great" work of literature is its ability to have an effect on the reader. In the same way, it is this affective power of fiction, drama, and poetry that helps to explain the survival of those works we regard as classics. Dostoevsky's *Crime and Punishment,* Shakespeare's *King Lear,* and Wordsworth's *Prelude,* for example, survive as classics because they have offered generations of readers the opportunity to clarify and perhaps even modify their views of life and also because they shed light on the complexity and ambiguity of human existence, including the reader's own.

READING FOR AESTHETIC PLEASURE

Literature can also be read for the sheer aesthetic pleasure we take in good craftsmanship of any kind. "A thing of beauty is a joy forever" is a phrase the poet John Keats has given us; well-ordered and well-chosen words are one of the few forms of immortality. Despite its other uses, a poem, a play, or a novel is a self-contained work of art, with a definable and describable structure and texture: it can be approached and appreciated on terms that are uniquely its own. What distinguishes literature from other forms of artistic expression is its reliance on structure and style in language. Sensitive and experienced readers will respond to well-chosen words, though they may not be initially conscious of exactly what they are responding to, or why. When that response is a positive one, we speak of our sense of pleasure or delight, in much the same way that we respond to a painting, a piece of sculpture, or a musical composition. If we push our inquiry further and try to analyze our response, we begin to move in the direction of literary criticism.

Rumor to the contrary, literary criticism is not an exercise in human ingenuity that professors of English engage in for its own sake. Neither is the word *criticism* to be confused with the kind of negativism and fault finding we sometimes encounter in caustic book reviews. The fact of the matter is that the more we learn about how to approach a story, poem, or play, the greater our appreciation of a truly great work becomes, and greater still the sense of pleasure and enjoyment we can derive from it. Literary criticism is nothing more, or less, than an attempt to clarify, explain, and evaluate our experience with a given literary work. Properly understood and properly employed, literary criticism allows us to raise and then answer, however tentatively, certain basic questions about an author's achievement and about the ways in which he or she achieved it. It also allows us to form some judgments about the relative merit or quality of the work as a whole.

Literary criticism is the inevitable by-product of the reading process itself, for if we take that experience seriously, then criticism of some sort becomes inevitable. The only question is whether the judgments we form will be sensible ones. Literary criticism begins the moment we close our book and start to reflect on what we have just read. At that moment, to be sure, we have a choice. If we have been engaged in light reading, say in a detective story, where our interest and curiosity are satisfied once the solution to the crime is revealed and the criminal apprehended, we may simply put the book aside without a second thought and turn to weightier matters. Such an act, in itself, is a judgment. But if our reading has moved us intellectually or emotionally, we may find ourselves pausing to measure, explore, or explain our responses. If, in turn, we choose to organize and define those responses and to communicate them to someone else—to a parent, a roommate, or a close friend—we have in that moment become a literary critic.

The nature of literary criticism and the role of the critic have been simplified in this example for the sake of making a point; however, the illustration is a perfectly valid one. Criticism is the act of reflecting on, organizing, and then articulating, usually on paper, our response to a given literary work. Such an activity does not, however, take place in a vacuum. Like all organized fields of academic study, the study of literature rests on at least three key assumptions that critics and readers must be willing to accept. Literary criticism, first of all, presupposes that a work of literary art contains certain significant relationships and patterns of meaning that the reader-critic can recover and share. Without such prior agreement, of course, there can be no criticism, for by definition there would be nothing worthy of communication. Second, literary criticism presupposes the ability of the reader-turned-critic to translate his experience of the work into intellectual terms that can be communicated to and understood by others. Third, literary criticism presupposes that the critic's experience of the work, once organized and articulated, will be generally compatible with the experience of other readers. This is not to imply that critics and other readers will always see eye to eye, for of course they do not and never will. It *is* to say that to be valid and valuable the critic's reading of a work must accord, at least in a general way, with what other intelligent readers over a reasonable period of time are willing to agree on and accept.

To move from this general consideration of the function of literary criticism to the ways in which it can profitably be applied to the study of a given work of fiction, poetry, or drama is our task in the pages that follow. The approach we have chosen is an *analytical* one that attempts to increase the understanding and appreciation of literature by introducing students to the typical devices, or *elements,* that comprise a story, a poem, or a play and to the way in which these elements relate to each other and to the work as a whole. Such an approach has much to recommend it to the student coming to the formal study of literature for the first time.

To begin with, the analytical approach provides a critical vocabulary of such key terms as *point of view, character, image, scene,* and *protagonist.* Such a set of generally agreed-upon definitions is essential if we are to discuss a work intelligently. Without the appropriate vocabulary we cannot organize our responses to a work or share them. A common vocabulary allows us to move our discussion from one literary work to another—it allows us to discuss literature, not individual and isolated literary works. The theory and vocabulary of the elements of literature, along with their application to literary analysis, are neither remote nor arcane. They are the working tools of authors, critics, and intelligent readers. Their great virtue is the common ground they provide for discussing, describing, studying, and ultimately appreciating a literary work.

A second advantage of the analytical approach follows from the first. In order to identify and describe the various elements in a text and their interrelationship, we must ask and then attempt to answer certain basic questions about the text itself: What is the story's point of view and how does it influence our knowledge of the characters?

What are the central images of the poem and how do they relate to one another? How do each of the play's scenes contribute to our understanding of the protagonist? Such questions and their answers help us not only to determine what the work says and means but also to form value judgments about how effectively (or ineffectively) the author has used his or her material.

The elements of literature presented and discussed in the sections that follow constitute a modest catalog. Each relates to one or more of the three major genres: fiction, poetry, and drama. Although the elements have no particular order of importance—some are more significant in one work than in another, without affecting the relative merit of the works themselves—they do offer a logical sequence for their examination. Some elements are more obvious than others; a discussion of fiction, for example, may begin conveniently with the three elements that create a fictional story (*plot, character,* and *setting*), followed by those that govern an author's interpretation and handling of the story (*point of view, theme, symbol and allegory,* and *style and tone.*)

The analytical method, it should be noted, is just one of a number of approaches taken by critics in their exploration and study of literature. It is true that by focusing our attention exclusively on the literary work we run the risk of minimizing, or ignoring altogether, many other factors that might otherwise contribute to our understanding. With the analytical method, for example, we tend to overlook the author's intention in writing the work, the relationship between the work and the author's life and experience, or the even broader relationship between the work and the historical culture in which it was written and to which it was originally directed. The analytical method also tends to ignore the vital relationship of literature to human experience in general and to the reader's own experience in particular. All of these subjects and others are tempting approaches to literary study and are worthy of exploration. The beginner, however, must resist the temptation, at least temporarily, and give priority to literary analysis, for before we can profitably turn to the larger implications of a literary work, that work itself must be understood.

I
Fiction

1

What Is Fiction?

When we speak of *fiction,* most of us are referring to the short story and the novel—the two genres that have dominated Western literary culture since the late eighteenth century. Broadly defined, however, the term *fiction* refers to any narrative, in prose or in verse, that is wholly or in part the product of the imagination. As such, plays and narrative poems (poems that tell a story) can be classified as fiction, as can folktales, parables, fables, legends, allegories, satires, and romances—all of which contain certain fictional elements. When we talk about fiction in this sense then, we are talking about a way of treating subject matter, not about fiction as genre (the short story and the novel): we are, that is, making a statement about the relationship between the created world of a given work and the real world of objective experience.

The precise relationship between fiction and life has been debated extensively among critics and authors since classical times. Such a distinction can at times be troublesome, as for example when we recognize that some works we refer to as fiction describe a real time and place and contain information about events and people that historians can document as authentic. Most modern critics agree, however, that whatever its apparent factual content or *verisimilitude,* fiction is finally to be regarded as a presentation or imitation of life and not to be confused with a literal transcription of life itself. Fiction organizes and refines the raw material of fact to emphasize and clarify the significance of fact. The world of fiction is a re-created world apart, a world of the possible or the probable, rather than the actual. It is governed by its own rules and internal completeness. To the extent that we find such a world credible or believable, it is because in character and in event that world has been made to be consistent and coherent within itself. Consider the relationship between Daniel Defoe's shipwrecked hero and his real-life original, Alexander Selkirk:

> The "Truth" of *Robinson Crusoe* is the acceptability of the things we are told, their acceptability in the interest of the effects of the narrative, not their correspondence with any actual facts involving Alexander Selkirk or another. . . . That is "true" or "internally necessary" which completes or accords with the rest of the experience, which cooperates to arouse our ordered response. . . .[1]

The writer of fiction, on the other hand, may deliberately choose not to deal with the world of our everyday experience at all. His chosen manner of treatment may be symbolic or allegorical rather than realistic; the tone may be comic, satiric, or ironic, rather than serious. The writer of fiction, in short, is free to exercise tremendous freedom in his choice of subject matter and the fictional elements at his disposal, and he is free to invent, select, and arrange those elements so as to achieve any one of a number of desired effects. In every instance, the measure of a writer's success depends on just how well or how poorly he or she has succeeded in unifying the story and controlling its impact; it does not depend on how closely or faithfully life is mirrored or copied. "The only obligation to which in advance we [as readers] may hold a novel, without incurring the accusation of being arbitrary," to quote Henry James, "is that it be interesting. . . . We must grant the artist his subject, his idea, his *donnée:* our criticism is applied only to what he makes of it."[2]

[1] I. A. Richards, *Principles of Literary Criticism* (New York: Harcourt, Brace and Company, 1928), p. 269.

[2] Henry James, "The Art of Fiction," *The Art of Fiction and Other Essays by Henry James* (New York: Oxford University Press, 1948), pp. 8, 14.

2

The Elements of Fiction

PLOT

"Story" vs Plot

"Let us define plot," E. M. Forster wrote:

> We have defined a story as a narrative of events arranged in their time-sequence. A plot is also a narrative of events, the emphasis falling on causality. "The king died, and then the queen died of grief" is a plot. The time-sequence is preserved, but the sense of causality overshadows it. Or again, "The queen died, no one knew why, until it was discovered that it was through grief at the death of the king." This is a plot with mystery in it, a form capable of high development. It suspends the time-sequence, it moves as far away from the story as its limitations will allow. Consider the death of the queen. If it is in a story we say: "And then?" If it is in a plot we ask: "Why?" That is the fundamental difference between these two aspects of the novel. A plot cannot be told to a gaping audience of cavemen or to a tyrannical sultan or to their modern descendant the movie-public. They can only be kept awake by "And then—and then—" they can only supply curiosity. But a plot demands intelligence and memory also.[1]

[1] E. M. Forster, *Aspects of the Novel and Related Writings* (New York: Harcourt Brace and Company, 1927), pp. 130–131.

Forster's remarks help us to understand the essential nature of fictional plot. The incidents of plot, he reminds us, however lifelike and "real" they may seem to the reader, are not to be confused with the kind of random and indeterminate incidents that punctuate our everyday experience. In ordinary life we live through a sequence of events of varying duration linked only by the temporal order of their occurrence. At the same time, events that will ultimately concern us but of whose very existence we are unaware, are taking place elsewhere. If some of these events have a greater magnitude and significance than others, and if a logical and necessary relationship does indeed exist between them, such facts are usually only apparent upon subsequent reflection—a process that, as Forster notes, calls upon both "intelligence and memory."

The creator of a fictional plot deliberately makes such an overview of experience possible. The term *plot* implies just such an overview; it implies the controlling intelligence of an author who has winnowed the raw facts and incidents at his disposal and then ordered and arranged them to suggest or expose their causal relationship. In Forster's example, the moment that grief is established as the motive for the death of the queen, two apparently disparate and merely coincidental events become linked together as cause and effect. At that very same moment the author has also radically altered the existing relationship between the reader-onlooker and the events themselves. While they remained apparently unrelated, the death of the king and the subsequent death of the queen in and of themselves were events capable of arousing little more than curiosity. However, once an appeal has been made to the "intelligence and memory" of the reader, through establishing a causal relationship, passive curiosity gives way to active participation and involvement. What was once just a story—a direct, unedited rendering of experience—has been rearranged and translated into a potentially interesting and exciting plot.

The Elements of Plot

When we refer to the plot of a work of fiction, then, we are referring to the *deliberately arranged sequence of interrelated events* that constitute the basic narrative structure of a novel or a short story. Events of any kind, of course, inevitably involve people, and for this reason it is virtually impossible to discuss plot in isolation from character. Character and plot are, in fact, intimately and reciprocally related, especially in modern fiction. In "The Art of Fiction" Henry James asks, "What is character but the determination of incident? What is incident but the illustration of character?" In the sense that James intended it, a major function of plot can be said to be the representation of characters in action, though as we will see the action involved can be internal and psychological as well as external and physical.

In order for a plot to begin, some kind of catalyst is necessary. An existing equilibrium or stasis must be broken that will generate a sequence of events, provide the plot direction, and focus the attention of the reader. Most plots originate in some significant *conflict*. The conflict may be either external, in which the *protagonist* (also referred to as the *hero*[2] or the focal character) is pitted against some object outside himself, or internal, in which case the issue to be resolved is one inside the protagonist's psyche or personality. External conflict may reflect a basic opposition between man and nature (such as in Jack London's famous short story "To Build a Fire" or Ernest Hemingway's *The Old Man and the Sea*) or between man and society (as in Herman Melville's "Bartleby the Scrivener"). It may also take the form of an opposition between man and man (between the protagonist and a human adversary, the *antagonist*), as for example in most detective fiction, in which the sleuth is asked to match wits and sometimes muscle with an archcriminal. Internal conflict, on the other hand, is confined to the protagonist. In this case, the opposition is between two or more elements within the protagonist's own character, as in Joseph Conrad's "The Secret Sharer," when a young captain must conquer his insecurity and self-doubt to become master of his ship.

Most plots, it should be noted, contain more than one conflict. In "The Secret Sharer," for example, while the basic conflict takes place within the protagonist, its resolution depends on the captain's decision to risk running his vessel aground (that is, to pit himself against his natural environment). In some cases, however, these multiple conflicts are presented in a way that makes it extremely difficult to say with absolute certainty which is the most decisive. It should be noted as well that the conflict of a story may exist prior to the formal initiation of the plot itself, rather than be explicitly dramatized or

[2] In general, *protagonist* is a better term than *hero;* the latter implies a set of admirable and positive qualities that many protagonists do not have.

presented in an early scene or chapter. Some conflicts, in fact, are never made explicit by the author or the characters and must be inferred by the reader from what the characters do or say as the plot unfolds. Conflict, then, is the basic opposition, or tension, that sets the plot of a novel or short story in motion; it engages the reader, builds the suspense or mystery of the work, and arouses expectation for the events that are to follow.

The plot of the traditional short story is often conceived of as moving through five distinct sections or stages, which can be diagramed roughly as follows:

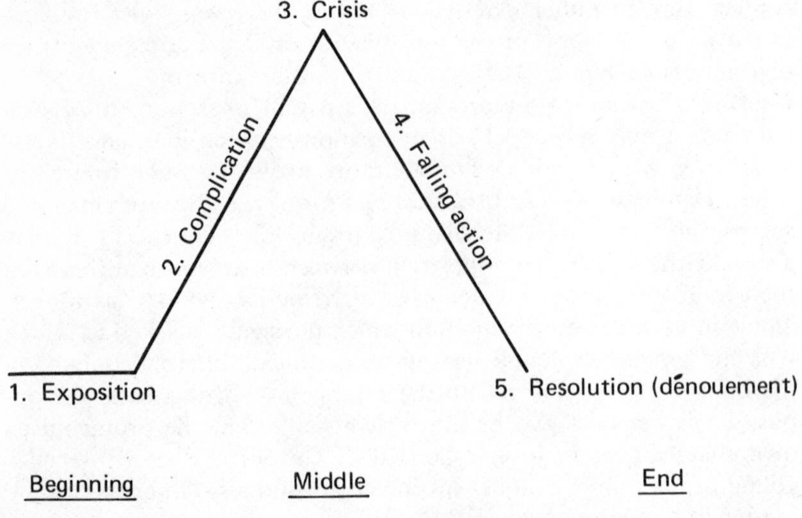

In some novels this five-stage structure is repeated in many of the individual chapters while the novel as a whole builds on a series of increasing conflicts and crises. Such a structure is found both in such classics of fiction as Flaubert's *Madame Bovary* and in the adventure thrillers of Alistair MacLean.

EXPOSITION. The exposition is the beginning section in which the author provides the necessary background information, sets the scene, establishes the situation, and dates the action. It may also introduce the characters and the conflict, or the potential for conflict. The exposition may be accomplished in a single sentence or paragraph, or, in the case of some novels, occupy an entire chapter or more. Some plots require more exposition than others. A historical novel set in a foreign country several centuries ago obviously needs to provide the reader with more background information than a novel with a contemporary setting.

COMPLICATION. The complication, which is sometimes referred to as the rising action, breaks the existing equilibrium and introduces the characters and the underlying or inciting conflict (if they have not already been introduced by the exposition). The conflict is then developed gradually and intensified.

CRISIS. The crisis (also referred to as the climax) is that moment at which the plot reaches its point of greatest emotional intensity; it is the turning point of the plot, directly precipitating its resolution.

FALLING ACTION. Once the crisis, or turning point, has been reached, the tension subsides and the plot moves toward its appointed conclusion.

RESOLUTION. The final section of the plot is its resolution; it records the outcome of the conflict and establishes some new equilibrium or stability (however tentative and momentary). The resolution is also referred to as the *conclusion* or the *dénouement*, the latter a French word meaning "unknotting" or "untying."

Highly plotted works, such as detective novels and stories, which contain distinct beginnings, middles, and ends, usually follow such conventional plot development. In the case of Arthur Conan Doyle's Sherlock Holmes stories, for example, the *exposition* is usually presented succinctly by the faithful Dr. Watson:

> One summer night, a few months after my marriage, I was seated by my own hearth smoking a last pipe and nodding over a novel, for my day's work had been an exhausting one. My wife had already gone upstairs, and the sound of the locking of the door some time before told me that the servants had also retired. I had risen from my seat and was knocking out the ashes of my pipe, when I suddenly heard the clang of the bell. . . . I went out into the hall and opened the door. To my astonishment, it was Sherlock Holmes who stood upon my step.
>
> "Ah, Watson," said he, "I hoped that I might not be too late to catch you."
>
> —from "The Crooked Man," Arthur Conan Doyle (1893)

The *complication* comes almost at once. The crime is reported, and with Holmes's famous "Come, Watson, the game is afoot," the period of rising action and suspense begins. Holmes, of course, is the *hero-protagonist;* Professor Moriarty, or some other suitably sinister villain like Dr. Grimesby Roylott ("The Adventure of the Speckled Band"), is the *antagonist.* For a time at least, the conflict of will and intellect seems almost even. Once Holmes solves the crime or mystery, the *crisis,* or climax, has been reached. The suspense and tension drop away, and the plot enters into the *falling action,* which is devoted to Holmes's detailed explanation of his method of detection. The *resolution* is short and belongs either to Watson ("A few words may suffice to tell the little that remains"—"The Final Problem") or to Holmes:

> And that's the story of the Musgrave Ritual, Watson. They have the crown down at Hurlstone—though they had some legal bother, and a considerable sum to pay before they were allowed to retain it. I am sure that if you mentioned my name they would be happy to show it to you. Of the woman nothing was ever heard, and the probability is that she got away out of England, and carried herself, and the memory of her crime, to some land beyond the seas.
>
> —from "The Musgrave Ritual," Arthur Conan Doyle (1893)

Although the terms *exposition, complication, crisis, falling action* and *resolution* are helpful in understanding the relationship among the parts of some kinds of narrative, all plots, unfortunately, do not lend themselves to such neat and exact formulations. Even when they do, it is not unusual for critics and readers to disagree among themselves about the precise nature of the conflict—whether, for example, the protagonist is more in conflict with society than he is with himself—or about where the major crisis, or turning point, of the narrative actually occurs. Nor is there any special reason that the crisis should occur at or near the middle of the plot. It can occur at any moment. In many of the short stories in James Joyce's *Dubliners,* the crisis—in the form of a sudden illumination that Joyce called an epiphany—occurs at the very end of the story, and the falling action and the resolution are dispensed with altogether. Exposition and complication can also be omitted in favor of a plot that begins *in medias res.* In much modern and contemporary fiction the plot consists of a "slice of life" into which we enter on the eve of crisis, and the reader is left to infer beginnings and antecedents—including the precise nature of the conflict—from what he or she is subsequently able to learn.

This is the case in such famous Hemingway short stories as "Hills Like White Elephants" and "A Clean, Well-Lighted Place," in which the author chooses to eliminate not only the traditional beginning, but also the ending in order to focus our attention on a more limited moment of time, the middle, which takes the form of a single self-contained episode. Both stories are lightly plotted: there is very little description and almost no action. The reader overhears a continuous dialogue between two characters—a nameless man and woman in the first story, an older waiter and a younger one in the second. Conflict and complication in each case are neither shown nor prepared for, but only revealed; the situation and the "story" are to be understood and completed through the active participation of the reader. Such stories are sometimes referred to as plotless, in order to suggest that the author's emphasis and interest have been shifted elsewhere, most frequently to character or idea.

The difficulty of conceptualizing plot in a schematic way becomes even more complicated when dealing with works, usually novels, that have more than one plot. Many novels contain one or more *subplots* that reinforce by contrast or parallel the main plot. Some novels even contain a double plot as in Thackeray's *Vanity Fair,* where we are asked to follow the careers of both the selfish adventuress Becky Sharp and the ingenuous Amelia Sedley. As Amelia's fortunes sink, Becky's rise; then follows a reversal in which Amelia's rise is paralleled by Becky's slow but inevitable decline.

Selectivity

In deciding how much plot to include in a given work, how much emphasis to give individual episodes, and how these episodes are to be related to one another, the author's selectivity comes fully into play. In general, the shorter the narrative, the greater the degree of selectivity that will be required. The very economy of the short story, for example, limits the amount of plot that can be included, a limitation of treatment that usually can be avoided in the longer novel. But no matter how much space there is at the writer's disposal, it is not possible to tell the reader everything that "happened" to the characters. (James Joyce once contemplated writing a short story recording everything that happened during a single day in the lives of Stephen

Dedalus and Leopold Bloom. The result was *Ulysses,* which grew to 767 pages and even then covered only twenty-one and a half hours.) In constructing the plot, the author will of necessity be forced to select the incidents or events that are most relevant to the story to be told. Those incidents that are most significant will be emphasized and expanded into full-fledged dramatic scenes by using such devices as description, dialogue, and action. Other incidents will be given relatively less weight and emphasis through deliberate subordination. In the latter case, the author may shorten the dramatic elements of the scene or eliminate them altogether in favor of summary—in favor of telling, rather than showing. All these episodes, major or minor, need not advance the plot in precisely the same way or at the same pace or speed, although the reader does have the right to expect that each will contribute in some way to a completed story.

The Ordering of Plot

The customary way of ordering the several episodes in a plot is to present them in a linear, chronological fashion to approximate the order of their occurrence in time. Chronological plotting can be handled in a variety of ways. It can be tightly controlled, as in the conventional five-stage detective story sketched previously. This is also the method in many historical novels, in which the separate episodes are linked closely and visibly in a firm cause-effect relationship, to give the impression of historical verisimilitude—"the way it was." Each episode logically and inevitably unfolds from the one that preceded it, thereby generating a momentum that drives the plot forward toward its appointed resolution. Chronological plot structure can also be loose, relaxed, and episodic. In Henry Fielding's *Tom Jones* and Mark Twain's *Huckleberry Finn,* the plots are composed of a series of separate and largely self-contained *episodes,* resembling so many beads on a string. The unifying element is the protagonist, as he wanders into and out of a series of adventures that, in their totality, initiate him to life and provide his moral education.

A third type of chronologically arranged plot is encountered in psychological novels, such as James Joyce's *Ulysses,* Virginia Woolf's *To the Lighthouse,* and William Faulkner's *The Sound and the Fury,* in which the reader's attention is centered on the protagonist's unfolding state of mind as it wrestles with some internal conflict or problem. Here the interest is in the passage of "psychological time" which, in these three novels, is presented through a technique called stream of consciousness. Reflecting the twentieth-century interest in psychology, *stream of consciousness* attempts to give the illusion of the actual workings of the human mind by recording the continuous and apparently random flow of ideas, feelings, sensations, associations, and perceptions as they impact and register on the protagonist's consciousness. The technique is difficult to sustain; and its effectiveness has been much debated among literary critics, in part because of the burden that it imposes on the reader's patience and perceptivity.

Finally, it is important to recognize that, even within plots that are mainly chronological, the temporal sequence is often deliberately broken and the chronological parts rearranged for the sake of emphasis and effect. Recall the two Hemingway stories cited here in which we encounter the characters in the middle of their "story" and must infer its chronological antecedents. In this case and in others, although the main direction of the plot may be chronological and forward, the author is under no obligation to begin at the beginning. Hemingway has us begin in the middle of things; other authors may begin at the end and then, having intrigued and captured us, work backward to the beginning and then forward again to the middle. In still other cases, the chronology of plot may shift backward and forward in time, as for example in Charles Dickens's classic, *A Christmas Carol.*

Perhaps the most frequently and conventionally used device for interrupting the flow of a chronologically ordered plot is the *flashback*, a summary or fully dramatized episode framed by the author in such a way as to make it clear that the events being discussed or dramatized took place at some earlier period of time. Flashbacks are often crucial to our understanding of the story, for they introduce us to information that would otherwise be unavailable and thus increase our knowledge and understanding of present events.

The key point to remember about plot is that it is open to infinite variety. An author is under no obligation whatsoever to make his plot conform to any scheme or pattern but his own. The only requirement that the writer of fiction dares not shirk is that the plot be interesting.

Evaluating Plot

Having studied a given story or novel to see how the author has arranged and made use of the elements of plot, we should be ready to evaluate his or her success. The customary test of a plot's effectiveness is its unity: the degree to which each episode and the place it occupies in the narrative structure of the work bear in some necessary and logical (or psychological) way upon the resolution of the initial conflict. In the process, one can also raise questions about the plausibility of a given episode or, for that matter, about the plausibility of the plot as a whole—that is, whether the events and their resolution are guilty of violating our sense of the probable or possible. The violation of plausibility—which is, in turn, a violation of the basic intelligence of the reader—is a quality we often associate with popular commercial fiction, in which a happy ending seems to be grafted on a plot for the sake of convenience and propriety, when everything that preceded pointed in the opposite direction.

One frequently used test of plausibility involves the author's use of *chance* (events that occur without apparent cause or sufficient preparation) and *coincidence* (the accidental occurrence of two events that have a certain correspondence). Although chance and coincidence do occur in real life, their use in literature becomes suspect if they seem to be merely an artificial device for arranging events or imposing a resolution. Such events used inappropriately do not carry with them the logic of their own conviction and thus tend to mar or even destroy a plot's plausibility and unity.

Analyzing Plot

In approaching a work of fiction for the first time, we can analyze the plot by attempting to answer such questions as the following:

1. What is the conflict (or conflicts) on which the plot turns? Is it external, internal, or some combination of the two?
2. What are the chief episodes or incidents that make up the plot? Is its development strictly chronological, or is the chronology rearranged in some way?
3. Compare the plot's beginning and end. What essential changes have taken place?
4. Describe the plot in terms of its exposition, complication, crisis, falling action, and resolution.
5. Is the plot unified? Do the individual episodes logically relate to one another?
6. Is the ending appropriate to and consistent with the rest of the plot?

7. Is the plot plausible? What role, if any, do chance and coincidence play?

CHARACTER

The relationship between plot and character is a vital and necessary one. Without character there would be no plot and, hence, no story. For most readers of fiction the primary attraction lies in the characters, in the endlessly fascinating collection of men and women whose experiences and adventures in life form the basis of the plots of the novels and stories in which they appear. Few of us reach literary maturity without having our favorites—Tom Jones and Parson Adams, Rip Van Winkle and Ichabod Crane, Heathcliff, Jane Eyre, Hester Prynne, Captain Ahab, Becky Sharp, Mr. Micawber and David Copperfield, Tom Sawyer and Huckleberry Finn, Nick Carraway and Jay Gatsby, Leopold Bloom, Nick Adams; the list goes on and on. Fiction presents us with an almost endless variety of memorable human beings, some who delight and amuse us, others who puzzle, intrigue, or terrify us. We can sympathize, or even empathize, with some of these characters in their open enjoyment of life, in their doubts and sorrows, in their loneliness and endless search for value and meaning. Other characters only appall us with their greed, their burning hatred and desire for revenge, or their ability to manipulate others coldly for selfish ends.

Part of the fascination with the characters of fiction is that we come to know them so well, perhaps at times too well. In real life we come to know people for the most part only on the basis of externals—on the basis of what they say and what they do; the essential complexity of their inner lives can only be inferred, if at all, after years of close acquaintance. Fiction, on the other hand, often provides us with direct and immediate access to that inner life—to the intellectual, emotional, and moral complexities of human personality that lie beneath the surface. And even when the author withholds that access, he usually provides sufficient information to allow us to make judgments about the internal makeup of the men and women to whom we are introduced. In either case, however, the ability to make such judgments—the ability to interpret correctly the evidence the author provides—is always crucial to our understanding.

When we speak of character in terms of literary analysis, we are concerned essentially with three separate but closely connected activities. We are concerned, first of all, with being able to establish the nature and personalities of the characters themselves, and with our ability to understand the major identifying intellectual, emotional, and moral qualities. Second, we are concerned with the methods and techniques an author uses to create, develop, and present characters to the reader. Third, we are concerned with whether the characters so presented are credible and convincing. In evaluating the success of characterization, the final issue is a particularly crucial one, for although plot can carry a work of fiction to a point, it is a rare work whose final value and importance are not somehow intimately connected with just how convincingly the author has managed to portray the characters. Naturally, such an evaluation can only take place within the context of the novel or short story as a whole, which inevitably links character to the other elements of fiction.

Characters in Fiction

The term *character* applies to any individual in a literary work. For purposes of analysis, characters in fiction are customarily described by their relationship to plot, by the degree of development they are given by the author, and by whether or not they undergo significant character change.

The major, or central, character of the plot is the protagonist; his opponent, the character against whom the protagonist struggles or contends is the antagonist. The protagonist is usually easy enough to identify: he or she is the essential character without whom there would be no plot in the first place. It is the protagonist's fate (the conflict or problem being wrestled with) on which the attention of the reader is focused. The terms *protagonist* and *antagonist* do not, however, imply a judgment about the moral worth of either, for many protagonists and antagonists (like their counterparts in real life) embody a complex mixture of positive as well as negative qualities. For this reason they are more suitable terms than *hero, heroine,* or *villain,* which connote a degree of moral absoluteness that major characters in great fictional works, as opposed, say, to popular melodrama, simply do not exhibit.

Very often the title of the work identifies the protagonist: *Oedipus Rex, Hamlet, The Deerslayer, Madame Bovary, Ana Karenina, Sister Carrie,* and *Herzog* are examples. But titles can be deceptive. It can be argued that the protagonist of Herman Melville's "Bartleby the Scrivener" is not the enigmatic copyist, but rather the amiable and benevolent lawyer who is asked to cope with a bizarre individual whom he can finally neither understand nor reach.

The antagonist can be somewhat more difficult to identify, especially if he is not a human being, as with Herman Melville's great white whale in *Moby-Dick* or the marlin that challenges the courage and endurance of the old fisherman Santiago in Ernest Hemingway's *The Old Man and the Sea.* In fact, as was intimated earlier, the antagonist may not be a living creature at all, but rather the hostile social or natural environment with which the protagonist is forced to contend. The protagonist may not always manage to compete successfully with and defeat the antagonist, either; often, as in the case of Washington Irving's "The Legend of Sleepy Hollow" and Theodore Dreiser's *Sister Carrie,* just the opposite is true.

To describe the relative degree to which fictional characters are developed by their creators, E. M. Forster distinguishes between what he calls flat and round characters. *Flat* characters are those who embody or represent a single characteristic, trait, or idea, or at most a very limited number of such qualities. Flat characters are also referred to as type characters, as one-dimensional characters, or, when they are distorted to create humor, as caricatures. "The really flat character," Forster notes, "can be expressed in one sentence such as 'I never will desert Mr. Micawber.' There is Mrs. Micawber—she says she won't desert Mr. Micawber; she doesn't, and there she is. Or: 'I must conceal, even by subterfuges, the poverty of my master's house.' There is Caleb Balderstone in [Sir Walter Scott's] *The Bride of Lammermoor."* [3] Fiction is full of such individuals, and they are almost always immediately recognizable—by their incompleteness, by the oddity of their appearance, by their mannerisms, or by the recurring words they utter. For this reason, as is the case in many of Dickens's novels, they often serve as convenient vehicles for humor and satire. These characters and their deeds are always predictable and never vary, for as Forster notes, they are not changed by circumstance.

Flat characters are usually minor actors in the novels and stories in which they appear, but not always so. For example, Montressor and Fortunato are the protagonist and antagonist, respectively, in Edgar

[3] Forster, op. cit., p. 104.

Allan Poe's "The Cask of Amontillado." Yet they are both flat characters: Montressor, who leads the unsuspecting Fortunato to be walled up in his family crypt, embodies nothing but cold-blooded revenge. And Fortunato, who is dressed in the cap and motley of the jester, complete with bells, is quite literally a fool. Flat characters have much in common with the kind of *stock characters* who appear again and again in certain types of literary works: the rich uncle of domestic comedy, the hard-boiled private eye of the detective story, the female confidante of the romance, and the mustachioed villain of old-fashioned drama.

Round characters are just the opposite. They embody a number of qualities and traits and are complex multidimensional characters of considerable intellectual and emotional depth who have capacity to grow and change. Major characters in fiction are usually round characters, and it is with the very complexity of such characters that most of us become engrossed and fascinated. The terms *round* and *flat* do not automatically demand invidious comparison. Each kind of character has its uses in literature—witness Poe's successful use of flat characters to dramatize the theme of revenge in "The Cask of Amontillado." And even when they are minor characters, as they usually are, flat characters often are convenient devices to draw out and help us to understand the personalities of characters who are more fully realized. Finally, round characters are not necessarily more alive or more convincing than flat ones. If they are, it is because the author has succeeded in making them so.

Characters in fiction can also be distinguished on the basis of whether they demonstrate the capacity to develop or change as the result of their experiences. *Dynamic characters* exhibit this capacity; *static characters* do not. As might be expected the degree and rate of character change varies widely, even among dynamic characters. In some works, the development is so subtle that it may go almost unnoticed; in others, it is sufficiently drastic and profound as to cause a total reorganization of the character's personality or system of values and beliefs. Change in character may come slowly and incrementally over many pages and chapters, or it may take place with a dramatic suddenness that surprises, and even overwhelms, the character. With characters who fully qualify as dynamic, such change, however and whenever it occurs, can be expected to alter subsequent behavior in some significant and demonstrable way.

Dynamic characters include the protagonists in most novels, which by virtue of their very size and scope provide excellent vehicles for illustrating the process of change. So-called initiation novels, such as *David Copperfield, Huckleberry Finn,* and *The Great Gatsby,* are examples. In each case the author has arranged the events of plot so that they reveal the slow and painful maturation of the young protagonist coming into contact with the world of adult experience. Short stories can also illustrate character change, as in the case of Hawthorne's young country rustic Robin Molineux in "My Kinsman, Major Molineux," who journeys to colonial Boston in search of his kinsman only to undergo an ordeal that leaves him on the threshold of maturity. What that maturity consists of, Hawthorne refuses to say, but there can be little doubt that by the story's conclusion Robin has passed into and through a significant emotional and spiritual crisis.

Static characters leave the plot as they entered it, largely untouched by the events that have taken place. Although static characters tend to be minor ones, because the author's principal focus is elsewhere, this is not always the case. Hazel Morse, the protagonist of Dorothy Parker's story "Big Blonde" is a static character whose essential quality is her incapacity to change. Through a succession of men friends and lovers she fails to be anything other than a "good sport." Parker's theme, therefore, is tied to the idea of stasis and passivity. The reader waits for Hazel Morse to exert herself and take charge of her own destiny, only to discover at the end that Hazel is unable to manage even her own suicide. But protagonists like Hazel Morse are comparatively rare; for the most part, an author creates static characters as *foils* to emphasize and set off by contrast the development taking place in others.

Methods of Characterization

In presenting and establishing character, an author has two basic methods or techniques at his disposal. One method is *telling,* which relies on exposition and direct commentary by the author. In telling—a method preferred and practiced by many older fiction writers—the guiding hand of the author is very much in evidence. We learn and look only at what the author calls to our attention. The other method is the indirect, dramatic method of *showing,* which involves the author's stepping aside, as it were, to allow the characters to reveal themselves directly through their dialogue and their actions.

With showing, much of the burden of character analysis is shifted to the reader, who is required to infer character on the basis of the evidence provided in the narrative. Telling and showing are not mutually exclusive, however. Most authors employ a combination of each, even when the exposition, as in the case of most of Hemingway's stories, is limited to several lines of descriptive detail establishing the scene.

Most modern authors prefer showing to telling, but neither method is necessarily better or more fruitful than the other. As with so many other choices that the writer of fiction is called on to make, the choice of a method of characterization depends on a number of different circumstances, including the author's temperament, the particular literary conventions of the period in which he or she is writing, the size and scope of the work, the degree of distance and objectivity the author wishes to establish between himself and the characters, the author's literary and philosophical beliefs about how a sense of reality can best be captured and conveyed to the reader, and, of course, the kind of story the author wishes to tell. All these factors heavily influence the technique of characterization; collectively they determine why and how the author does what he does. And all these factors are worthy of consideration in the course of literary discussion and analysis.

Direct methods of revealing character—characterization by telling—include the following:

CHARACTERIZATON THROUGH THE USE OF NAMES. Names are often used to provide essential clues that aid in characterization. Some characters are given names that suggest their dominant or controlling traits, as, for example, Edward Murdstone (in Dickens's *David Copperfield*) and Roger Chillingsworth (in Hawthorne's *The Scarlet Letter*). Both men are the cold-hearted villains their names suggest. Other characters are given names that reinforce (or sometimes are in contrast to) their physical appearance, much in the way that Ichabod Crane, the gangling schoolmaster in Irving's "The Legend of Sleepy Hollow," resembles his long-legged namesake. Names can also contain literary or historical allusions that aid in characterization by means of association. The name *Ethan Brand*, referring to the wandering lime burner who gives his name to Hawthorne's short story, contains an allusion to the mark or brand of Cain, a legacy of guilt that the outcast Brand shares with his Biblical counterpart. One must also, however, be alert to names used ironically that characterize through inversion. Such is the case with the foolish Fortunato of Poe's "The Cask of Amontillado," who surely must rank with the most *un*fortunate of men.

CHARACTERIZATION THROUGH APPEARANCE. Although in real life most of us are aware that appearances are often deceiving, in the world of fiction details of appearance (what a character wears and how he looks) often provide essential clues to character. Take, for example, the second paragraph of "My Kinsman, Major Molineux," in which Hawthorne introduces his protagonist to the reader:

> He was a youth of barely eighteen years, evidently country-bred, and now, as it should seem, upon his first visit to town. He was clad in a coarse gray coat, well worn, but in excellent repair; his under garments were durably constructed of leather, and fitted tight to a pair of serviceable and well-shaped limbs; his stockings of blue yarn were the incontrovertible work of a mother or a sister; and on his head was a three-cornered hat, which in its better days had perhaps sheltered the graver brow of the lad's father. Under his left arm was a heavy cudgel formed of an oak sapling, and retaining a part of the hardened root; and his equipment was completed by a wallet, not so abundantly stocked as to incommode the vigorous shoulders on which it hung. Brown, curly hair, well-shaped features, and bright, cheerful eyes were nature's gifts, and worth all that art could have done for his adornment.
>
> —from "My Kinsman, Major Molineux," Nathaniel Hawthorne (1832)

The details in the paragraph tell us a good deal about Robin's character and basic situation. We learn that he is a "country-bred" youth nearing the end of a long journey, as his nearly empty wallet suggests. His clothes confirm that he is relatively poor. Yet Robin is clearly no runaway or rebel, for his clothes though "well worn" are "in excellent repair," and the references to his stockings and hat suggest that a loving and caring family has helped prepare him for his journey. The impression thus conveyed by the total paragraph, and underscored by its final sentence describing Robin's physical appearance, is of a decent young man on the threshold of adulthood who is making his first journey into the world. The only disquieting note—a clever bit of foreshadowing—is the reference to the heavy oak cudgel that Robin has brought with him. He will later brandish it at strangers in an attempt to assert his authority and in the process reveal just how inadequately prepared he is for coping with the strange urban world in which he finds himself.

As in Hawthorne's story, details of dress and physical appearance should be scrutinized closely for what they may reveal about character. Details of dress may offer clues to background, occupation, economic and social status, and perhaps, as with Robin Molineux, even a clue to the character's degree of self-respect. Details of physical appearance can help to identify a character's age and the general state of his physical and emotional health and well-being: whether the character is strong or weak, happy or sad, calm or agitated. Appearance can be used in other ways as well, particularly with minor characters who are flat and static. By common agreement, certain physical attributes have become identified over a period of time with certain kinds of inner psychological states. For example, characters who are tall and thin are often associated with intellectual or aesthetic types who are withdrawn and introspective. Arthur Dimmesdale and Roger Chillingsworth, the two major male characters in *The Scarlet Letter,* share these traits, as does the pallid recluse Roderick Usher, in Poe's "The Fall of the House of Usher." Portly or fat characters, on the other hand, suggest an opposite kind of personality, one characterized by a degree of laziness, self-indulgence, and congeniality, as in the case of Fielding's Parson Adams or Dickens's Tony Weller. Such convenient and economical short cuts to characterization are perfectly permissible, of course, as long as they result in characters who are in their own way convincing.

CHARACTERIZATION BY THE AUTHOR. In the most customary form of telling the author interrupts the narrative and reveals directly, through a series of editorial comments, the nature and personality of the characters, including the thoughts and feelings that enter and pass through the characters' minds. By so doing the author asserts and retains full control over characterization. The author not only directs our attention to a given character, but tells us exactly what our attitude toward that character ought to be. Nothing is left to the reader's imagination. Unless the author is being ironic—and there is always that possibility—we can do little more than assent and allow our conception of character to be formed on the basis of what the author has told us. Consider the following passages:

> In that same village . . . there lived . . . a simple good-natured fellow by the name of Rip Van Winkle. . . . I have observed that he was a simple good-natured man; he was, moreover, a kind neighbor and an obedient henpecked husband. Indeed, to the latter circumstance might be

owing that meekness of spirit which gained him such universal popularity. . . . The great error in Rip's composition was an insuperable aversion to all kinds of profitable labor. . . . In a word, Rip was ready to attend to anybody's business but his own; but as to doing family duty and keeping his farm in order, he found it impossible.

—from "Rip Van Winkle," Washington Irving (1819)

He was a newcomer in the land, a *chechaquo* [a tenderfoot], and this was his first winter. The trouble with him was that he was without imagination. He was quick and alert in the things of life, but only in the things, and not in the significances. Fifty degrees below zero meant eighty-odd degrees of frost. Such fact impressed him as being cold and uncomfortable, and that was all. It did not lead him to meditate upon his frailty as a creature of temperature, and upon man's frailty in general, able only to live within certain narrow limits of heat and cold; and from there on it did not lead him to the conjectural field of immortality and man's place in the universe. . . . That there should be anything more to it than that was a thought that never entered his head.

—from "To Build a Fire," Jack London (1908)

There was a woman who was beautiful, who started with all the advantages, yet she had no luck. She married for love, and the love turned to dust. She had bonny children, yet she felt they had been thrust upon her, and she could not love them. They looked at her coldly, as if they were finding fault with her. And hurriedly she felt she must cover up some fault in herself. Yet what it was that she must cover up she never knew. Nevertheless, when her children were present, she always felt the centre of her heart go hard. This troubled her, and in her manner she was all the more gentle and anxious for her children, as if she loved them very much. Only she herself knew that at the centre of her heart was a hard little place that could not feel love, no, not for anybody.

—from "The Rocking-Horse Winner," D. H. Lawrence (1932)

In each of the preceding examples, the general orientation of the character's personality has been fixed by the author once and for all—the author provides us with a given and then proceeds to construct a plot that illustrates such characters in action.

By contrast, there are essentially two methods of indirect characterization by showing: characterization through dialogue (what characters say) and characterization through action (what characters do). Unlike the direct methods of characterization already discussed, showing involves the gradual rather than the immediate establishment of character. Such a process requires rather than excludes the active participation of the reader and in so doing calls upon what Forster called "intelligence and memory."

CHARACTERIZATION THROUGH DIALOGUE. Real life is quite literally filled with talk. People are forever talking about themselves and between themselves, communicating bits and pieces of information. Not all of this information is important or even particularly interesting; much of it smacks of the kind of inconsequential small talk we expect at a cocktail party; it tells us relatively little about the personality of the speaker, except, perhaps, whether he or she is at ease in social situations. Some light fiction reproduces dialogue as it might occur in reality, but the best authors trim everything that is inconsequential. What remains is weighty and substantial and carries with it the force of the speaker's attitudes, values, and beliefs. We pay attention to such talk because it is interesting and, if we are attempting to understand the speaker, because it may consciously or unconsciously serve to reveal his innermost character and personality.

The task of establishing character through dialogue is not a simple one. Some characters are careful and guarded in what they say: they speak only by indirection, and we must infer from their words what they actually mean. Others are open and candid; they tell us, or appear to tell us, exactly what is on their minds. Some characters are given to chronic exaggeration and overstatement; others to understatement and subtlety.

It is a rare work of fiction, whose author does not employ dialogue in some way to reveal, establish, and reinforce character. For this reason the reader must be prepared to analyze dialogue in a number of different ways: for (a) what is being said, (b) the identity of the speaker, (c) the occasion, (d) the identity of the person or persons the speaker is addressing, (e) the quality of the exchange, and (f) the speaker's tone of voice, stress, dialect, and vocabulary.

a. *What is being said.* To begin with, the reader must pay close attention to the substance of the dialogue itself. Is it small talk, or is the subject an important one in the developing action of the plot? In terms of characterization, if the speaker insists on talking only about himself or only on a single subject, we may conclude that we have either an egotist or a bore. If the speaker talks only about others, we may merely have a gossip and busybody.
b. *The identity of the speaker.* Obviously, on balance, what the protagonist says must be considered to be potentially more important (and hence revealing) than what minor characters say, although

the conversation of a minor character often provides crucial information and sheds important light on the personalities of the other characters (and on his or her own) as well.

c. *The occasion.* In real life, conversations that take place in private at night are usually more serious and, hence, more revealing than conversations that take place in public during the day. Talk in the parlor, that is, is usually more significant than talk in the street or at the theater. On the whole, this is probably also true in fiction as well, but the reader should always consider the likelihood that seemingly idle talk on the street or at the theater has been included by the author because it is somehow important to the story being told.

d. *The identity of the person or persons the speaker is addressing.* Dialogue between friends is usually more candid and open, and thus more significant, than dialogue between strangers. The necessary degree of intimacy is usually established by the author in setting a scene or through the dialogue itself. When a character addresses no one in particular, or when others are not present, his speech is called a *monologue,* although, strictly speaking, monologues occur more frequently in drama than in fiction.[4]

e. *The quality of the exchange.* The way a conversation ebbs and flows is important, too. When there is real give and take to a discussion, the characters can be presumed to be open-minded. Where there is none, one or more of the characters are presumably opinionated, doctrinaire or close-minded. Where there is a certain degree of evasiveness in the responses, a character may be secretive and have something to hide.

f. *The speaker's tone of voice, stress, dialect, and vocabulary.* The speaker's tone of voice (either stated or implied) may reveal his attitude toward himself (whether, for example, he is confident and at ease or self-conscious and shy) and his attitude toward those with whom he is speaking. His attitude to others may, for example, be either warm and friendly or cold, detached, and even hostile. Moreover, the reader must also be alert to suggestions of irony in the speaker's voice, which would suggest that what is being said is quite the opposite from what is actually meant. Fi-

[4] A specialized form of monologue is the stream-of-consciousness technique, in which the author enters the mind or consciousness of his character and directly expresses unfolding thoughts and emotions. Stream of consciousness implies a recognition that speech is inadequate to communicate inner psychological life.

nally, dialect, stress, and word choice all provide important clues to character: they may reflect the character's origin, education, occupation, or social class.

In evaluating what a given character says about himself and others one always faces (in the absence of the clarifying comments of the author) the problem of reliability and trustworthiness. Deliberate deception as well as unconscious self-deception always lurk as distinct possibilities in fiction, as in life. Although determining reliability and veracity can be difficult, most authors provide clues. When one character is contradicted in whole or in part by another, the accumulated evidence on both sides must be carefully weighed and examined. One can also test reliability by looking at the character's subsequent conduct or behavior to see if what he does somehow contradicts what he says. Finally, there is always the appeal to the subsequent events of the plot itself to see whether those events tend to support or contradict the character's statements. Any number of fictional plots turn, in fact, on the failure of one character to understand the personalities of others. The badly frightened Swede in Stephen Crane's "The Blue Hotel," for example, is so steeped in the folklore of the frontier West that he convinces himself that his companions are conspiring to rob or to murder him, a misapprehension that triggers a chain of violent events that costs the Swede his life.

CHARACTERIZATION THROUGH ACTION. Character and action, as we have noted, are often regarded as two sides of the same coin. To quote Henry James again: "What is character but the determination of incident? What is incident but the illustration of character?" James' premise is a widely shared one: conduct and behavior are logical and necessary extensions of psychology and personality. Inner reality can be measured through external event. What a given character *is* is revealed by what that character *does*. In short, the single most important and definitive method of presenting and revealing character is through action.

To establish character on the basis of action, it is necessary to scrutinize the several events of the plot for what they seem to reveal about the characters, about their unconscious emotional and psychological states as well as about their conscious attitudes and values. Some actions, of course, are inherently more meaningful in this respect than others. A gesture or a facial expression usually carries with it less significance than some larger and overt act. But this is not always the case. Very often it is the small and involuntary action, by very virtue of its spontaneous and unconscious quality, that tells us more about a character's inner life than a larger, premeditated act reflecting decision and choice. In either case, whether the action is large or small, conscious or unconscious, it is necessary to identify the common pattern of conduct and behavior of which each separate action is a part. One helpful way of doing so is on the basis of *motive,* the attempt to trace certain effects back to their underlying causes. If we are successful in doing so, if a consistent pattern of motivation appears, then it is fairly safe to assume that we have made some important discoveries about the character. To be sure, we must always allow for the gratuitous or motiveless act—we must not, that is, assume that for every action there is immediate or adequate preparation.

Robin Molineux's responses to the events that befall him provide a good example of character revealed through action. Robin's adventure is a journey of moral and psychological initiation, a rite of passage from youth to adulthood, innocence to maturity, and ignorance to knowledge. Ironically, the provincial capital that Robin enters is on the brink of a political revolution whose first victim is none other than the very kinsman whom Robin is seeking. For all his self-proclaimed "shrewdness," Robin and his cudgel are no match for the disorienting world of the city, whose crooked and narrow streets are incomprehensible to all but the initiated. Robin is not among the knowing. His country ways and naive-because-untested expectations leave him open and vulnerable to the world of the city, a world filled with danger, hostility, temptation, and elemental human violence. Through one event after another, including a meeting with a group of conspirators whose password Robin can neither understand nor return, Robin's ignorance, inadequacy, and lack of preparation are exposed. Taken together, the events of the plot, and Robin's response to them, reveal his essential character and prepare him for the climax of the story; his smug self-confidence is undermined while his confusion, anxiety, doubt, and sense of his own helplessness increase.

Evaluating Character

Having identified, on the basis of the evidence presented by the author, the essential nature and personality of the characters in the work, we must also be prepared to evaluate how successful the author has been in their creation. Although it is unreasonable to expect that the characters of fiction will necessarily be close approximations of the kind of people that we know—for part of the joy of fiction is having the opportunity to meet new people—we can expect the author's creations to be convincing and credible on their own terms. If they are not, such characters can be counted as relative failures, for our interest in them will surely flag.

What we chiefly require in the behavior of fictional characters, however, is *consistency*. Characterization implies a kind of unspoken contract between author and reader; and the reader has the right to expect that a character, once established, will not then behave in ways contrary to his or her nature. The principle of consistency by no means implies that characters in fiction cannot undergo development and change, for, as we have noted, the plots of many works are organized precisely upon just such a possibility. It is, rather, to say that, when a character undergoes change, such change should be consistent in some basic and identifiable way with the character and his circumstances. In seeking to test for consistency, we most frequently fall back upon motivation and ask ourselves whether the motive for a particular action or series of actions is adequate, justified, and probable, given what we know about that character. If the question can be answered in the affirmative, even in the context of behavior that at first glance seems puzzling or confusing, the principle of consistency has not been violated.

Analyzing Character

1. Who is the protagonist of the work and who (or what) is the antagonist? Describe the major traits and qualities of each.
2. What is the function of the work's minor characters?
3. Identify the characters in terms of whether they are flat or round, dynamic or static.
4. What methods does the author employ to establish and reveal the characters? Are the methods primarily of showing or of telling?
5. Are the actions of the characters properly motivated and consistent?
6. Are the characters of the work finally credible and interesting?

SETTING

Fiction can be defined as character in action at a certain time and place. The first two elements of this equation, character and action, have already been discussed. Now we turn our attention to *setting,* a term that, in its broadest sense, encompasses both the physical locale that frames the action *and* the time of day or year, the climactic conditions, and the historical period during which the action takes place. At its most basic, setting helps the reader visualize the action of the work, and thus adds credibility and an air of authenticity to the characters. It helps, in other words, to create and sustain the illusion of life, to provide what we call *verisimilitude.* There are, however, many different kinds of setting in fiction and they function in a variety of ways.

Some settings are relatively unimportant. They serve as little more than incidental and decorative backdrops, not unlike the wood and canvas sets we have grown accustomed to expect in modern situational comedies, which have little or no necessary relationship to either the plot or the characters. Some settings, on the other hand, are intimately and necessarily connected with the shape, meaning, and unity of the total work and our understanding of it. It is with these that as critics we must be chiefly concerned. "Scene," remarks British author Elizabeth Bowen, "is only justified in the novel where it can be shown, or at least felt, to act upon action and character; in fact, where it has dramatic use."[5] Although we may disagree with Ms. Bowen, in the sense that any setting can be justified as long as it is appropriate, her basic argument is a valid one. The most important fictional settings are those that are "dramatic," those that are organic, essential, and directly relevant to the work considered as a whole.

In order to understand the purpose and function of setting, the reader must pay particular attention to the descriptive passages in which the details of settings are introduced. Generally speaking, unless such passages are intended merely as local color, the greater their weight and apparent emphasis, the greater their importance and relevance to the total work. In most short stories and in many novels, setting is established at or near the beginning of the work as a means

[5] Elizabeth Bowen, *Pictures and Conversations* (New York: Alfred A. Knopf, 1975), p. 178.

of orienting the reader and framing the action that is to follow. Where the emphasis on setting in such passages is at best slight and perfunctory, as it is, for example, in most of Hemingway's short stories, or where the setting once established is then referred to again only incidently, if at all, one can assume that setting as such is secondary to the author's other concerns and purposes. If, on the other hand, the emphasis on setting in early passages is full and substantial, and if similar references to setting reoccur periodically as a kind of echoing refrain, one can reasonably assume that setting is designed to serve some larger function in relationship to the work as a whole.

The quality of the language by which the author projects setting provides another clue as to his or her intention. When that intention is to invest the setting with a photographic vividness that appeals essentially to the reader's eye, the details of setting will be rendered through language that is concrete and denotative. The author will pile concrete detail on top of concrete detail in an attempt to provide the illusion of a stable external reality. On the other hand, the author may want us to "feel" rather than simply "see" the setting, as is the case when setting is to be used as a means of creating mood and atmosphere. In that case the appeal will be to the reader's imagination and emotions through language that is connotative, emotionally heightened, and suggestive. The author will, that is, manipulate the poetic qualities of language to elicit from the reader, in advance, the desired and appropriate response. Often the author will want the reader *both* to see and feel the setting and to that end will use the resources of language to achieve both effects simultaneously.

The Functions of Setting

Setting in fiction is called on to perform a number of desired functions. Setting may serve (1) to provide background for the action; (2) as an antagonist; (3) as a means of creating appropriate atmosphere; (4) as a means of revealing character; and (5) as a means of reinforcing theme. These functions must not, however, be thought of as mutually exclusive. In many works of fiction, setting can and does serve a number of different functions simultaneously.

SETTING AS BACKGROUND FOR ACTION. To quote Elizabeth Bowen once more: "Nothing can happen nowhere." For this reason, if for no other, fiction requires a setting or background of some kind, even if it only resembles the stage set of a daytime television soap opera. Sometimes this background is extensive and highly developed, as in the historical novels of Sir Walter Scott, where setting—in the form of costume, manners, events, and institutions, all peculiar to a certain time and place—is rendered in minute detail to give a sense of "life as it was." In other cases, as in many modern short stories, setting is so slight that it can be dispensed with in a single sentence or two or must be inferred altogether from dialogue and action. When we speak of setting as background, then, we have in mind a kind of setting that exists by and large for its own sake, without any clear relationship to action or characters, or at best a relationship that is only tangential and slight.

To see whether setting acts as an essential element in the fiction, or whether it exists merely as decorative and functionless background, we need ask ourselves this: Could the work in question be set in another time and another place without doing it essential damage? If the answer is yes, then the setting can be said to exist as decorative background whose function is largely irrelevant to the purpose of the work as a whole.

SETTING AS ANTAGONIST. Setting in the form of nature can function as a kind of causal agent or antagonist, helping to establish plot conflict and determine the outcome of events. The Yukon wilderness with which Jack London's nameless tenderfoot tries unsuccessfully to contend in "To Build a Fire" is one example of a setting that functions as antagonist; the "tumultuous" and "snarling" sea in Stephen Crane's "The Open Boat" is another. Undoubtedly, the most famous example of setting as an agent that shapes and determines the lives and fate of those who come within its presence is Hardy's menacing Egdon Heath in *The Return of the Native*. The overpowering physical, "titanic" personality of the Heath is established immediately, in the first chapter ("A Face on Which Time Makes but Little Impression"), well before the reader is introduced to the characters or the plot:

> The most thorough-going ascetic could feel that he had a natural right to wander on Egdon: he was keeping within the line of legitimate indulgence when he laid himself open to influences such as these. Colours and beauties so far subdued were, at least, the birthright of all. Only in summer days of highest feather did its mood touch the level of gaiety. Intensity was more usually reached by way of the solemn than by way of the

brilliant, and such a sort of intensity was often arrived at during winter darkness, tempests, and mists. Then Egdon was aroused to reciprocity; for the storm was its lover, and the wind its friend. Then it became the home of strange phantoms; and it was found to be the hitherto unrecognized original of those wild regions of obscurity which are vaguely felt to be compassing us about in midnight dreams of flight and disaster, and are never thought of after the dream till revived by scenes like this.

—from *The Return of the Native,* Thomas Hardy (1878)

Egdon Heath, as Hardy makes clear, is no mere neutral backdrop to action, but a sinister, almost human (or even superhuman) force, intimately connected with the lives of its inhabitants. He speaks of the "influences" of the Heath and personifies its qualities ("the storm was its lover, and the wind its friend") to suggest a dominating presence whose influence is ever present and inescapable. As one well known critic has correctly observed, "This dynamic use of scene to determine the lives of the characters . . . is technically the most interesting thing in the book."[6] And one might add, it is the most impressive as well.

SETTING AS A MEANS OF CREATING APPROPRIATE ATMOSPHERE. Thomas Hardy's Egdon Heath serves his novel not only as a causative agent but as a means of establishing atmosphere. Hardy, of course, is not alone. Many authors manipulate their settings as a means of arousing the reader's expectations and establishing an appropriate state of mind for events to come. Consider, for example, the opening paragraph of Washington Irving's "Rip Van Winkle":

Whoever has made a voyage up the Hudson must remember the Kaatskill Mountains. They are a dismembered branch of the great Appalachian family, and are seen away to the west of the river, swelling up to a noble height and lording it over the surrounding country. Every change of season, every change of weather, indeed every hour of the day, produces some change in the magical hues and shapes of these mountains, and they are regarded by all the good wives, far and near, as perfect barometers. When the weather is fair and settled, they are clothed in blue and purple, and print their bold outlines on the clear evening sky; but sometimes, when the rest of the landscape is cloudless, they will gather a hood of gray vapor about their summits, which in the last rays of the setting sun will glow and light up like a crown of glory.

—from "Rip Van Winkle," Washington Irving (1819)

[6] Edward Wagenknecht, *Cavalcade of the English Novel* (New York: Henry Holt and Company, 1943), p. 361.

The emphasis here on setting is deliberate. The lordly Kaatskills, as Irving paints them, not only dominate the scene, but lend it a magical quality with their ever-changing hues and shapes. Later, Irving will explicitly refer to them as "these fairy mountains" and portray them as an isolated world apart, thus preparing the reader for Rip's marvelous encounter with the strange little men, dressed in "antique Dutch fashion," from whose flagons he will share a drink.

No author is more adept at using setting to create atmosphere than Edgar Allan Poe. In the following passage from "The Fall of the House of Usher," the narrator first enters Roderick Usher's room. Notice how Poe not only provides the details of setting, but tells the reader just how to respond to them:

> The room in which I found myself was very large and lofty. The windows were long, narrow, and pointed, and at so vast a distance from the black oaken floor as to be altogether inaccessible from within. Feeble gleams of encrimsoned light made their way through the trellissed panes, and served to render sufficiently distinct the more prominent objects around; the eye, however, struggled in vain to reach the remoter angles of the chamber, or the recesses of the vaulted and fretted ceiling. Dark draperies hung upon the walls. The general furniture was profuse, comfortless, antique, and tattered. Many books and musical instruments lay scattered about, but failed to give any vitality to the scene. I felt that I breathed an atmosphere of sorrow. An air of stern, deep and irredeemable gloom hung over and pervaded all.
>
> —from "The Fall of the House of Usher," Edgar Allan Poe (1839)

The room, which Poe skillfully makes us both see and feel, is as "inaccessible" and "gloomy" as its owner and as such establishes an appropriate mood that anticipates and foreshadows our eventual meeting with Roderick himself.

SETTING AS A MEANS OF REVEALING CHARACTER. Very often the way in which a character perceives the setting, and the way he or she reacts to it, will tell the reader more about the character and his state of mind than it will about the actual physical setting itself. This is particularly true of works in which the author carefully controls the point of view. In "My Kinsman, Major Molineux," for example, there is no indication that the outlandishly attired conspirators, who move easily through Boston's streets, are confused in the slightest by the city. Yet Robin Molineux, Hawthorne's young protagonist, most certainly is. For Robin the city is scarcely real; he is "almost ready to believe that a spell was on him." The dark "crooked and narrow" streets seem to lead nowhere, and the disorienting moonlight, so perfect for the carrying out of clandestine activities, serves only to make "the forms of distant objects" fade away "with almost ghostly indistinctness, just as his eye appeared to grasp them." As Hawthorne presents it, the urban landscape mirrors perfectly Robin's growing sense of isolation, loneliness, frustration, and confusion.

An author can also use setting to clarify and reveal character by deliberately making setting a metaphoric or symbolic extension of character. Roderick Usher's "inaccessible" room is a perfect representation of its owner-occupant. So, too, with the entire house. As Poe's nameless narrator rides toward the House of Usher, he notes its "insufferable gloom," its "vacant eye-like windows," the "minute fungi . . . hanging in fine tangled web-work from the eaves," its advanced state of decay, and, finally, the "barely perceptible fissure" extending the full length of the house "until it became lost in the sullen waters of the tarn." As the reader soon discovers, Roderick Usher and his house are mirror images of one another. Roderick is as remote and gloomy as the house itself: his eyes, like the windows, are vacant and lifeless; his hair has the same gossamer consistency as the fungi growing from the eaves; and there is within him the same perceptible and fatal fissure. As the action of the story proceeds to make clear, Roderick and his house are in an advanced state of internal disintegration. Setting and character are one; the house objectifies, and in this way serves to clarify, its master. It is only fitting, therefore, that at Roderick's death the melancholy House of Usher should collapse into the "deep and dank tarn."

SETTING AS A MEANS OF REINFORCING THEME. Setting can also be used as a means of reinforcing and clarifying the theme of a novel or short story. In Hardy's *The Return of the Native,* for example, Egdon Heath not only serves as an antagonist and as a means of creating and sustaining atmosphere, but also as a way of illustrating Hardy's vision of the role of blind causality in an unfriendly universe. Stephen Crane, who shared many of Hardy's beliefs in naturalism, utilizes setting in a similar way in his story "The Blue Hotel." The setting of Crane's story is introduced in the very first sentences:

> The Palace Hotel at Fort Romper was painted a light blue, a shade that is on the legs of a kind of heron, causing the bird to declare its position

> against any background. The Palace Hotel, then, was always screaming and howling in a way that made the dazzling winter landscape of Nebraska seem only a grey swampish hush. It stood alone on the prairie, and when the snow was falling the town two hundred yards away was not visible.
>
> —from "The Blue Hotel," Stephen Crane (1898)

The reader subsequently discovers that this setting has direct thematic relevance to Crane's conception of the relationship between man and nature, as the author-narrator makes clear:

> We picture the world as thick with conquering and elate humanity, but here, with the bugles of the tempest pealing, it was hard to imagine a peopled earth. One viewed the existence of man then as a marvel, and conceded a glamour of wonder to these lice which were caused to cling to a whirling, fire-smitten, ice-locked, disease-stricken, space-lost bulb. The conceit of man was explained by this storm to be the very engine of life. One was a coxcomb not to die in it.

In a fundamentally indifferent universe, mankind's survival largely depends on a capacity for self-assertion, much in the way that the blue hotel asserts its lonely presence against the stark, inhospitable Nebraska landscape.

A Note on Setting in Time

In most of the preceding examples we have emphasized the physical aspects of setting at the expense of the temporal ones. But the time of day or time of year at which a given event or series of events occurs can also contribute importantly to setting as well, as in the case of historical novels. The fact that the events of Hawthorne's "My Kinsman, Major Molineux" take place at night is a highly relevant part of the setting, for darkness is traditionally an appropriate cover for deeds of conspiracy and violence. In Poe's "The Cask of Amontillado," the action takes place not only in the evening, but "during the supreme madness of the carnival season" in the dark crypts beneath Montressor's palazzo. Poe could scarcely have conjured up a more effective setting in which to dramatize the way insanity emerges from beneath the surface of apparent respectability to consummate its single-minded desire for vengeance. Many of the most climactic moments of fiction, in fact, seem to take place at night (note, for example, the scaffold scene in *The Scarlet Letter*) as if to suggest that it is after the rest of the world is asleep that we stand most ready to reveal the essential truths about ourselves to the world.

In much the same way, certain seasons of the year lend themselves more to certain kinds of events than to others. Poe's narrator arrives at the House of Usher on "a dull, dark, and soundless day in the autumn of the year," a period we normally associate with the coming of winter and of death. Winter also is an appropriate setting for the action of Crane's "The Blue Hotel," for the howling storm which swirls around the hotel is perfectly in keeping with the physical violence that soon overtakes and destroys the Swede. Authors will often use the cycle of the year and the cycle of the day to establish settings precisely *because* of the traditional association with the successive cycles in human life: spring-morning-youth; summer-noon-maturity; fall–afternoon (or twilight)–declining years; winter-night-death.

Analyzing Setting

1. What is the work's setting in space and time?
2. How does the author go about establishing setting? Does the author want the reader to see *or* feel the setting; or does the author want the reader both to see *and* feel it? What details of the setting does the author isolate and describe?
3. Is the setting important? If so, what is its function? Is it used to reveal, reinforce, or influence character, plot, or theme?
4. Is the setting an appropriate one?

POINT OF VIEW

A story must have a plot, characters, and a setting. It must also have a storyteller: a narrative voice, real or implied, that presents the story to the reader. When we talk about narrative voice, we are talking about *point of view,* the method of narration that determines the position, or angle of vision, from which the story is told. The nature of the relationship between the narrator and the story, the teller and the tale, is always crucial to the art of fiction. It is the means by which the author presents and shapes his materials and by which the reader's knowledge, interest, and sympathy are focused and controlled. It also governs the reader's access to the story and determines just how much he can know at any given moment about what is taking place. So crucial is point of view that, once having been chosen, it will color and shape the way in which everything else is presented and perceived, including plot, character, and setting. Alter or change the point of view, and you alter and change the story.

The choice of point of view is the choice of who is to tell the story, who talks to the reader. It may be a narrator outside the work (*omniscient* point of view); a narrator inside the work, telling the story from a *limited omniscient* or *first-person* point of view; or apparently no one (*dramatic* point of view). As we will see in the subsequent discussion, these four basic points of view, and their variations, involve at the extreme a choice between omniscient point of view and dramatic point of view—a choice that involves, among other things, the distance that the author wishes to maintain between the reader and the story and the extent to which the author is willing to involve the reader in its interpretation. As the author moves away from omniscience along this spectrum of choices, he progressively surrenders the ability to see into the minds of his characters. However, the question of point of view, perhaps more so than any element of fiction that we have examined so far, is as complex and complicated as it is important; the discreet categories summarized here only begin to account for the possibilities that readers will encounter in their adventures with fiction.

Omniscient Point of View

With the omniscient point of view (sometimes also referred to as panoramic, shifting, or multiple point of view), the narrator firmly imposes himself between the reader and the story, and retains full and complete control over the narrative. By definition, the omniscient narrator is an all-knowing presence. From a vantage point outside the story, the narrator is free to tell us much or little, to dramatize or summarize, to interpret, speculate, philosophize, moralize or judge. He or she can tell us directly what the characters are like and why they behave as they do; record their words and conversations and dramatize their actions; or enter their minds to explore directly their innermost thoughts and feelings. The narrator can move the reader from one event to the next, being just as explicit (or evasive) as he wishes about their significance and meaning; he can skip backward and forward in time, now dramatizing, now summarizing as he chooses. When the omniscient narrator speaks to us in his own voice, there is a natural temptation to identify that voice with the author's. Sometimes such an identification is warranted; at other times it may not be, for the voice that tells the story and speaks to the reader, although it may seem to reflect the author's beliefs and values, is as much the author's creation as any of the characters in the story.

Omniscient narration frequently occurs in eighteenth- and nineteenth-century novels—Fielding's *Tom Jones* and Thackeray's *Vanity Fair* are good examples. In the latter, the narrator frankly assumes the role of puppeteer, "the Manager of the Performance," in a manner that may seem offensive and condescending to modern readers who are used to a more realistic treatment:

> But my kind reader will please to remember that this history has "Vanity Fair" for a title, and that Vanity Fair is a very vain, wicked, foolish place, full of all sorts of humbugs and falsenesses and pretensions. And while the moralist, who is holding forth on the cover (an accurate portrait of your humble servant), professes to wear neither gown nor bands, but only the very same long-eared livery in which his congregation is arrayed; yet, look you, one is bound to speak the truth as far as one knows it, whether one mounts a cap and bells or a shovel-hat; and a deal of disagreeable matter must come out in the course of such an undertaking.
>
> —from *Vanity Fair,* William Makepeace Thackeray (1848)

In our own discussions, we have seen the commentary of the omniscient narrator in Crane's "The Blue Hotel," where men are compared to lice clinging to "a whirling, fire-smitten, ice-locked, disease-stricken, space-lost bulb." In Hawthorne's "My Kinsman, Major Molineux," an omniscient narrator introduces the story with a lengthy paragraph of historical "remarks . . . as a preface to the following adventures" and then suggests that "The reader, in order to avoid a long and dry detail of colonial affairs, . . . dispense with an account of the train of circumstances that had caused much temporary inflammation of the popular mind." Though the story that follows is narrated principally from Robin's point of view, the omniscient narrator is ever in the wings. At the story's climactic moment, he breaks in to record the reaction of the moon to Robin's catharsis: "The Man in the Moon heard the far bellow. 'Oho,' quoth he, 'the old earth is frolicsome to-night!' "

A more typical example of the omniscient point of view is found in the following passage from Hardy's *The Mayor of Casterbridge.* It occurs at the very beginning of the seventh chapter as Elizabeth-Jane and her mother arrive at the Three Mariners Inn:

> Elizabeth-Jane and her mother had arrived some twenty minutes earlier. Outside the house they had stood and considered whether even this homely place, though recommended as moderate, might not be too serious in its prices for their light pockets. Finally, however, they had found courage to enter, and duly met Stannidge the landlord; a silent man, who drew and carried frothing measures to this room and to that, shoulder to shoulder with his waiting-maids—a stately slowness, however, entering into his ministrations by contrast with theirs, as became one whose service was somewhat optional. It would have been altogether optional but for the orders of the landlady, a person who sat in the bar, corporeally motionless, but with a flitting eye and quick ear, with which she observed and heard through the open door and hatchway the pressing needs of customers whom her husband overlooked though close at hand. Elizabeth and her mother were passively accepted as sojourners, and shown to a small bedroom under one of the gables, where they sat down.
>
> —from *The Mayor of Casterbridge,* Thomas Hardy (1886)

In a single paragraph the narrator summarizes and thus advances the action, provides details of setting, and reveals the state of mind of four characters, in turn.

Some critics draw a distinction between omniscient methods that permit their narrators to comment freely in their own voices, using "I" or the editorial "we," (*editorial* omniscience) and those that present the thoughts and actions of characters without such overt editorial intrusions (*neutral* or *impartial* omniscience). Crane and Thackeray in the examples cited are clearly among the former; Hardy, at least in the passage here, is among the latter.

Although there is an observable direction in modern literature away from using omniscience—in part because of an intellectual temperament that tends to distrust, and even deny, absolutes, certainties, and all-knowing attitudes—twentieth-century authors continue to debate its value and to exploit its advantages. Like so many of the critical choices that the writer of fiction is called on to make, however, the choice of point of view is finally a matter of appropriateness. The omniscient point of view, while inappropriate to a Hemingway story, is certainly very appropriate to large, panoramic novels like Tolstoy's national epic *War and Peace,* where an omniscient mode of narration is used to suggest the complexity and scope of Russian life itself.

The great advantage of the omniscient point of view, then, is the flexibility it gives its "all-knowing" narrator, who can direct the reader's attention and control the sources of information. As we move away from omniscient telling in the direction of showing, the narrator progressively surrenders these advantages. In choosing to move inside the framework of the work to merge his or her identity with that of one of the characters (limited omniscient or first-person point of view) or to give up all identity (dramatic point of view), the narrator restricts the channels through which information can be transmitted to the reader; as a result, the reader is involved more and more directly in the task of interpretation.

Limited Omniscient Point of View

With limited omniscient (sometimes referred to as third person or selective omniscient) point of view, the narrator retains the right of immediate access to the work but moves the point of view inside by selecting a single character to act as the center of revelation. What the reader knows and sees of events is always restricted to what this focal character can know or see; however, this point of view differs significantly from the first-person point of view, which we will discuss later. At times the reader may be given direct access to this character's own "voice" and thoughts, insofar as these are reproduced through dialogue or presented dramatically through monologue or stream of consciousness. On all other occasions, the reader's access is indirect: it is the narrator's voice that tells the story and transmits the action, characterization, description, analysis, and other informing details upon which the reader's understanding and interpretation depend. Although the focal character is a visible presence within the story in a way that a fully omniscient narrator is not, at any moment that character is only as available and accessible to the reader as the narrator will permit.

The character chosen as narrative center, and often referred to through the use of a third-person pronoun as *he* or *she,* may be the protagonist or some other major character. Often, however, the assignment is given to a minor character who functions in the role of an an onlooker, watching and speculating from the periphery of the story and only minimally involved, if at all, in its action. Once chosen, it is this character's mind and eyes that become the story's angle of vision and point of entry for the reader. Henry James aptly refers to this character in his critical essays and prefaces as "the reflector" or "mirroring consciousness," for it is through the prism of his or her conscious mind that the story is filtered and reflected.

The advantages of the limited omniscient point of view are the tightness of focus and control that it provides and the intensity of treatment that it makes possible. These advantages explain why the limited omniscient point of view is so admirably suited to the short story, whose restricted scope can accommodate full omniscience and multiple points of entry only with great difficulty. The limited omniscient point of view predominates in Hawthorne's "My Kinsman, Major Molineux," as seen, for example, in the previously-quoted passage describing Robin's physical appearance and clothing. It is used with good effect as well in another of Hawthorne's famous tales, "Young Goodman Brown," in which the author is interested in the way in which the conviction of sin can totally influence and distort an individual's outlook. In order to chronicle Goodman Brown's progressive disillusionment with the world, climaxed by his conviction that his fellow townspeople, and even his wife Faith, are numbered among the Devil's disciples, the narrator positions himself at Goodman's shoulder and reveals the world as it takes shape before Goodman's innocent eyes. Whether or not Goodman Brown's night in the forest is dream or reality finally makes no difference; Goodman is convinced beyond redemption that the Devil is correct: that "Evil is the nature of mankind." Goodman's naïve and untested faith is destroyed; his vision of life is darkened; and he goes to his grave a gloomy, distrustful, and lonely man. The limited omniscient point of view serves Hawthorne's purposes well, for it is Brown's personal vision of the way that things *appear to be*—rather than the way that things actually *are*—that is at the center of Hawthorne's story.

The limited omniscient point of view also works particularly well as a means of creating and sustaining irony because it can exploit the disparity between what the focal character thinks he or she knows and the true state of affairs. Henry James, whose novels and stories make heavy use of a third-person "reflector" in the form of a "finely aware and richly responsible" character who prides himself on these traits, is an excellent case in point. In "The Tree of Knowledge," for example, a story that as its title suggests, turns on "knowledge" and "knowing," the reflector is the middle-aged bachelor Peter Brench, who has dedicated his life to making sure that Mrs. Mallow and her son Lancelot are kept ignorant of the "Master's" lack of artistic talent. Brench, James tells us, is an individual who "had judged himself once for all": "It was one of the secret opinions . . . of Peter Brench that his main success of life would have consisted in his never having committed himself about the work, as it was called, of his friend Morgan Mallow." As it turns out, Peter Brench's heroic gesture has been an unnecessary one, for Mrs. Mallow and Lancelot know only too well that the Master's talent is impoverished. For years they have successfully kept from Brench the very knowledge he would keep from *them.* The irony of the situation is made possible by James's ability to narrate the story from Peter Brench's point of view while slowly revealing to the reader the exact degree of Peter's false assumptions.

First-Person Point of View

The use of first-person point of view places still another restriction on the voice that tells the story. As already noted, the movement from full to limited omniscience essentially involves the narrator's decision to position himself inside rather than outside the story and to limit his omniscience to a single character. First-person point of view retains this inside position, but goes one step further by locating the point of view in a character who addresses the reader directly, without an intermediary.

First-person point of view thus combines the advantages and restrictions of limited omniscience with its own. As with limited omniscience, first-person narration is tightly controlled and limited in its access to information. The first-person narrator, like his limited omniscient counterpart, while free to speculate, can only report information that falls within his own firsthand knowledge of the world or what he comes to learn secondhand from others.[7] First-person narration, however, assumes the still greater burden of its own subjectivity. The only thoughts and feelings that first-person narrators experience directly are their own, and once the authority for the story has been shifted to their shoulders there is a danger that their thoughts and feelings—the way they perceive the world—will become colored by subjective prejudices and biases of which they are

[7] Some authors get around this limitation by introducing letters, diaries, and journals into their narratives, thus giving the narrator (and the reader) direct and immediate access to the thoughts and feelings of others. Samuel Richardson's *Pamela* (1740) and *Clarissa* (1748) and Bram Stoker's *Dracula* (1897) are good examples of the use of this device and as a result are sometimes referred to as epistolary novels. The problem with works that rely heavily on such written documentation is mainly one of credibility: are men and women, caught up in adventures of one sort or another, willing and able to sit down to compose their thoughts and feelings on paper? Pamela, for example, writes six letters on her wedding day!

not fully, if at all, aware. The implications of this uncorrected subjectivity are crucially important, for it means that the reader can never expect to see characters and events as they actually are but only as they *appear* to be to the mediating consciousness of the "I"-narrator who stands between the reader and the work. For this reason it is always necessary to pay particular attention to the character that fills that role—to his or her personality; built-in biases, values, and beliefs; and degree of awareness and perceptivity—in order to measure his reliability as a narrator.[8] In this respect, of course, first-person point of view closely resembles the perspective from which each of us views our own life and times. Like the protagonist-narrator, we can *see* everything that falls within our line of vision, but we can only *know* the content of our own mind, and we must be constantly alert to the influences, large and small, that shape and possibly distort our outlook on the world.

First-person point of view has its advantages, however, not the least of which is the marvelous sense of immediacy, credibility, and psychological realism that autobiographical storytelling always carries with it. "Call me Ishmael," begins Herman Melville's *Moby-Dick;* the reader is at once addressed in a conversational tone as a friend worthy of confidence by one who is about to tell us directly in his own person about his adventures in pursuit of a white whale. Ishmael's invitation to share with the reader his own unedited experiences is a seductive one. If the appeal is accepted—and there is little reason, at least initially, why it should not be—the reader and his sympathies are at once engaged on behalf of the narrator and his story, and the illusion is created that subsequent participation and discovery will be joint ones. No other point of view is more effective in its capacity for eliciting the reader's direct intellectual and emotional involvement in the teller and the tale.

First-person narrators are usually identified and differentiated on the basis of their degree of involvement with the events of the plot. They may be protagonists, like Mark Twain's Huckleberry Finn, who tell the stories of their own lives and adventures. In such works, the protagonist-narrator is always firmly in control of the content, pace, and method of presentation. Certain events will be fully or par-

[8] It is also true, of course, that the *author's* biases can and often do color the writing. In first-person point of view, these biases may be an intentional element in the plot. In other points of view, they may be unintentional, but equally important.

tially dramatized as the protagonist witnessed them; others will be transmitted to the reader indirectly through the use of summary and comment. Protagonist-narrators, not surprisingly, tend to dominate their works to the disadvantage of other characters, and by continually calling attention to their own presence, and to their own thoughts and feelings, fully characterize themselves in the process. To the extent that such characters are perceptive and intelligent and able to make sense of the events in which they participate, their stories frequently, as in the case of Huckleberry Finn's, illustrate their growth and maturation. Where such sensitivity and intelligence are lacking, the protagonist-narrator becomes at once a ready-made subject for irony.

Protagonist-narrators may narrate events ostensibly as they take place, as in Daniel Defoe's *Robinson Crusoe,* or in leisurely retrospect, with the narrator looking backward over a period of time on adventures that have already been concluded, as Pip does in Charles Dickens's *Great Expectations.* In retrospective views, the extent to which the narrator has managed in the interim to achieve appropriate distance and objectivity can be an issue, as well. The unnamed protagonist-narrator of James Joyce's "Araby," for example, looking backward at his own boyish romanticism has clearly not reached such a position of objectivity. In calling himself "a creature driven and derided by vanity," he is clearly judging himself too harshly for an act that an older, and a presumably wiser, adult would be willing to excuse as part of the inevitable process of growing up. In addition, to the extent that life-endangering situations are at stake, protagonist-narration offers little real suspense over the eventual outcome; that the protagonist is able to tell his or her story means that, at the very least, as with Melville's Ishmael, "I only am escaped alone to tell thee."

A particularly good example of the way in which protagonist-narrators are established as the narrative authority of their works is found in the opening lines of Mark Twain's *Huckleberry Finn:*

> You don't know about me, without you have read a book by the name of *The Adventures of Tom Sawyer,* but that ain't no matter. That book was made by Mr. Mark Twain, and he told the truth, mainly. There was things which he stretched, but mainly he told the truth. That is nothing. I never seen anybody but lied, one time or another, without it was Aunt Polly, or the widow, or maybe Mary. Aunt Polly—Tom's Aunt Polly, she

is—and Mary, and the Widow Douglas, is all told about in that book—which is mostly a true book; with some stretchers, as I said before.
—from *The Adventures of Huckleberry Finn,* Mark Twain (1885)

In this brief passage, Huck succeeds in achieving a number of important things on behalf of his creator. We are introduced to the protagonist, or, rather, he introduces himself to us, and in a way that makes him at once credible and convincing. This is achieved in part by Huck's declaration of his own candor and honesty, but partly too by the slightly ungrammatical backwoods idiom in which he speaks: a "voice" that strikes us as highly appropriate for a largely self-educated rural youth raised in Mark Twain's nineteenth-century Missouri. Huck's speech is a very important part of his characterization; and Mark Twain has clearly succeeded—where other authors often fail—in creating characters who "talk like they ought to." By alluding specifically to the author, "Mr. Mark Twain," Huck also creates the illusion—so necessary with first-person narrative—that author and character are distinct and separate; and, in this case, that Huck has an identity of his own, quite apart from the man who wrote *The Adventures of Tom Sawyer.* (The intelligent reader, in his role as critic, will of course see such an assertion for the convention that it is.)

What Huck says and the confidential and intimate way in which he says it are deliberately calculated to engage the reader's sympathy and trust. And what better way to engage the reader than by generously allowing that while Mark Twain "mainly . . . told the truth" in *Tom Sawyer,* there were some "stretchers" because "I never seen anybody but lied, one time or another." The implication and invitation are clear: If, as Huck assures us, *The Adventures of Tom Sawyer* is "mostly a true book," we can count on the veracity of the present work, for Huckleberry Finn, who knows a "stretcher" when he sees one, will be in charge. The opening paragraph thus serves Mark Twain's purposes well: it establishes immediacy and intimacy because it purports to be a firsthand account of experience without the intervention or analysis of an outside narrator; and it marks the beginning of a growing acquaintance with Huckleberry Finn, a character who invites our belief because of his self-proclaimed awareness and sensitivity where matters of truth are concerned.

Not all protagonist-narrators tell their own stories. Sometimes the protagonist-narrator is charged with the responsibility of telling someone else's story, as Nick Carraway, the protagonist of Fitzgerald's *The Great Gatsby,* is charged with the responsibility of telling Jay Gatsby's. Because the narrative focus is shifted elsewhere, the characterization of such narrators will be less fully developed than that of a Huckleberry Finn. In the end, however, the purpose of Fitzgerald and Mark Twain is very much the same: to record the impact of the story being told upon the growth and maturation of the narrator.

First-person narrators are frequently not the protagonist at all, but rather characters whose roles in the plot are clearly secondary. They may, in fact, have almost no visible role in the plot and exist primarily as convenient devices for transmitting the narrative to the reader. Such is the case with the nameless narrator of Poe's "The Fall of the House of Usher" and Sherlock Holmes's indefatigable sidekick and biographer Dr. Watson. Narrators of this type will be, at best, only partially characterized and may remain little more than disembodied voices distinguishable only by the fact that they address the reader in the first person. Such narrators do, however, enjoy certain definite advantages. Often they have greater freedom of movement than the protagonist-narrator. From their positions at the periphery of the story they may move among and between the other characters with relative ease, using them as sources to acquire helpful information. First-person narrators who function other than as protagonists telling their own stories very often appear in the roles of *confidantes,* as genial and sympathetic personalities in whose wisdom and judgment (or presumed neutrality) others seem willing, or even desperate, to confide. Such is the lot of Nick Carraway, who tells the reader on the very first page of the novel that "I'm inclined to reserve all judgments, a habit that has opened up many curious natures to me and also made me the victim of not a few veteran bores." It is also true of Dr. Watson, who is the *foil* to whom Holmes can explain in meticulous detail his method of detection, thus building and heightening the suspense while allowing Holmes to keep his readers in the dark until the last about the problem-solving going on in his mind.

In their relationship to the other characters and to the action of the plot, first-person narrators may be either interested and involved or disinterested and detached. In either case, however, they are always subject to hidden biases and prejudices in their telling of the story. Minor characters serving as narrators, no less than major ones, must be watched constantly, especially if the reader has reason to suspect that they may be other than totally reliable guides to the truth of what they report.

STREAM OF CONSCIOUSNESS. We have already described stream of consciousness as the technique of characterization that renders *from the inside* the conscious or unconscious content of the human mind and the myriad of thoughts, perceptions, feelings, and associations that ebb and flow there. To the extent that an author chooses to locate the center of narrative authority exclusively inside the mind of a single character and to record external reality, including speech and action, only as it registers its impression upon that mind, stream of consciousness can also be used as a variation of first-person point of view. An excellent example is offered by the opening passage of William Faulkner's *The Sound and the Fury:*

> Through the fence, between the curling flower spaces, I could see them hitting. They were coming toward where the flag was and I went along the fence. Luster was hunting in the grass by the flower tree. They took the flag out, and they were hitting. Then they put the flag back and they went to the table, and he hit and the other hit. Then they went on, and I went along the fence. Luster came away from the flower tree and we went along the fence and they stopped and we stopped and I looked through the fence while Luster was hunting in the grass.
>
> —from *The Sound and the Fury,* William Faulkner (1929)

The speaker is Benjy Compson, the thirty-three-year-old idiot whose point of view dominates the first section of Faulkner's novel. But the voice that addresses the reader is not Benjy's speaking voice. Rather we are being made privy to the pattern of thought and sensation unfolding within Benjy's infantile mind as he stands in the Compson garden watching golfers through the fence.

Stream-of-consciousness technique used as first-person point of view is difficult to sustain over an extended period of time because of the heavy demands it makes on the author and reader alike. Not only does it fasten the story's angle of vision exclusively to the *inside* of a single mind, whose patterns of conscious and unconscious thoughts and feelings are frequently illogical and hard to follow, but, theoretically at least, it also effectively prevents the author from providing stage directions and clarifying comments and from asserting other forms of direct managerial control over the development of the narrative. To avoid these difficulties, and still take full advantage of the possibilities of stream-of-consciousness narration, authors will typically utilize either the omniscient or limited omniscient point of view, which, as already noted, allows the necessary external control, while making it possible to explore the content of the minds of one or more of the characters. This is the case with such well-known works as Virginia Woolf's *To the Lighthouse* and James Joyce's *The Portrait of the Artist as a Young Man,* which make extensive use of the stream-of-consciousness technique.

Dramatic Point of View

In the dramatic, or objective, point of view the story is told ostensibly by no one. The narrator, who to this point in our discussion has been a visible, mediating authority standing between the reader and the work, now disappears completely and the story is allowed to present itself dramatically through action and dialogue. With the disappearance of the narrator, telling is replaced by showing, and the illusion is created that the reader is a direct and immediate witness to an unfolding drama.[9] Without a narrator to serve as mentor and guide, the reader is left largely on his own. There is no way of entering the minds of the characters; no evaluative comments are offered; the reader is not told directly how to respond, either intellectually or emotionally, to the events or the characters. The reader is permitted to view the work only in its externals, from the outside. Although the author may supply certain descriptive details, particularly at the beginning of the work, the reader is called on to shoulder much of the responsibility for analysis and interpretation. He or she must deduce the circumstances of the plot, past and present, and how and why the characters think and feel as they do on the basis of their overt behavior and conversation.

In its relationship to the reader, dramatic point of view is often compared to the perspective from which we observe a film or a stage play. As with dramatic point of view, the viewer, sitting in the audience, has no way of penetrating the minds of the characters and is

[9] The words *ostensibly* and *illusion* are used advisedly here, for a narrative voice is almost always present somewhere in the story, if only to provide a few brief sentences of description or stage direction. In truth, the narrator never totally disappears in a work of fiction, and the task of the critic is to know where and when he makes his presence felt.

left to infer their mental or emotional states from the dialogue (or monologue) and the action. The plot unfolds in scenes before the viewer, whose angle of vision is fixed by the seat in which he or she sits; there is no one at the viewer's shoulder, or at the foot or the side of the stage, to provide additional information and to say where, in particular, his wandering eyes should focus. To be sure, this analogy, although helpful, is by no means perfect. The writer of fiction, whose medium is language, selects and arranges language within the confines of a printed page and exercises far greater control than either the filmmaker or dramatist in focusing the reader's attention and, through the quality of the words themselves, manipulating the reader's response.

Dramatic point of view appeals to many modern and contemporary writers because of the impersonal and objective way it presents experience and because of the vivid sense of the actual that it creates. Ernest Hemingway is its leading exemplar. The dramatic mode dominates Hemingway's short stories and novels where it is used to illustrate and reinforce the Hemingway "code," with its emphasis on psychological and emotional detachment and self-control.

The following passage of dramatic narration occurs at the beginning of Hemingway's famous short story "The Killers."

> The door of Henry's lunch-room opened and two men came in. They sat down at the counter.
>
> "What's yours?" George asked them.
>
> "I don't know," one of the men said. "What do you want to eat, Al?"
>
> "I don't know," said Al. "I don't know what I want to eat."
>
> Outside it was getting dark. The streetlight came on outside the window. The two men at the counter read the menu. From the other end of the counter Nick Adams watched them. He had been talking to George when they came in.
>
> "I'll have a roast pork tenderloin with apple sauce and mashed potatoes," the first man said.
>
> "It isn't ready yet."
>
> "What the hell do you put it on the card for?"
>
> "That's the dinner," George explained. "You can get that at six o'clock."
>
> —from "The Killers," Ernest Hemingway (1927)

The action unfolds dramatically. The few concrete, factual details are introduced without comment; and the action and the characters are allowed to present themselves directly to the reader without benefit of an intervening narrator. The effect is one of pure showing. At first glance, the scene seems quite insignificant. It is only in retrospect, after we have learned that the two men who enter Henry's diner are hired killers, that we see why Hemingway has written about them at all. And even then, the casualness of their entrance is what makes the scene so chilling; we feel that they should have acted differently, that only absolutely amoral men would remain so bored and indifferent while anticipating a murder. All this, of course, is part of Hemingway's artistry.

Reliable and Unreliable Narrators

In analyzing the point of view of a given work of fiction, the reader is often forced to confront the question of the relative trustworthiness or reliability of the narrator. With omniscient point of view, the question of reliability is usually not a troublesome one, for when the narrator is placed outside the work and aids directly in its analysis and interpretation, his reliability can be largely assumed. Much the same thing is true with the dramatic point of view, where there is no apparent narrator present. When, however, the narrative voice is positioned inside the work and belongs to a character who is more or less directly involved in the action, the question of the narrator's reliability often becomes pertinent indeed.

Reliability, it should be understood, is not a matter of whether the reader happens to agree with the narrator's views or opinions. We can choose to agree or not with such views, but our agreement or lack thereof will not fundamentally effect how we view and understand the work. Reliability refers to something far more serious, for an unreliable narrator who is allowed to go undetected and uncorrected can distort our understanding of the work even as he distorts the author's own intention, attitudes, and meaning.

Sometimes, of course, an unreliable narrator is a stylistic device used by the author to create a thematic point. When this is so, the author usually provides somewhere a clear indication of the narrator's unreliability. The failure to do so will result in ambiguity and even unintelligibility, as, for example, in Henry James's celebrated chiller *The Turn of the Screw,* in which the reliability of the governess-narrator is an issue James allows to go unresolved. If the governess is a reliable narrator, we have a genuine ghost story on our hands; if she is not, we are dealing with a neurotic woman who is responsible for the death of an innocent child. James does not tell us which version of the governess is correct.

The question of reliability most often arises with perfectly honest and well-intentioned narrators who make every effort to tell the truth of things insofar as they are able to perceive it. Sincerity and good intentions are one thing; reliability is another. Such narrators may prove to be unreliable because they are ignorant or because they commit an error in judgment by drawing the wrong conclusions from the facts available. They may also prove to be unreliable because they are victims of their own self-deception. Whatever the cause, once the reader begins to suspect that the narrator is unreliable, a note of ambiguity or irony is introduced into the work.

To overcome the problem of an unreliable narrator, the reader must first of all be able to identify the narrator's existence; and having done so, the reader must be able to supply, on his own, an alternative perspective which will allow him to view the work correctly. Sometimes the necessary correction can be made by analyzing and attempting to understand the intellectual and moral qualities of the narrator or by studying carefully what the other characters have to say about him or her. Winterbourne, the first-person narrator of Henry James's short novel *Daisy Miller,* is a case in point. A Europeanized American, Winterbourne errs in judging the moral character of his fellow countryman because he has "lived too long in foreign parts." His outlook has become corrupted by his Old World view of human nature, and he is unable to understand, much less appreciate, the genuine innocence and spontaneity of a young American girl who simply does in Rome as she would do at home in Schenectady. Winterbourne confuses manners with morality; as a result, the impression of Daisy that the reader receives from him for much of the story is a misleading one. Only by understanding Winterbourne, and what he has become, can the reader correct his opinion of Daisy Miller and see her for the radical, if foolish, innocent that she is. James's fiction is filled with misguided and misguiding narrators like Winterbourne, and his example has been followed by many modern and contemporary writers who use the fallible narrator as a device for the deliberate creation of irony.

Winterbourne, like Peter Brench in "The Tree of Knowledge," largely corrects his own reliability as a narrator by coming to see the extent to which he has been blinded by his own biases and false assumptions. Other narrators never reach such self-knowledge, and our problem as readers is further compounded when we are unable to establish reliability or unreliability conclusively by studying their characters or by studying the evidence offered by others. On such occasions the reader will have to look to the other norms of the work, to the implied or expressed values that help to determine its meaning and theme, or to the vision of life it offers. Where such norms can be said to be different from those the narrator presents or affirms, that narrator is likely to be a fallible and unreliable one.

Unfortunately, authors writing fiction do not have textbook definitions in front of them. If they did, and if they followed them, the task of analyzing point of view would be greatly simplified. The essential problem with point of view, as we noted earlier, is that the separate categories we have outlined often do not occur in a pure and undiluted form. *Moby-Dick* begins with Ishmael telling his own story in the first person. Toward the middle of the book, Ishmael disappears from sight and Ahab emerges to dominate the story. At that point, the narrative structure takes on the qualities of a Shakespearean play, complete with stage directions. In Melville's case, the violation of consistency can hardly be construed a weakness, and what is true of *Moby-Dick* is true, to a greater or lesser extent, of many other works of fiction as well.

Analyzing Point of View

1. What is the point of view? Is the point of view consistent throughout the work or does it shift in some way?
2. Where does the narrator stand in relation to the work? Where does the reader stand?
3. To what sources of knowledge or information does the point of view give the reader access? What sources of knowledge or information does it serve to conceal?
4. If the work is told from the point of view of one of the characters, is the narrator reliable? Does his or her personality, character, or intellect affect an ability to interpret the events or the other characters correctly?
5. Given the author's purposes, is the chosen point of view an appropriate and effective one?
6. How would the work be different if told from another point of view?

THEME

Theme is one of those critical terms that mean very different things to different people. To some, who think of literature mainly as a vehicle for teaching, preaching, propagating a favorite idea, or encouraging some form of correct conduct, theme may mean the moral or lesson that can be extrapolated from the work, as with one of Aesop's fables or Parson Weems' famous (and, sadly, apocryphal) story about George Washington and the cherry tree. Theme is also used sometimes to refer to the basic issue, problem, or subject with which the work is concerned: for example, "the nature of man," "the discovery of truth," or "the initiation into adulthood." In this sense, a number of short stories—Poe's "The Cask of Amontillado," Crane's "The Blue Hotel," and Hemingway's "The Killers,"—may all be said to deal in common with the theme of violence. Or, we may speak of theme as a familiar pattern or motif that occurs again and again in literature, say the journey theme found in works as different and similar as Cervantes's *Don Quixote,* Henry Fielding's *Tom Jones,* Mark Twain's *Huckleberry Finn,* Virginia Woolf's *To the Lighthouse,* John Steinbeck's *The Grapes of Wrath,* and James Dickey's *Deliverance.*

When we speak of theme in connection with the critical analysis of a literary work, however, we usually have a broader and more inclusive definition in mind. In literature, theme is the central idea or statement about life that unifies and controls the total work. By this definition, then, the theme is not the issue, or problem, or subject with which the work deals, as violence is the subject of Stephen Crane's "The Blue Hotel." Rather, theme is the comment or statement the author makes about that subject as it necessarily and inevitably emerges from the interplay of the various elements of the work.

Theme in literature, whether it takes the form of a brief and meaningful insight or a comprehensive vision of life, can be said to represent the vehicle an author uses to establish a relationship with the larger world in which he or she lives and works. It is the author's way of communicating and sharing ideas, perceptions, and feelings with his readers or, as is so often the case, of probing and exploring with them the puzzling questions of human existence, most of which do not yield neat, tidy, and universally acceptable answers. Although we cannot, as critics, judge a work solely on the basis of the quality of the ideas presented (or on their degree of complexity or sophistication), it is also true that one of the marks of a great work of literature—a work that we generally regard as a "classic"—is the significance of its theme; and that an author's ability to construct a work whose various elements work together to yield a significant theme is an important test of the quality of that author's mind and art.

"What does it mean?" "What is the author trying to say?" "What *is* the theme of the work?" These are the questions that students are often most eager and impatient to discuss. Why, then, one may properly ask, did we not begin our discussion of fiction by discussing theme? Why delay its introduction until after having considered plot, character, setting, and point of view?

We have done so for a reason that has very much to do not only with the nature of theme, but with the nature of fiction itself. We have organized our discussion to illustrate the fact that a work of fiction consists of a number of crucial elements *in addition* to theme; that the identification and understanding of these other elements—particularly the interaction of character and incident—can be as important to the story as theme, or more so; and that any discussion of theme, by definition, must be prepared to take those other elements into account. Theme, that is, does not exist as an intellectual abstraction that an author superimposes on the work like icing on a cake (although, at times, there is a temptation to treat it as such); theme is organically and necessarily related to the work's total structure and texture. This is the point made by Flannery O'Connor, herself one of America's most important twentieth-century writers of fiction, using one of her typically homely metaphors:

> People talk about the theme of a story as if the theme were like a string that a sack of chicken feed is tied with. They think that if you can pick out the theme, the way you pick the right thread in the chicken-feed sack, you can rip the story open and feed the chickens. But this is not the way meaning works in fiction. . . . The meaning of a story has to be embodied in it, has to be made concrete in it. A story is a way to say something that can't be said any other way, and it takes every word in the story to say what the meaning is.[10]

Theme in fiction is discoverable to the extent that we are willing as critics to subject its various elements—its "every word"—to the process of analysis and interpretation.

[10] Flannery O'Connor, "Writing Short Stories," in *Mystery and Manners* (New York: Farrar, Straus and Giroux, 1969), p. 96.

Three more important points about theme in fiction need to be made. First of all, as an element of fiction, theme may be less prominent and less fully developed in some works than in others. This is especially true in the case of detective, gothic, and adventure fiction, where the author wants primarily to entertain by producing mystification, inducing chills and nightmare, or engaging the reader in a series of exciting, fast-moving incidents.

Such works may not have a demonstrable theme at all, at least in the sense in which we have defined the term. To identify the theme of a detective story with the idea that "crime doesn't pay" is not only to confuse theme with moral, but in all probability to misinterpret where the author has chosen to place the work's emphasis. One must, however, be careful. Many works of humor and satire—for example, the short stories of James Thurber or the novels of Sinclair Lewis—while they make us smile, and perhaps laugh, do have thematic content and offer the reader significant, and in Lewis's case very serious, insights into modern and contemporary life. Much the same thing is often true of gothic fiction, where, in the hands of genuine artists like Poe, Faulkner, and John Fowles (*The Collector*), melodrama and terror are used not for their own sake but to probe the recesses of the human soul.

Second, it is entirely possible that intelligent readers and critics will differ, at times dramatically, on just what the theme of a given work is. It is on the basis of such disagreements that the reputations of literary critics are frequently made, or discredited. Critical disagreements often occur when the elements of the work are arranged in a way that yields two, or more, acceptable, yet mutually exclusive, statements. A case in point is "Young Goodman Brown," Hawthorne's story of a young Puritan who leaves his wife of three months (appropriately named Faith) and embarks on a nighttime journey into the forest to keep a prearranged appointment with the Devil. As he makes his way through the woods, first alone and then in the company of a stranger (presumably the Devil) who resembles his own father, Goodman Brown becomes increasingly convinced that his fellow townspeople, and finally even Faith, are members of the Devil's unholy communion. The story climaxes in a lurid rite of initiation, in which Goodman Brown cries out: "My Faith is gone! . . . There is no good on earth, and sin is but a name. Come Devil! for to thee is the world given."

In the aftermath, Brown's faith is destroyed; he shrinks from the bosom of his wife and goes to his grave convinced that "Evil is the nature of mankind." The final theme of the story, however, is anything but clear. Hawthorne's tale is made deliberately ambiguous through the use of a limited omniscient point of view: the narrator refuses to commit himself as to whether what Goodman Brown thinks he sees is really happening or whether it is merely the figment of Brown's distorted imagination.

As a result, the story has been analyzed by its various critics to yield a multitude of possible themes, all of them plausibly rooted in the facts of the story as the critics have interpreted those facts. Some have accepted Goodman Brown's own interpretation as the definitive statement of Hawthorne's theme; others have argued that Hawthorne is attempting to illustrate the failure of belief and the effects of moral scepticism. The story has also been variously interpreted as an attack on the hypocrisy of Puritan society, as an attack on Calvinistic theology, and as a psychoanalytic study of arrested sexual development that has nothing at all to do with the question of religious faith. As recently as 1966, Paul J. Hurley, in presenting yet another reading of the story, announced that "The critical controversy which has centered on Hawthorne's 'Young Goodman Brown' seems to have reached an impasse."[11] But impasse or not, the following decade, 1966–1976, produced at least forty-three new discussions of the story, and the debate goes on.[12] Nor does Hawthorne's story stand alone as an example of protracted (and, one might add, finally inconclusive) literary debates.

Third and last, the theme of a given work need not be in accord with the reader's particular beliefs and values. On those grounds many of us would surely object to a reading of Hawthorne's story that concluded its theme to be the assertion that mankind is inherently evil and goodness is an illusion. To be sure, we are under no obligation as readers to accept a story's theme as it is presented to us, especially if we believe that it violates the truth of our own experience and that of others. But we must remember that although literature is full of ideas that may strike us, at least initially, as unpleasant, controversial, or simply wrong-headed, literary sophistication and

[11] Paul J. Hurley, "Young Goodman Brown's 'Heart of Darkness,'" *American Literature,* 37:410 (January 1966).

[12] As determined from the bibliography in the *Instructor's Supplement* to James H. Pickering's *Fiction 100: An Anthology of Short Stories,* 2nd ed. (New York: Macmillan Publishing Company, 1978), pp. 70–73.

plain common sense should warn us against dismissing them out of hand. Stories such as Hawthorne's survive, in part at least, because of the fresh and startling ideas and insights they offer. Such ideas and insights have the power to liberate our minds and our imaginations and to cause us to reflect critically about our own values, beliefs, and assumptions. At the very least, before rejecting an author's ideas, we owe it to the author and to ourselves to make certain that we understand why we reject them.

An author's ideas, as they are embodied in the theme, may be *unconvincing* on still other, more important, grounds. An author's theme may be unconvincing because the work itself fails to substantiate that theme, because the interplay of the elements of the story as we experience and analyze them may not support or justify the theme that author apparently wanted us to draw from it. If, that is to say, the reader can sometimes fail to do full justice to an author, an author may, on occasion, fail equally to do full justice by his reader.

Identifying Theme

When we attempt to identify the theme of a work of fiction we are attempting to formulate in our own words the statement about life or human experience that is made by the total work. The task is often far from easy, because it necessarily involves us in the analysis of a number of elements in their relationship to one another and to the work as a whole. Part of the value of attempting to identify theme is that it forces us to bring together and to understand the various aspects of the work, in the process of which we may notice things we had previously ignored or undervalued. We will be successful in the task to the extent that we are willing to be open-minded and objective and resist the temptation to pay attention to some rather than all the elements of the work, or, what is worse, to read into them what simply is not there. The identification of theme, then, is a way to validate our understanding, to focus our response, and to make the work finally and fully our own.

The ideas that constitute a work's theme may be relatively commonplace ones that easily fall within the framework of our own experience. They may also be fairly complex and abstract—somewhat hard to understand and put into words—either because we have not encountered them before or because they relate to concepts that are in themselves inherently difficult. Some themes are topical in nature (that is, they involve ideas that are valid only in relation to a specific time and place, or to a specific set of circumstances); others are universal in their application. On some occasions the theme may be explicitly stated by one of the characters (who serves as a spokesman for the author) or by the author in the guise of an omniscient narrator. Even though such explicit statements must be taken seriously into account, a degree of caution is also necessary, for as we know characters and narrators alike can be unreliable and misleading. In most cases, however, theme is not stated but implied by the work's total rendering of experience; it is only gradually revealed through the treatment of character and incident and by the progress and movement of the story. This is particularly true of works in which theme is tied to the revelation of character and takes the form of a statement about that character and/or what that character may imply about people or life in general.

Because different kinds of works will yield different themes in different ways, there is no one correct approach to identifying theme. The following suggestions and comments, however, may prove helpful:

a. It is important in considering theme to avoid confusing it with the work's subject or situation. Theme is the abstract, generalized statement or comment that the work makes about a concrete subject or situation. It is also true that unless we are first successful in establishing the subject, or establishing the work's basic situation, we are unlikely to be able to establish its theme. Begin then with the subject or situation; once that is identified, we are in a position to formulate a thematic statement about the work.

   Take the case of Hawthorne's "Young Goodman Brown." Its subject, as the title suggests, is the young Puritan himself (at some point it will be necessary to consider whether his name implies that he is intended to represent a type of untested goodness, an everyman figure). We will then want to ask ourselves a series of questions about what happens to him in the course of the story. What visible changes take place in his situation, in his character, or in both? What does he discover and learn as a result of his experiences? Now we are in a position to propose a theme for the story. In this case we might say (and remember, the same basic theme can be stated in a variety of ways) that Hawthorne's theme is an illustration of the unfortunate and permanent effects of the conviction of sin upon a man (and, perhaps, all mankind, if the theme is to be made universal) who has failed, in his innocence, to arrive at a mature adult understanding of the world and of mankind's basic capacity for both good and evil. Other readers of Hawthorne's story will arrive at different interpretations; we must be prepared to defend our view in the form of a critical analysis that will relate all the significant aspects of the story—especially character, event, and point of view—in support of our interpretation of the story's theme.

b. We must be as certain as we can that our statement of theme does the work full justice. There is always the danger, that is, of either understating the theme by failing to discover its total significance, or of overstating and enlarging it beyond what the elements of the story can be said to support, thus making the work appear more universally applicable than it is. The danger of the latter is probably greater than the danger of the former. Authors, like all intelligent people, know that universal, all-embracing statements about life are frequently refuted by the experiences of individuals, and they will usually restrict their claims accordingly. They know that there are very few generalizations about experience that will hold true under every circumstance. Authors also know that most of the really important questions about human existence do not yield easy, formulistic answers. As readers we must be careful not to credit literary works with solutions and answers where such issues and questions are only being explored or where only tentative answers are being proposed.

On the other hand, there is a danger of not seeing the full thematic significance of a work. We fail to grasp a work's total implications by being inattentive in our reading. If we ignore the final two pages of Fitzgerald's *The Great Gatsby*, or skim them in the belief that all is said and done, then we might be tempted to say that the theme of the novel is the danger of founding one's idealism on false gods, as Gatsby does in his belief that he can recapture the past by regaining Daisy Buchanan. At one level, at least, it is certainly true that this is the novel's theme: the author's implied comment on the situation that we have watched unfold through Nick Carraway's eyes. But in those final two pages Fitzgerald deliberately gives his theme (and his book) a much wider implication by deliberately equating Gatsby's dream with the American continent, "the last and greatest of all human dreams." In this way, the theme of *The Great Gatsby* becomes Fitzgerald's statement about the failure of the American Dream itself.

c. We defined theme as a "statement about life that unifies and controls the total work"; thus, the test of any theme that we may propose is whether it is fully and completely supported by the work's other elements. If our statement of theme leaves certain elements or details unexplained, or if those elements and details fail to confirm our statement, then unless the work itself is flawed, chances are we have been only partially successful in our identification.

d. The title which an author gives the work often suggests a particular focus or emphasis for the reader's attention. Frequently, the title of a work serves to identify and confirm the work's protagonist or essential character. Titles may also provide clues about theme. Joseph Conrad's "Heart of Darkness" refers not only to the uncharted center of Africa, the "dark" continent, but to the capacity for evil that exists in the human heart, a title relevant to both the plot situation and the theme of Conrad's story. As usual, however, titles can be as deceptive or misleading in their relation to theme as to anything else. The title of Charles Dickens's novel *Great Expectations,* for example, is in a sense clearly ironic, for Pip can reach maturity only *after* he renounces his "great expectations" and the false assumptions and values upon which they are based.

e. As readers get more and more involved with literary study they want to know more about the life and personality of the authors they read. Biographical and autobiographical explorations are helpful and illuminating—as are the personal statements an author makes about his or her life and work in prefaces, letters, journals, notebooks, and critical writings—and can tell us a great deal about the author, the times in which he lived and wrote, and the relationship between the author and the work. They can also tell us something about the author's *intentions.* Although there is a great and natural temptation to take the author at his word (for what is that word, really, but a type of expert testimony), conclusions about theme that are erected on the author's own statement need careful critical evaluation. Authors are as fallible as the rest of us in explaining motive, and in some cases may be the least reliable of guides as to what their work finally means. D. H.

Lawrence is certainly correct in this respect, when he reminds us in his *Studies in Classic American Literature* (1923), "Never trust the artist. Trust the tale."

Analyzing Theme

1. Does the work have a theme? Is it stated or implied?
2. What generalization(s) or statement(s) about life or human experience does the work make?
3. What elements of the work contribute most heavily to the formulation of the theme?
4. Does the theme emerge organically and naturally, or does the author seem to force the theme upon the work?
5. What is the value or significance of the work's theme? Is it topical or universal in its application?

SYMBOL AND ALLEGORY

Symbol

A symbol, according to Webster's Dictionary, is "something that stands for or suggests something else by reason of relationship, association, convention, or accidental resemblance . . . a visible sign of something invisible." Symbols, in this sense, are with us all the time, for there are few words or objects that do not evoke, at least in certain contexts, a wide range of associated meanings and feelings. For example, the word *home* (as opposed to *house*) conjures up feelings of warmth and security and personal associations of family, friends, and neighborhood, the American flag suggests country and patriotism. Human beings, by virtue of their capacity for language, are symbol-making creatures. As Melville's Ishmael muses in the famous "Doubloon" chapter of *Moby-Dick:* "And some certain significance lurks in all things, else all things are little worth, and the round world itself but an empty cipher, except to sell by the cartload, as they do hills about Boston, to fill up some morass in the Milky Way."

Most of our daily symbol making and symbol reading is unconscious and accidental, the inescapable product of our experience as human beings. In literature, however, symbols—in the form of words, images, objects, settings, events and characters—are often used deliberately to suggest and reinforce meaning, to provide enrichment by enlarging and clarifying the experience of the work, and to help to organize and unify the whole. William York Tindall likens a literary symbol to "a metaphor one half of which remains unstated and indefinite."[13] The analogy is a good one. Although symbols exist first as something literal and concrete within the work itself, they also have the capacity to call to mind a range of invisible and abstract associations, both intellectual and emotional, that transcend the literal and concrete and extend their meaning. A literary symbol brings together what is material and concrete within the work (the visible half of Tindall's metaphor) with its series of associations (that "which remains unstated and indefinite"); by fusing them, however briefly, in the reader's imagination, new layers and dimensions of meaning, suggestiveness, and significance are added.

The identification and understanding of literary symbols require a great deal from the reader. They demand awareness and intelligence: an ability to detect when the emphasis an author places on certain elements within the work can be legitimately said to carry those elements to larger, symbolic overtones, and when the author means to imply nothing beyond what is literally stated. They also make demands on the reader's maturity and sophistication, for only when we are sufficiently experienced with the world will the literal and concrete strike an appropriate symbolic chord. If, that is to say, we have not had the occasion to think much or think deeply about life and experience it is not likely that we will be able to detect, much less understand, the larger hidden meanings to which symbols point. As Tindall observes, "What the reader gets from a symbol depends not only upon what the author has put into it but upon the reader's sensitivity and his consequent apprehension of what is there."[14]

However, there are dangers as well. Although the author's use of symbol may be unconscious as well as conscious, ours is an age in which the conscious and deliberate use of symbolism defines much of our literary art, as the criticism of the past forty years amply bears witness. There is, consequently, a tendency among students of literature, especially beginning students, to forget that all art contains a mixture of both the literal and the symbolic and to engage in a form

[13] William York Tindall, *The Literary Symbol* (New York: Columbia University Press, 1955), p. 12.

[14] Ibid., p. 17.

of indiscriminate "symbol hunting" that either unearths symbols and symbolic meanings where none are intended or pushes the interpretation of legitimate symbols beyond what is reasonable and proper. Both temptations must be avoided.

It is perfectly true, of course, that the meaning of any symbol is, by definition, indefinite and open-ended, and that a given symbol will evoke a slightly different response in different readers, no matter how discriminating. Yet there is an acceptable range of possible readings for any symbol beyond which we must not stray. We are always limited in our interpretation of symbols by the total context of the work in which they occur and by the way in which the author has established and arranged its other elements; we are not free to superimpose—from the outside—our personal and idiosyncratic meanings simply because they appeal to us. Finally, in working with symbols we must also be careful to avoid the danger of becoming so preoccupied with the larger significance and meaning that we forget the literal importance of the concrete thing being symbolized. Moby Dick, for all he may be said to represent to Ahab, Ishmael, Starbuck, Flask, Stubb, Herman Melville, and finally to the reader, is still a whale, a living, breathing mammal of the deep that is capable of inflicting crushing damage on those who pursue him too closely.

Symbols are often classified as being traditional, original, or private, depending on the source of the associations that provide their meanings. *Traditional symbols* are those whose associations are the common property of a society or a culture and are so widely recognized and accepted that they can be said to be almost universal. The symbolic associations that generally accompany the forest and the sea, the moon and the sun, night and day, the colors black, white and red, and the seasons of the year are examples of traditional symbols. They are so much a part of our culture that we take their significance pretty much for granted. A special kind of traditional symbol is the *archetype,* a term that derives from anthropologist James G. Frazer's famous study of myth and ritual *The Golden Bough* (1890–1915) and the depth psychology of Carl Jung. (Jung holds that certain symbols are so deeply rooted in what were the repeated and shared experiences of our common ancestors—he refers to them as the "collective unconsciousness" of the human race—as to evoke an immediate and strong, if unconscious, response in any reader.) Hawthorne's use of blackness in "Young Goodman Brown," with its obvious overtones of mystery, evil, and satanism, is an example of an archetypal symbol. The very initiation ceremony that Goodman hastens to attend also has archetypal significance; Frazer discovered that such rites exist everywhere in the cultural patterns of the past and continue to exert a powerful influence on the patterns of our behavior.

Original symbols are those whose associations are neither immediate nor traditional and that derive their meaning, largely if not exclusively, from the context of the work in which they are used. Melville's white whale is an original symbol, for while whales are often associated in the popular imagination with brute strength and cunning, Moby Dick assumes his larger, metaphysical significance (for Ahab he is the pasteboard mask behind which lurks the pent-up malignity of the universe) only within the contextual limits of Melville's novel. Outside that novel, Moby Dick is just a whale.

Private symbols restrict the source of their meaning even more than original symbols. Just as all of us have certain objects in our lives that call to mind a variety of private associations (in the way a family heirloom does), certain authors employ symbols that are the products of their own peculiar and idiosyncratic systems of philosophy or belief, as is the case with a number of the symbols found in the poetry of William Blake and William Butler Yeats. Private symbols, by virtue of their source, are esoteric and largely unintelligible, except to those whom the author—or that author's critics and interpreters—has succeeded in educating. Fortunately, most of the symbols that the average reader encounters are either traditional or original. The presence of traditional symbols, it should be noted, does not mean that we are free to ignore the framing context of the work and to impose from the outside one pattern or another as we see fit. Traditional symbols, for all their accompanying associations, must always be established by the context of the work and find their significance inside the work, not beyond it.

Symbols operating at the level of individual words and combinations of words called images are crucial to the art of poetry, and for their discussion the reader is referred to the discussion of poetry that follows. In this section, we will briefly consider how writers of fiction employ symbols in conjunction with setting, plot, and character.

SETTING AND SYMBOL. In a number of the examples used in the preceding section on setting—Hardy's Egdon Heath, Crane's snow-surrounded blue hotel, Roderick Usher's house, and the city streets through which Robin Molineux roams in search of his kinsman—we noted how the details of setting are used functionally, to extend, clarify, and reinforce the author's larger intention and meaning. We also called attention to the ways in which authors employ the seasons of the year and the time of day because of the traditional associations they have for the reader. Those identifications are not arbitrary ones, for in each of the works cited the author deliberately calls attention to the setting, not once but on several occasions, in a way that suggests that it is integrally related to his larger purposes. In the case of Hardy and Crane, it is to call attention to the thematic implications of the work; in the case of Poe and Hawthorne, it is to help reveal the personalities of their characters. Setting in fiction that goes beyond mere backdrop is often used in such symbolic ways. Symbolic settings are particularly useful to authors when they frame and encompass the events of plot and thus provide the work as a whole with an overarching pattern of unity.

One further example of the symbolic use of setting should suffice. F. Scott Fitzgerald begins the second chapter of *The Great Gatsby* with a lengthy description of a barren wasteland—"a valley of ashes"—that lies halfway between West Egg, Long Island, where Nick Carraway lives, and New York City. In the middle of this desolate landscape stands a weatherbeaten billboard depicting a gigantic pair of eyes framed by an "enormous" pair of yellow spectacles and advertising the services of one Doctor T. J. Eckleburg. Nick surmises that the eyes and spectacles are the work of "some wild wag of an occulist [who] set them there to fatten his practice in the borough of Queens, and then sank down himself into eternal blindness, or forgot them and moved away." Their strategic location in the story, and the fact that they are referred to throughout the work, suggests that the brooding eyes of Doctor Eckleburg and the ash-filled expanse on which they look out are functionally related to the novel and are intended to signal some larger meaning. One of the characters ironically likens them to the eyes of God who "sees everything." In the context of the novel, however (and remember, where symbolism is concerned, context is always crucially important), Doctor Eckleburg's eyes would hardly seem to represent such a benign and hopeful view of things. Rather, they are generally interpreted as symbolizing Fitzgerald's fatalistic view of modern life, a view that at once calls to mind the wasteland of T. S. Eliot's famous poem.

Plot and symbol. Single events of plot, large or small, or plots in their entirety often function symbolically. *Moby-Dick* is literally filled with examples of the former, and in each of the cases cited here Melville deliberately calls the reader's attention to the event by setting it off in a brief, appropriately titled chapter that forces the reader to consider its larger significance. In Chapter XXX ("The Pipe"), Ahab hurls his pipe into the sea ("This thing is meant for sereneness, to send up mild white vapors among mild white hairs, not among iron-grey locks like mine. I'll smoke no more—"), an act that suggests Ahab's lack of inner tranquility and his growing social isolation from the members of his crew. In confirmation of this interpretation, the alert reader will recall two earlier scenes in the Spouter-Inn at New Bedford, where Ishmael and his new-found friend, the giant harpooner Queequeg, share a pipe together in celebration of the ancient ritual of friendship and solidarity. Later in the novel (Chapter CXVIII, "The Quadrant"), as the Pequod approaches its appointed rendezvous with the great white whale, Ahab seizes the ship's quadrant and smashes it ("no longer will I guide my earthly way by thee"), a symbolic gesture signaling the monomaniacal captain's arrogant assertion of his own power and omnipotence; from that moment onward, the destiny of ship and crew is to be squarely in his own hands.

In both examples, Melville encourages his reader to seek larger significance and meaning in what might otherwise be overlooked as small and apparently insignificant actions. And in both examples, our ability to interpret these actions correctly—to see their symbolic importance—increases our understanding of Captain Ahab. In most instances, however, the author will not be so obliging. Although it is certainly true that even the most commonplace action or event—even to the level of a gesture, if it is spontaneous and unconscious—can carry symbolic meaning, it is often difficult, at least upon first reading, to tell for certain whether symbolism is involved. Its symbolic character may not become clear until we have finished the work and look backward to see how the individual parts of the plot relate to the whole. In Hawthorne's "My Kinsman, Major Molineux," for example, it may not be clear until the end of the story that each of the separate incidents that punctuate Robin's journey in search of his kinsman form a chain of symbolic events that are an integral part of his ritual of initiation.

When the entire sequence of events that constitutes a plot falls into a symbolic pattern, as in "My Kinsman, Major Molineux" and "Young Goodman Brown," the events are often archetypal. Such a plot, that is, conforms to basic patterns of human behavior so deeply rooted in our experience that they recur ritualistically, time and time again, in the events of myth, folklore, and narrative literature. In fiction, perhaps the most frequently encountered archetypal pattern is the journey or quest, in which young men and women undergo a series of trials and ordeals that finally confirm their rite of passage from innocence to maturity. Such a pattern underlies not only the plots of the two Hawthorne stories cited here but a surprisingly large number of the other works used earlier as examples, including Fielding's *Tom Jones,* Melville's *Moby-Dick,* Dickens's *Great Expectations,* Conrad's "The Secret Sharer," Joyce's "Araby," Fitzgerald's *The Great Gatsby,* and Hemingway's "The Killers."

CHARACTER AND SYMBOL. Symbolism is frequently employed as a way of deepening our understanding of character. Some characters are given symbolic names to suggest underlying moral, intellectual, or emotional qualities. The name "Robin Molineux," for example, suggests springtime, youth, and innocence, while the name "Roger Chillingsworth" (Hester Prynne's husband in *The Scarlet Letter*) suggests cold intellectuality and lack of human warmth, in keeping with his demonic character. The objects assigned to characters function in the same way: the heavy oak cudgel that Robin carries with him into the city is a symbol of his youthful aggressiveness; Faith Brown's pink ribbons (which blend the traditional red of sin and sexuality with the traditional white of purity and innocence) confirm the ambiguity of her role in "Young Goodman Brown"; Ahab's ivory leg, the badge of his first encounter with Moby Dick, serves to objectify the psychic wound that gnaws at him from within; and Gabriel Conroy's preoccupation with galoshes in James Joyce's "The Dead" suggests his cautious and conservative nature.

Characters who undergo the kind of archetypal experiences discussed here are often referred to as archetypal characters. But while the personalities of major characters are often revealed and clarified through the use of symbols rooted in the language that describes them, their very complexity as human beings usually prevents their being defined by a single symbol. This is not true of minor characters, especially those who are flat and one-dimensional and are "constructed round a single idea or quality."[15] Fiction is filled with such individuals. Leggatt, the escaped convict who intrudes his presence on the insecure and untested young captain in Conrad's "The Secret Sharer" comes to symbolize the captain's subconscious self, or alter ego. Until Leggatt leaves the ship—until, that is, the captain's conscious and subconscious selves become integrated—the captain is prevented from attaining "that ideal conception of one's own personality every man sets up for himself secretly." Bartleby, the abject scrivener of Melville's story, can be said to symbolize a negative view of life which recoils before a universe which he either cannot or will not accept. By the time the story begins, Bartleby has weighed the world by his own obscure standards and found it unacceptable. But unlike the aggressive, openly defiant Captain Ahab, Bartleby's resistance takes the form of an ever-increasing passivity and solitude, as symbolized by the lofty brick wall beyond his window and his own "dead wall reveries." And, finally, in Shirley Jackson's story "The Lottery," Old Man Warner, who has participated in the lottery on seventy-six previous occasions and has become its chief defender ("There's always been a lottery"), symbolizes blind subservience to an established ritual that has long since ceased to have a rational purpose.

Symbolism thus enhances fiction by holding "the parts of a literary work together in the service of the whole"[16] in such a way as to help readers organize and enlarge their experience of the work. This is not to say that a work of fiction containing symbolism is inherently better than or superior to one that does not. Nor is it to say that the use of symbolism in and of itself can make a given work successful. It is to say that symbolism, when employed as an integral and organic part of the language and structure of a work of fiction, can stimulate and release the imagination—which is, after all, one of the chief goals of any form of art.

Allegory

Allegory is a technique for expanding the meaning of a literary work by having the characters, and sometimes the setting and the

[15] Forster, loc. cit. pp. 103–104.
[16] Tindall, op. cit., p. 16.

events, represent certain general abstract ideas, qualities, or concepts, usually moral, religious, or political in nature. Unlike symbolism,[17] the abstractions of allegory are fixed and definite and tend to take the form of simple and specific ideas that, once identified, can be readily understood. Because they remain constant, they also are easily remembered. In their purest form, works of allegory operate consistently and simultaneously at two separate but parallel levels of meaning: one located inside the work itself, at the concrete surface level of plot and character; the other, outside the work, at the level of the particular ideas or qualities to which these internal elements point. Such works function best when these two levels reinforce and complement each another: we read the work as narrative, but we are also aware of the ideas that lie beyond the concrete representations. Allegories tend to break down when the author's focus and emphasis shifts in the direction of the abstract, when we have reason to suspect that the characters, for example, exist only for the sake of the ideas they represent. At such times, our interest in the narrative inevitably falls away and we tend to read the work for the message or thesis it promotes.

In the most famous sustained prose allegory in the English language, John Bunyan's *The Pilgrim's Progress* (published in two parts, in 1678 and 1684), the didactic impulse always latent within allegory is very clear. *Pilgrim's Progress* is a moral and religious allegory of the Christian soul in search of salvation. It tells the story of an individual, appropriately named "Christian," who, warned by the Evangelist to leave his home in the City of Destruction, sets off with his pack (containing his load of worldly sins) to seek the Celestial City (heaven). His road, however, is a long and difficult one, and at every turn Christian meets individuals and obstacles whose names and personalities (or characteristics) embody the ideals, virtues, and vices for which they stand: Mr. Worldly Wiseman (who dwells in the town of Carnal-Policy), Mistrust, Timorous, Faithful (who tells about his own encounters with Pliable, Discontent, Shame, and Talkative), Giant Despair (who holds Christian prisoner for a time in Doubting Castle), the Slough of Despond, the Valley of the Shadow of Death, Hill Difficulty, and so on.

[17] Allegory and symbolism are not antithetical; in fact, allegory can be said to be a simplified form of symbolism. Allegory, like symbolism, functions as a type of metaphor, but in the case of allegory, the two halves of the metaphor are stated and definite.

Although such works of pure allegory as Bunyan's *Pilgrim's Progress* and Edmund Spenser's *The Faerie Queene* are relatively rare, many works make extended use of allegory (Jonathan Swift's *Gulliver's Travels,* Nathaniel Hawthorne's *The Scarlet Letter,* William Golding's *The Lord of the Flies,* and George Orwell's *Animal Farm*), and many more make occasional use of allegory, not infrequently combined with symbolism. As a fictional mode of presentation, however, allegory is unquestionably out of favor among modern and contemporary authors and critics, for reasons that have to do with the nature of allegory itself. First of all, the didacticism of allegory and its tendency toward a simplified, if not simplistic, view of life is suspect in a world where there is very little common agreement about truth and the validity of certain once universally respected ideas and ideals. Second, the way allegory presents character is simply not in keeping with the modern conception of fictional characterization. In allegory the characters, and the ideas and ideals those characters embody, are presented as given. The modern author, on the other hand, prefers to build characters and to develop and reveal their personalities gradually, in stages, throughout the course of the work. And, finally, twentieth-century critics, tend to be intolerant of any literary work whose meaning is not totally contained within the structure of the work.

Hawthorne's "Young Goodman Brown" contains clear instances of allegory. Goodman Brown's name, and the names of several of the minor characters (Old Goody Cloyse and Deacon Gookin) suggest, perhaps ironically, that they are to be counted among the religiously upright. And the name of Goodman Brown's wife, Faith, as her husband's comments consistently remind us, is intended to represent the traditional religious faith that Brown forsakes for the purposes of his journey into the forest and then loses entirely: "after this one night I'll cling to her skirts and follow her to heaven;" "Faith kept me back a while;" "With heaven above and Faith below, I will yet stand firm against the devil!"; "My Faith is gone". Some critics, in fact, insist that the entire story is to be read and interpreted allegorically as an illustration of the theological doctrines of Puritan Calvinism. The same kind of allegorical reading has been suggested for "My Kinsman, Major Molineux." Read as an historical and political allegory of America's coming of age and maturation as a young and independent nation, Robin can be said to represent colonial America and his kinsman, the British colonial authority that must be displaced and overthrown. Both Robin and colonial America share a number of common characteristics: both have rural, agrarian origins; both are young and strong, yet insecure and self-conscious because they are untested and inexperienced in the ways of the world; both are pious and proud (even arrogant) and given to aggressive behavior; and both have a reputation, deserved or not, for native "shrewdness." Just as Robin learns that he can "rise in the world without the help of [his] . . . kinsman, Major Molineux," so colonial America realizes that it can achieve its destiny as a mature and independent nation without the paternalistic control of Great Britain.

Although most modern writers prefer symbolism to allegory as a technique for enlarging the meaning of their works, allegory continues to make an occasional appearance in modern and contemporary fiction, particularly among such writers as C. S. Lewis, George Orwell, and William Golding whose work is underscored by a strong philosophical, political, or religious vision. The names of many of the fictional creations of Flannery O'Connor, who confessed that she felt "more of a kinship with Hawthorne than with any other American writer," openly hint that they exemplify the kind of abstractions we associate with allegory (Joy Hopewell, Mrs. Freeman, Manley Pointer, Grandmother Godhigh, Mrs. Chestny, Mr. Head, Mrs. Cope, Mr. Cheatam, Mr. Greenleaf, Mrs. May). When authors like Flannery O'Connor do employ allegorical names, they usually take care not to allow the names to carry the full burden of characterization. O'Connor's characters are far more complex individuals than the single qualities of their names suggest.

Analyzing Symbol and Allegory

1. What symbols or patterns of symbolism (or allegory) are present in the work? Are the symbols traditional, original or private?
2. What aspects of the work (e.g., theme, setting, plot, characterization) does the symbolism (allegory) serve to explain, clarify, or reinforce?
3. Does the author's use of symbolism (allegory) seem contrived or forced in any way, or does it arise naturally out of the interplay of the story's major elements?

STYLE AND TONE

Style

The distinctive quality of literature that sets it apart from all other forms of artistic expression is its reliance on language. Using words is the writer's craft. They are the writer's means of recovering and objectifying experience; they are his or her means of presenting, shaping, and controlling subject matter. Language is also the means by which the writer controls and influences the reader: in responding to literature we are always responding *to* and *through* the author's words. The literary critic must pay close attention to those words, not only because they convey the sum and substance of the author's message—the story he wishes to tell—but because they provide important clues to the author's emotional and psychological life, beliefs, and attitudes and to the way in which he perceives and experiences himself and the world around him.

When we talk about an author's words and the characteristic ways he uses the resources of language to achieve certain effects, we are talking about *style*. In its most general sense, style consists of *diction* (the individual words an author chooses) and *syntax* (the arrangement of those words into phrases, clauses, and sentences), as well as such devices as rhythm and sound, allusion, ambiguity, irony, paradox, and figurative language. The latter elements of style are crucial to the art of poetry; they are discussed in the following section. We will touch on them here, in order to establish that the language of fiction, no less than the language of poetry and drama, is distinguished by the author's ability to make full and effective use of the language at his or her command.

Each writer's style is unique. "Every writer," British critic David Lodge notes in his *Language of Fiction,* "displays his own unique 'signature' in the way he uses language, something which all his works, however diverse, have in common, and which distinguishes them from the work of any other writer. . . ."[18] One test of the distinctiveness of an author's style is its ability to resist paraphrase. The test is relatively simple. Take a passage from any well-regarded work and rephrase it. Although the underlying ideas may remain the same, the words themselves will probably register a quite different effect on

[18] David Lodge, *Language of Fiction: Essays in Criticism and Verbal Analysis of the English Novel* (London: Routledge and K. Paul, 1966), p. 50.

you. Much the same dilemma is faced by the translator, who attempts to reproduce faithfully the stylistic qualities of an author's poetry or prose. The words may have translatable equivalents, but what they often lack in translation are the emotional qualities and nuances of their originals. "We are conscious, reading him in a language not his own," Henry James observed of an attempt to translate Turgenev from the Russian, "of not being reached by his personal tone, his individual accent." The reason, of course, takes us back to the very medium of the writer. That medium, Lodge observes, "differs from the media of most other arts—pigment, stone, musical notes, etc.—in that it is never virgin: words come to the writer already violated by other men, impressed with meanings derived from the world of common experience."[19] In the case of Ivan Turgenev, that experience, the product of a certain man living at a certain time and place, goes far toward explaining the origin of those distinctive elements of style that apparently eluded his translator.

By examining the style of a work of fiction we are seeking as critics to accomplish a number of objectives. First of all, we are seeking to isolate and identify those distinctive traits and characteristics that comprise the author's "signature." Second, we are interested in understanding the effects produced by particular stylistic devices and techniques and how these effects influence our response to the work's other elements—particularly character, incident, setting, and theme—and to the work as a whole. Third, we are attempting, by way of evaluation, to arrive at a judgment based on a consideration of just how effectively the author has managed to integrate form and content. This examination is an attempt to measure just how well an author has succeeded in a given work with the style he or she has chosen. It is not intended to demonstrate, or even imply, the inherent superiority of one author's style—or one kind of style—over another, although comparisons can of course be made.

DICTION. Although words are usually meaningful only in the context of other words, stylistic analysis begins with the attempt to identify and understand the type and quality of the individual words that comprise an author's basic vocabulary. When used in connection with characterization, words are the vehicles by which a character's ideas, attitudes, and values are expressed. Words convey the details

[19] Ibid., p. 47.

of outer appearance and inner state of mind. In dialogue they reflect the speaker's intelligence and sophistication, general level of conscious awareness, and socioeconomic, geographical, and educational background. When used to describe incidents, words help to convey the narrator's (or author's) attitude toward those events and the characters involved in them. When used to describe setting, words help to create and sustain an appropriate atmosphere.

The analysis of diction includes the following considerations: the *denotative* (or dictionary) meaning of words, as opposed to their *connotative* meaning (the ideas associated with or suggested by them); their degree of concreteness or abstractness; their degree of allusiveness; the parts of speech they represent; their length and construction; the level of usage they reflect (standard or nonstandard; formal, informal, or colloquial); the imagery (details of sensory experience) they contain; the figurative devices (simile, metaphor, personification) they embody; their rhythm and sound patterns (alliteration, assonance, consonance, onomatopoeia). In studying diction, we also need to pay close attention to the use of repetition: the way key words recur in a given passage or series of passages in such a way as to call special attention to themselves.

SYNTAX. When we examine style at the level of syntax, we are attempting to analyze the ways the author arranges words into phrases, clauses, and finally whole sentences to achieve particular effects. Although syntax is determined partly by the lexical content (or meaning) of the words and partly by the basic grammatical structure of the language, every writer enjoys considerable freedom to shape and control the syntactic elements of style. In looking at an author's syntax we want to know how the words have been arranged and particularly how they deviate from the normal and expected.

Although one can study syntactic units smaller than the sentence—for example individual phrases that call attention to themselves by their length, construction, and placement—syntax is probably most easily approached and analyzed in sentences. Such an approach mirrors most closely the writing process itself, for sentences are the major units of thought, and it is on the crafting of sentence that most authors concentrate their creative energies. Sentences can be examined in terms of their length—whether they are short, spare, and economical or long and involved; in terms of their form—whether they are simple, compound, or complex; and in terms of their construction—whether they are *loose* (sentences that follow the normal subject-verb-object pattern, stating their main idea near the beginning in the form of an independent clause), *periodic* (sentences that deliberately withhold or suspend the completion of the main idea until the end of the sentence), or *balanced* (sentences in which two similar or antithetical ideas are balanced).

Each type of sentence will have a slightly different effect on the reader. Long, complicated sentences slow down and retard the pace of a narrative, whereas short, simple sentences hasten it. Loose sentences, because they follow the normal, predictable patterns of speech, tend to appear more natural and less contrived than either periodic or balanced sentences, particularly when they are used in the creation of dialogue. Moreover, the deliberate arrangement of words within individual sentences or groups of sentences can result in patterns of rhythm and sound (pleasant or unpleasant) that establish or reinforce feeling and emotion. Although an author will usually vary the kinds of sentences used in order to avoid monotony (unless that is the intention), certain syntactic patterns will dominate and become characteristic of that author's style.

Because stylistic analysis is generally carried out by isolating and examining one or more representative passages from a given work, the following five examples may prove illustrative.

> I was born in the year 1632, in the City of York, of a good family, tho' not of that country, my father being a foreigner of Bremen, who settled first at Hull. He got a good estate by merchandise, and leaving off his trade, lived afterward at York, from whence he had married my mother, whose relations were named *Robinson,* a very good family in that country, and from whom I was called *Robinson Kreutznaer;* but by the usual corruption of words in England, we are now called, nay, we call our selves, and write our name Crusoe, and so my companions always call'd me.
>
> —from *The Life and Adventures of Robinson Crusoe,* Daniel Defoe (1719)

Stylistic Analysis: In this first paragraph of the novel, the narrator (Robinson Crusoe) is intent on establishing his voice and identity as a real person with a family history. It is composed of two loose, fairly intricate sentences (one in some editions) in which the main clause is followed by a series of phrases and clauses that add concrete and denotative facts and detail, by way of additional information. The single exception to this emphasis on fact is the repetition of the judgmental adjective *good* ("good family," "good estate," "good family"), which is intended to lend an impression of stability and respectability to an otherwise neutral description, whose details are irrelevant to the story that Defoe wants to tell.

The style is simple and straightforward, much as you would expect from someone trying to persuade us that he is a real person worthy of belief. Note, for example, how Crusoe scrupulously catches himself in mid-sentence in order to set the record straight: "we are now called, nay, we call ourselves." The reader is being skillfully imposed upon by the author's calculated use of language: once we are willing to believe in the fundamental honesty and sincerity of the narrator—a man who pays close attention to facts and who obviously lacks verbal pretension—we are likely to accept pretty much at face value the authenticity of the exciting adventures that are to follow.

> During the whole of a dull, dark, and soundless day in the autumn of the year, when the clouds hung oppressively low in the heavens, I had been passing alone, on horseback, through a singularly dreary tract of country; and at length found myself, as the shades of evening drew on, within view of the melancholy House of Usher. I know not how it was—but, with the first glimpse of the building, a sense of insufferable gloom pervaded my spirit. I say insufferable; for the feeling was unrelieved by any of that half-pleasurable, because poetic, sentiment, with which the mind usually receives even the sternest natural images of the desolute or terrible.
>
> —from "The Fall of the House of Usher," Edgar Allan Poe (1839)

Stylistic Analysis. In this first paragraph of the story, the unnamed narrator, Roderick Usher's boyhood acquaintance, first approaches the melancholy and decaying house. Poe's obvious intent is to establish, from the outset, the appropriate setting and atmosphere for the story—one that will simultaneously arrest the reader's attention and evoke an appropriate emotional response. The opening sentence, surely one of the most famous in all of American literature, is a long, periodic one, in which a series of rhythmic phrases and clauses are deliberately arranged to suspend, until the very end, and so prepare the way for, the object of the narrator's search. Within the sentence, Poe carefully intensifies his visual details with adjectives and adverbs and reinforces their effect through the use of alliteration and onomatopoeia. The second and third sentences, which record the narrator's response to the scene, continue to invite the reader to respond in the same way. Poe's emotion-charged prose is clearly excessive (note the use of such words as "oppressively," "dreary," "melancholy," "insufferable," "half-pleasurable," "sternest," "desolute," and "terrible"), yet its very excess effectively establishes the mood that is to dominate and surround the story from beginning to end.

> I was pretty tired, and the first thing I knowed, I was asleep. When I woke up I didn't know where I was, for a minute. I set up and looked around, a little scared. Then I remembered. The river looked miles and miles across. The moon was so bright I could a counted the drift logs that went a slipping along, black and still, hundred of yards out from shore. Everything was dead quiet, and it looked late, and *smelt* late. You know what I mean—I don't know the words to put it in.
>
> —from *The Adventures of Huckleberry Finn,* Mark Twain (1885)

Stylistic Analysis. When Ernest Hemingway wrote in his *Green Hills of Africa* (1935) that "All modern American literature comes from one book by Mark Twain called *Huckleberry Finn,*" he was referring to the realism of Mark Twain's style, which differs so markedly from the heavy, formal, "literary" prose of writers like Poe. The defining qualities of Mark Twain's style—which does, clearly, look ahead to the twentieth century—are very much in evidence in this passage. Huck Finn is speaking in a voice and manner appropriate to a largely self-educated rural adolescent. Note his informal, colloquial language, with its small grammatical flaws, his simple, uncomplicated, relaxed sentences, and the sparse, yet vivid, imagery he uses to describe the moonlit river—all of which convey the impression of something real, honestly reported. His final confession of inadequacy, although hardly necessary, is perfectly in keeping with a character who constantly refuses to falsify his experience of the world.

> The narrow creek was like a ditch: tortuous, fabulously deep; filled with gloom under the thin strip of pure and shining blue of the heaven. Immense trees soared up, invisible behind the festooned draperies of the creepers. Here and there, near the glistening blackness of the water, a twisted root of some tall tree showed amongst the tracery of small ferns, black and dull, writhing and motionless, like an arrested snake. The short words of the paddlers reverberated loudly between the thick and somber walls of vegetation. Darkness oozed out from between the trees, through the tangled maze of the creepers, from behind the great fantastic and unstirring leaves; the darkness, mysterious and invincible; the darkness scented and poisonous of impenetrable forests.
>
> —from "The Lagoon," Joseph Conrad (1897)

Stylistic Analysis. Conrad's style differs markedly from Mark Twain's. Although Conrad's sentences are relatively short, the general impression created by the diction and syntax is one of density—as dense as the forest he describes. His aim here is to establish a setting and atmosphere that are exotic, strange, and ominous, and he does so by creating, chiefly by means of rich and evocative adjectives, a series of near-poetic images that appeal to sight, sound, and smell. His adjectives are striking: "tortuous," "pure and shining," "immense," "festooned," "glistening," "twisted," "black and dull, writhing and motionless," "thick and somber," "tangled," "fantastic and unstirring," "mysterious and invincible," "impenetrable." His style, in short, is perfectly in keeping with his own famous statement: "My task which I am trying to achieve is, by the power of the written word, to make you hear, to make you feel—it is, before all, to make you *see*."

"What's he going to do?"
"Nothing."
"They'll kill him."
"He must have got mixed up in something in Chicago."
"I guess so," said Nick.
"It's a hell of a thing."
"It's an awful thing," Nick said.
They did not say anything. George reached down for a towel and wiped the counter.
"I wonder what he did?" Nick said.
"Double-crossed somebody. That's what they kill them for."
"I'm going to get out of this town," Nick said.
"Yes," said George. "That's a good thing to do."
"I can't stand to think about him waiting in the room and knowing he's going to get it. It's too damned awful."
"Well," said George, "you better not think about it."

—from "The Killers," Ernest Hemingway (1927)

Stylistic Analysis. In this concluding passage from Hemingway's story, Nick Adams has just returned to the diner after failing to persuade the ex-prize fighter Ole Andreson to flee the two mobsters who want to kill him. For Nick, who is young and still unwilling to accept the inevitability of such brutality, the experience is overpowering and too much to bear. His instinctive reaction is to flee. For the older and wiser George, however, there are other, safer ways to cope: " 'Well,' said George, 'you better not think about it.' "

This is the celebrated Hemingway style at its best: an economical, terse, "masculine" style, characterized by short, simple sentences and active verbs; an informal, commonplace vocabulary of short, denotative words; the absence of unnecessary adjectives and adverbs; an emphasis on dialogue; and a concentration on particular concrete images that record the surface level of experience. For Hemingway, style is more than simple mannerism: it is his response to twentieth-century life, in which reality is painful and is to be endured by imposing tight order and control on actions and emotions. In Hemingway's fiction, emotion remains largely beneath the surface of events; it is expressed indirectly and is understated (" 'It's a hell of a thing.'/'It's an awful thing,' Nick said."), because to expose one's feelings is to risk the possibility of psychic injury.

The preceding examples illustrate how style can be used to serve characterization (Defoe and Mark Twain), the creation of setting and atmosphere (Poe and Conrad), and the reinforcement of theme (Hemingway). They also illustrate the dynamic, changing nature of the language of fiction itself. In comparing the style of Poe to the style of Hemingway, for example, we can see a movement toward less formality and more concrete diction, as well as a simpler syntax; the differences reflect the modern tendency toward realism in fiction. Generalizations about style can be dangerous, however, as examples from more contemporary fiction would make clear. Style is a highly personal, and sometimes a highly idiosyncratic, matter, open to endless opportunities for innovation and experimentation. Although some fictional styles are easier to read and understand than others, and although all readers sooner or later come to express stylistic preferences, there is, finally, no one style that is best or most appropriate. The critic's job is not to state preferences but to render judgments: to try to understand the distinctive elements that comprise an author's style, the various effects that those elements create, and the way in which they serve to reveal and reinforce the other elements of the work.

Tone

All of us are familiar with the term *tone* as it is used to characterize the special qualities of accent, inflection, and duration in a speaker's voice. From early childhood on we learn to identify and respond to these elements of speech. For example, a mother can tell her child to "Come here!" in a manner that is angry, threatening, concerned, amused, sympathetic, or affectionate, simply by altering her tone of voice. In each case, the mother's meaning is the same—she wants her child to come. However, the relationship she creates with her auditor (the child) will differ dramatically according to her tone. Tone, then, is a means of creating a relationship or conveying an attitude. The particular qualities of a speaking voice are unavailable to a writer in creating tone, but to a certain extent rhythm and punctuation can substitute for a speaker's accent and inflection, while word order and word choice can influence tone as easily in prose as in speech.

Just as the tone of the mother's voice communicates her attitude of anger or concern, so tone in fiction is frequently a guide to an author's attitude toward the subject or audience. For example, one recognizes at once the friendly, informal, and folksy tone of Huck Finn's introduction to his adventures:

> You don't know about me, without you have read a book by the name of *The Adventures of Tom Sawyer,* but that ain't no matter.

Huck wants to make us his friends, so he writes just as he would speak, without striving for grammatical perfection. As soon as he realizes that we might be put off by the sense of self-importance in his allusion to *The Adventures of Tom Sawyer,* he reassures us that it "ain't no matter" if we have failed to read the book. The tone and content of the sentence combine to indicate that Huck wants us to like him and that he wants to like us.

In contrast, in Mark Twain's preface to *Huckleberry Finn* his tone is threatening at the same time that it is ironic and humorous:

> NOTICE
>
> Persons attempting to find a motive in this narrative will be prosecuted; persons attempting to find a moral in it will be banished; persons attempting to find a plot in it will be shot.
>
> BY ORDER OF THE AUTHOR
> Per G. G., CHIEF OF ORDNANCE

We are not accustomed to such threats from authors, and our first reaction might be shock—after that, perhaps confusion. Why should Mark Twain make threats that are obviously exaggerated and impossible to carry out? Why, indeed, except to attract our attention to the novel's motive, moral, and plot. We may be amused by the author's obvious antipathy to literary critics and literary criticism, but we may also feel slightly goaded, a bit more eager to look for a motive, moral, and plot anywhere we damned well please! And after a moment we may recognize that Mark Twain's purpose in including this notice must have been to obtain just such a reaction; he forbids us to examine his book's literary meaning in order to suggest ironically that it does have serious literary purposes. Thus, although Huck's tone has accurately reflected his attitude toward the reader, it is doubtful that the same is true of Mark Twain's "Notice." His tone is ironic and he means just the opposite of what he says.

As these examples indicate, an author's tone is linked closely to intention and meaning; the tone must be inferred from a close and careful study of the various elements within the work, including plot, character, setting, point of view, and style.[20]

No matter how hard an author tries to mask his attitudes and feelings, and to hide his presence within the work, perhaps by taking refuge somewhere behind the narrative voice that tells the story, the author's tone can be inferred by the choices he makes in the process of ordering and presenting his material: by what is included and emphasized and what, by contrast, is omitted. In such choices lie what Wayne Booth refers to as "the implicit evaluation which the author manages to convey behind his explicit presentation."[21] The literary critic learns to look at such choices carefully—at the characters, incidents, setting, and details depicted; at the issues and problems that are raised and explored; at the style the author has employed; at every decision, in short, that the author has made—in order to infer from them the underlying attitudes and tone that color and control the work as a whole. The task is not at all an easy one, and for this reason tone is perhaps the most difficult and elusive of all the literary elements we have thus far discussed.

IRONY. When Huckleberry Finn steps forward to introduce himself, he is both frank and open, and there is little reason to believe

[20] It should be noted that the author-speaker who determines the tone of the work and to whom the reader responds may or may not be, and often is not, the historical author who wrote the work. The concept of the "implied author" and "the intricate relationship of the so-called real author with his various official versions of himself" are explored in Wayne C. Booth's *The Rhetoric of Fiction* (Chicago: University of Chicago Press, 1961). The distinction is, however, at times a difficult one, and for that reason can be left for more advanced literary study.

[21] Ibid., p. 74.

that he means anything other than what he says. The same thing, however, is not always true of Mark Twain himself, who is far more circumspect and cautious and prefers to adopt a posture of detachment and objectivity. Authors like Mark Twain recognize that life is not always simple or straightforward; that the affairs of men are full of surprises, ambiguities, contradictions, and complexities; and that appearances can and often do deceive. In order to reflect the puzzling, problematic nature of experience, such authors choose to approach their subjects indirectly, through the use of irony. They use techniques to create within a work two separate and contrasting levels of experience and a "disparity of understanding" between them.

The three types of irony that occur most frequently in literature are *verbal irony* (in which there is a contrast between what a speaker literally says and what he or she means); *irony of situation* (in which an event or situation turns out to be the reverse of what is expected or appropriate); and *dramatic irony* (in which the state of affairs known to the reader or the audience is the reverse of what its participants suppose it to be).

Verbal irony is easily enough recognized in speech because of the intonation of the speaker's voice. For example, when Mark Anthony refers to Brutus in Shakespeare's *Julius Caesar* as "an honorable man," few members of the audience are likely to misunderstand the irony in his statement. When used in fiction, however, verbal irony is sometimes more difficult to identify because it is conveyed exclusively through the author's style, through the words on the printed page. Sometimes the author helps the reader by means of repetition, as Hawthorne does in "My Kinsman, Major Molineux," where Robin, the uninitiated youth from the country, prides himself on his native "shrewdness." Shrewd, at least in the ways of the city, Robin is not, as he is reminded at the close of the story when the anonymous gentleman who has helped him through his evening vigil suggests that "as you are a shrewd youth, you may rise in the world without the help of your kinsman, Major Molineux."

Irony of situation, on the other hand, results from the careful manipulation of plot, point of view, setting and atmosphere. Robin's prolonged and frustrating search for his kinsman, for example, is rendered ironic by the fact that his arrival in Boston coincides exactly with a revolutionary plot whose chief object is the very individual who Robin believes will help him to rise in the world. Robin Molineux is but one in a long line of fictional characters whose expectations are altered or reversed by the events that overtake them. The situational irony in Hawthorne's story is sustained not only by the plot, but by the point of view, which reveals the true state of things only gradually both to Robin and the reader. In Shirley Jackson's "The Lottery," irony of situation is established by the ostensibly gay and lighthearted atmosphere and festive scene on the June morning on which the story opens and by Jackson's use of a detached and matter-of-fact dramatic point of view. Only as the events of the morning unfold does the reader come to grasp the underlying horror of ritualistic violence that the villagers are about to perpetrate on one of their own.

Dramatic irony, like irony of situation, depends on the use of plot, character, and point of view. An omniscient narrator, for example, will sometimes reveal information to the reader that his characters do not yet know; this allows the narrator to judge the subsequent actions of those characters and to anticipate the likely outcome of events. Dramatic irony can also be established by means of characters whose innocence and naivete cause them to misperceive or misinterpret events whose significance is perfectly clear to the reader. The plots of such works frequently turn on the matter of knowing or not knowing, as in Henry James's "The Tree of Knowledge," and result in outcomes that are either comic or tragic in their final implication.

As critics Robert Scholes and Robert Kellogg note, there are "In any example of narrative art . . . broadly speaking, three points of view—those of the characters, the narrator, and the audience." When any one of the three "perceives more—or less—than another, irony must be either actually or potentially present."[22] In any work of fiction, it is crucially important that we be able to determine if and how that potential has been exploited; to overlook or misinterpret the presence of irony can only lead to a misinterpretation of the author's attitudes and tone and the way he would have us approach and judge the work.

Analyzing Style and Tone

1. Describe the author's diction. Is the language concrete or abstract, formal or informal, literal or figurative? What parts of speech occur most often?

[22] Robert Scholes and Robert Kellogg, *The Nature of Narrative* (New York: Oxford University Press, 1966), p. 240.

2. What use does the author make of imagery; figurative devices (simile, metaphor, personification); patterns of rhythm and sound (alliteration, assonance, consonance, onomatopoeia); repetition; allusion?
3. Are the sentences predominantly long or short; simple, compound, or complex; loose, periodic, or balanced?
4. Describe the author's tone. Is it, for example, sympathetic, detached, condescending, serious, humorous, or ironic? How is the tone established and revealed?
5. What kind(s) of irony does the author use: verbal irony, irony of situation, dramatic irony? What purpose(s) does the irony serve?
6. What are the distinctive characteristics of the author's style? In what ways is the style appropriate to the work's subject and theme?

II
Poetry

3

What Is Poetry?

What is poetry? One modern poet, perhaps a little vexed by this question, replied that poetry, unlike prose, is a form of writing in which few lines run to the edge of the page. Although this half-facetious response may have been intended to force the questioner to formulate his own definition of poetry, it also expresses how difficult it is to distinguish between poetry and prose on any grounds other than their appearance on the printed page. All imaginative literature—whether poetry, prose, or drama—is primarily concerned with human feelings and attitudes. This is why literature is one of the humanities. And nearly all great literature tries to recreate human experiences that involve the reader emotionally and intellectually. What then makes poetry unique and important? What *is* poetry?

The question is not a new one, and answers to it do not come easily. Samuel Johnson, the great eighteenth-century lexicographer and critic, reflecting the frustration that many must feel in responding to the question, replied with his usual directness: "Why, Sir, it is much easier to say what it is not. We all know what light is; but it is not easy to *tell* what it is." For more than two thousand years, in fact, poets, philosophers, and literary critics have struggled in the telling without shedding much light. Nevertheless, a brief survey of some of their answers will help both to clarify the issues involved and to illustrate the major stages in the development and history of poetry.

POETRY AS ELEVATED OR LOFTY EXPRESSION

Although Aristotle in his *Poetics* (4th century B.C.) clearly linked mankind's enjoyment of poetry with our innate love of imitation and our sense of harmony and rhythm, he concluded that the reader's pleasure is largely governed by the relationship between the subject of the poem and the way in which that subject is treated. He noted, for example, that epic poems and romances, which depict men and women as more heroic than they are in reality, seem more effective when their diction is lofty but still clear. Unfortunately, many of Aristotle's followers transformed this observation into a rigid dictum that all serious poetry must be written in what is called the high style, a style characterized by rhetorical devices, inverted syntax, unfamiliar terms, and (to quote Aristotle) "everything remote from the ordinary."[1] The Aristotelian formula persisted unchallenged for centuries, and a good deal of inferior poetry was written in an effort to comply with it—some of the worst of it in direct imitation of the compound epithets found in Homer's poetry. Poets who fancied Homer's "wine-dark" sea and "rosy-fingered" dawn have given us in imitation such lame phrases as "sky-topp'd" hills, "daily-climbing" flocks, and "leaf-shaking" fear.

THE DIDACTIC PURPOSE OF POETRY

The first English refinement of Aristotelian, or classical, theory came in the fifteenth and sixteenth centuries when, as a result of the Reformation emphasis on the morally useful and didactic, poetry came to be viewed as "an art of imitation . . . with this end, to teach and delight."[2] Thus, many poems of the late medieval period and

[1] John Warrington, trans., *The Poetics* (London: J. M. Dent and Sons, 1963), p. 38.
[2] Sir Philip Sidney, *Apology for Poetry* (1583).

early Renaissance were accompanied by didactic commentaries in verse designed to force the poem's moral value explicitly upon the attention of its readers. Even so sensuous a poem as Ovid's *Metamorphoses,* which attempts to explain most natural phenomena in terms of the vicissitudes of love, was described in 1565 as a work that gives, for the trouble one takes in reading it,

> double recompense with pleasure and with gain:
> With pleasure through variety and strangeness of the things,
> With gain for good instruction which the understanding brings.
> —from *The XV Books Entytuled Ovid's Metamorphosis,*
> tr. Arthur Golding (1565)

This idea that poetry should instruct even as it entertains anticipates the kind of literature known as allegory, in which such English Renaissance writers as Edmund Spenser excelled and in which all the characters in a story (and sometimes its events and its setting, as well) represent abstract qualities. For example, in the first book of Spenser's *Faerie Queene* (1590), the Red Cross Knight, in addition to being the hero in the romantic episodes, also represents holiness and the Anglican church; his enemies, Duessa (a wicked enchantress) and Archimago (an evil wizard) stand for duplicity and hypocrisy, as well as the Roman Catholic church and the Pope. Similarly, the Faerie Queene is Elizabeth I of England; Duessa, her enemy, is Queen Mary of Scotland. Thanks to Spenser's allegory, the *Faerie Queene* can be read for its romantic adventures, its moral philosophy, its political commentary, its poetic beauty, or all four at once.

The concept of poetry as instruction did not, of course, originate in medieval England, nor did it disappear when poetry began to be viewed as a means of communicating pleasure rather than philosophy. Centuries earlier, the Roman poet Horace had already pronounced that poetry should be *utile et dulce*—"useful and sweet." And even as late as the nineteenth century, Percy Bysshe Shelley argued that "poets are the unacknowledged legislators of the world," in the sense that ideas first expressed by poets often become adopted by society as a whole. Yet, even by Shelley's time, this theory of poetry had been generally discredited, and few today would argue that didacticism is a central, or even a desirable, purpose of poetry. Most of us prefer to get our philosophy and our morality from other sources.

THE METAPHORIC AND METAPHYSICAL PURPOSES OF POETRY

In the last decade of the reign of Queen Elizabeth I, thanks to the influence of William Shakespeare and Christopher Marlowe, poetry was again redefined. In *A Midsummer Night's Dream,* Shakespeare argued that

> The poet's eye, in a fine frenzy rolling,
> Doth glance from heaven to earth, from earth to heaven;
> And, as imagination bodies forth
> The forms of things unknown, the poet's pen
> Turns them to shapes, and gives to airy nothing
> A local habitation and a name.
>
> —from *A Midsummer Night's Dream,*
> William Shakespeare (ca. 1595)

Literally, these lines describe the poet, pen in hand, in the act of composition. His eyes dart from the sky to his immediate surroundings as he struggles to put his thoughts into words. But when Shakespeare writes "the poet's eye," he also means to suggest "the poet's imagination"—thus, he is drawing an implied comparison between the movements of the eye and those of the imagination. Shakespeare is saying that, by definition, a poet is one who *sees* relationships, in this case relationships between earth and heaven and between mundane events and their philosophical implications. Many Elizabethan and Jacobean poets came to define their craft in just this way, so that Shakespeare's image of the poet's eye is a good example of imaginative Renaissance poetry and of what is meant by the term *metaphysical verse.* Although this phrase, coined from the suffix *meta* (meaning "beyond") and the root *physics,* has traditionally been used to describe the philosophical concerns and elaborate images in the work of such seventeenth-century poets as John Donne, Richard Crashaw, and Andrew Marvell, it really refers to any elaborate or far-fetched comparison, especially one with philosophical implications.

Of all the poets who employ the metaphysical comparison (or *conceit*), none is more famous than John Donne. In "A Valediction: Forbidding Mourning" he develops a series of elaborate comparisons to demonstrate the difference between true spiritual lovers and the passions of ordinary men and women:

A Valediction: Forbidding Mourning

As virtuous men pass mildly away,
  And whisper to their souls, to go,
Whilst some of their sad friends do say,
  The breath goes now, and some say, no;

So let us melt, and make no noise,
  No tear-floods, nor sigh-tempests move,
'Twere profanation of our joys
  To tell the laity our love.

Moving of th' earth brings harms and fears,
  Men reckon what it did and meant,
But trepidation of the spheres,
  Though greater far, is innocent.

Dull sublunary lovers' love
  (Whose soul is sense) cannot admit
Absence, because it doth remove
  Those things which elemented it.

But we by a love, so much refined
  That our selves know not what it is,
Inter-assured of the mind,
  Care less, eyes, lips, and hands to miss.

Our two souls therefore, which are one,
  Though I must go, endure not yet
A breach, but an expansion
  Like gold to airy thinness beat.

If they be two, they are two so
  As stiff twin compasses are two,
Thy soul, the fixt foot, makes no show
  To move, but doth, if th' other do.

And though it in the center sit,
  Yet when the other far doth roam,
It leans, and hearkens after it,
  And grows erect, as that comes home.

Such wilt thou be to me, who must
  Like th' other foot, obliquely run;
Thy firmness makes my circle just,
  And makes me end, where I begun.

—John Donne (1633)

Donne's intention in writing the poem just before his trip to the Continent in 1612 is to explain to his wife that their impending separation should be a mild and peaceful one. It is characteristic of the metaphysical style that each comparison, each metaphor or simile, leads to others. In this case, "melting" leads Donne to think of the transformation of ice to water, suggesting that perhaps his wife will "dissolve in tears" at their parting. In the second stanza, Donne goes on to forbid such conventional displays of sorrow—"tear-floods" and "sigh-tempests"—because " 'Twere profanation of our joys/ To tell the laity of our love." In other words, he is saying that any public display of sorrow at their parting will only draw attention to their relationship and thereby cheapen it. No longer will it have the ennobling quality of a religious ceremony (as implied by the words "profanation" and "laity"); instead it will resemble a common carnal love.

Donne's poem continues with a series of similarly striking metaphysical analogies (including, with the phrase "trepidation of the spheres," an allusion to the Ptolemaic system of astronomy) until it reaches an apparent paradox. Although he has begun the poem with the idea of a pious and gentle separation, he decides that there will be no final separation at all, only an attenuation, or stretching. This thought leads him to conclude the poem with two arresting metaphors in which he likens the relationship with his wife first to "gold to airy thinness beat" (sixth stanza) and then to the two legs of a drawing compass (seventh to ninth stanzas).

Donne's conception of parting—and this is the key point—changes in the course of the poem. Although he starts out explaining to his wife how she should react to their separation, he ends up by explaining to himself—and to all of us—how the constancy and purity of their love will keep them together. The kind of delightful discovery that Donne makes is precisely what renders his poetry, and that of many other poets, so exciting. If Donne had only repeated his initial metaphor in a series of ingenious but essentially unchanging comparisons, there would be very little point in reading past the first stanza. But in the process of writing, Donne's thoughts crystallize. As readers, we discover, through his changing metaphors and similes, the significance of his love—and of any spiritual love. It was precisely for this reason that Samuel Johnson, after expressing a number of reservations, ultimately praised the metaphysical conception of poetry: "If they [the metaphysical poets] frequently threw away their wit upon false conceits, they likewise sometimes struck out unexpected truths; if their conceits were far-fetched, they were often worth the carriage. To write on their plan it was at least necessary to read and think."[3]

POETRY AS CONCENTRATED PROSE

Dr. Johnson's rather restrained appreciation of metaphysical poetry helps to identify him as one of the characteristic spokesmen of the eighteenth-century during which poetry once again was redefined. No longer was poetry to be viewed as a form of pleasant instruction, as it had been in the medieval period, or startlingly metaphoric, as it had been in the Renaissance. Rather it was to be smooth, witty, and gracious, in keeping with the century's ideal of decorum and restraint. Alexander Pope, the greatest poet of the period, best defined the new ideal in his *Essay on Criticism* (1711):

> True wit is Nature to advantage dress'd;
> What oft was thought but ne'er so well expressed.

The emphasis here is on craft rather than creativity. Not surprisingly, many of the best poets of the age once again turned their attention to translation. John Dryden, for example, translated Virgil's *Aeneid* into English; while Pope spent some thirteen years working on translations of Homer's *Illiad* and *Odyssey.* When not engaged in translating the classics, eighteenth-century poets were inclined to imitate them. Pope's two most famous poems, *The Rape of the Lock* and *The Dunciad,* are both mock epics, and the century was full of ambitious but ill-advised attempts to imitate classical forms of poetry. Because of this emphasis on the translation and imitation of established classics, the eighteenth century is often called the neoclassical period.

As a result of the eighteenth-century taste for wit and grace in expression, most poets abandoned the elaborate rhetorical effects—"the fine frenzies"—common in medieval and Renaissance poetry. Instead, they sought to compress their thoughts, to waste no words, to create poetry that was as neatly trimmed as the formal gardens they loved to pace while composing it. The principal achievement of their poetic style was the closed couplet, an example of which is the

[3] G. B. Hill, ed., "Cowley" in *Lives of the English Poets* (Oxford: Clarendon Press, 1905), I, 20.

one by Pope just quoted. We will have more to say later about the closed couplet; for the moment it will suffice to note how supremely self-sufficient those two lines by Pope are. The first line is a metaphoric definition of wit, whereas the second line explains and modifies, even as it complements and balances, the first. Also note that the words employed are common ones—the ordinary, everyday language of men—and that the syntax follows a normal and expected pattern instead of reflecting the poet's traditional right to rearrange the standard word order of prose to meet the requirements of verse. These lines, in short, realize the eighteenth-century ideal that all language "must be genteel and neat—no pains taken."[4]

In reality, of course, this "new" conception of poetry was no more revolutionary than the didactic and metaphysical views discussed earlier. "A Valediction: Forbidding Mourning," for example, differs from prose in the number and range of its comparisons, but not its syntax. The sentences of the poem fall into the standard grammatical patterns of prose; and Donne shuns conventional poetic language in favor of a rather startling comparison between true lovers and a compass. The neoclassical poets, however, went well beyond Donne in seeking to make smoothness in diction and meter the measure of their verse. They held that poetry should be to prose as diamonds are to coal: the structure much the same, with a great difference in brilliance, weight, strength, and clarity. The view was endorsed by every major poet from Dryden to Wordsworth. To be sure, on many aspects of their craft these poets were in violent disagreement, but they could, nevertheless, all agree in principle with Wordsworth's assertion that the poet's goal should be to write "as far as was possible in a selection of language really used by men."

POETRY AS A VENT FOR EMOTIONS

No sooner had the eighteenth century developed the theory that poetry is nothing more than a crafted and refined version of standard language than the nineteenth century—an age of rebellion in literature as in politics—announced a new and partially contradictory definition. Indeed, only a few pages after advocating that poetry should be written in the "language really used by men," Wordsworth unex-

[4] Anthony à Wood, ca. 1675. From *Life and Times of Anthony à Wood,* collected from his diaries and other papers by Andrew Clark (Oxford: Oxford University Press, 1889–1900), II, p. 332.

pectedly endorsed the idea that "poetry is the spontaneous overflow of powerful feelings." Wordsworth, who was obviously a transitional poet, does not appear to have sensed any contradiction in expecting *uncommon* feelings to be expressed in *common* language. He also went on to deny that the emotional content of poetry demanded tear-floods, sigh-tempests, or any of the nymphs, fawns, and fairies traditionally used by poets, ranging from Ovid to Shakespeare, in an effort to give "to airy nothing a local habitation and a name."

Wordsworth's insistence on the poetic value of the language actually used by ordinary men was at heart antiromantic and not characteristic of the nineteenth century, for the word *romance,* by definition, recalls the language and feelings of the medieval adventure story or *romans.* Romance returns us to a world of high adventure, noble actions, archaic language, chivalry, courtliness, knights, dragons, and beautiful maidens. All of the poets in the generation after Wordsworth believed with Lord Byron that poetry is "the lava of imagination whose eruption prevents an earthquake" and that there is a "poetic" way of thinking that differs dramatically from prosaic thinking. It is typified by energy, emotion, excitement, and audacity.

In many respects, of course, the romantic definition of poetry was a return to the Renaissance ideal of highly metaphoric language, for romantic poets filled their lines with vibrant imagery. Indeed, such romantic poets as John Keats and Thomas Hood consciously imitated the Elizabethans. Hood, in fact, was the author of the most successful of the many attempts to conclude Christopher Marlowe's unfinished verse tale *Hero and Leander,* while Keats imitated the Elizabethans less in plot than in attitude, an attitude that is expressed well in his enthusiastic response to reading a translation of Homer by the sixteenth-century poet George Chapman:

On First Looking into Chapman's Homer

Much have I travell'd in the realms of gold,
And many goodly states and kingdoms seen:
Round many western islands have I been
Which bards in fealty to Apollo hold.
Oft of one wide expanse had I been told
That deep-browed Homer ruled as his demesne;
Yet did I never breathe its pure serene
Till I heard Chapman speak out loud and bold:
Then felt I like some watcher of the skies
When a new planet swims into his ken;
Or like stout Cortez when with eagle eyes

He stared at the Pacific—and all his men
Looked at each other with a wild surmise—
Silent, upon a peak in Darien.
—John Keats (1816)

This sonnet develops an analogy between Keats's pleasure in discovering a new imaginative world in Homer's poetry and the pleasure of an explorer like Cortez in sighting the Pacific Ocean from a mountain in Darien, a region in eastern Panama.[5] The similarity between Keats's bold comparison and Donne's metaphysical conceit is clear: Keats's images, like Donne's, range from earth to heaven and from mind to matter. Keats compares reading with traveling and the poet's "golden" words with the Inca's golden realms. The real curiosity in this poem, however, is Keats's sudden and brief change of imagery in the ninth and tenth lines, when he switches from his geographic metaphor to an astronomical one. He compares the pleasures of reading Homer to the sudden delight an astronomer might feel in discovering a new planet. Such an assertion makes the point that poetry can provide all the pleasure of an intellectual discovery and by doing so underscores the preoccupation of the romantic poets with transcendental "ideas" and the life of the mind. These poets were influenced by the eighteenth-century empirical philosophers—particularly Bishop Berkeley, who argued in *The Principles of Human Knowledge* "that all the choir of heaven, the furniture of the earth,—in a word all those bodies which compose the mighty frame of the world,—have not any subsistence without a mind." According to this view, nothing is certain to exist unless it can be perceived by the mind using the physical senses. Hence, thoughts are more "real" than objects, and poetry, because it is a form of concentrated thinking, is an important and justifiable philosophic pursuit.

The romantic's definition required that poetry be both emotional and introspective. To quote Keats again:

> Poetry should surprise by a fine excess and not by singularity. It should strike the reader as a wording of his own highest thoughts and appear almost as a remembrance. Its touches of beauty should never be halfway. The rise, the progress, the setting of imagery should, like the sun, come natural to him.
>
> —John Keats' letter to John Taylor, Feb. 27, 1818

[5] Actually, Balboa first stood on this mountain, as Keats was doubtless well aware. The sound of Cortez's name and the romantic associations that name conjures up explain and justify the historical inaccuracy.

To be sure, there are inaccuracies in this as in other definitions of poetry. Instead of being a fiery record of evanescent thoughts, most romantic poems, like those written in other periods, were meticulously crafted and repeatedly revised. Byron, for example, had implied that his poetry was tossed off in a feverish passion; in fact, all the original manuscripts of his poetry show signs of careful rewriting, and the same is true of the other romantic poets.

POETRY AS AN ORGANIC STRUCTURE

Early in the twentieth century, poets again redefined their art through new experiments with structure, content, and style. Walt Whitman and Gerard Manly Hopkins, writing in the last third of the nineteenth century in America and in England, respectively, had shaken poetry free from its dependence on fixed patterns of rhyme and meter. To these men, rhyme and meter were only two of the techniques useful in creating pleasing patterns of sound. Their *free verse* substituted balanced and parallel phrases for syllabic counting and replaced the rhyming words at the end of each line with other musical effects (alliteration, assonance, and dissonance) that were not new to English poetry but attained greater prominence in free verse. The result of the experimentation in poetic structure that took place during the first half of the twentieth century has led to many successes. Free verse is particularly effective when, as in the following poem by e.e. cummings, it uses the poem's structure on the printed page as a guide to its rhythms:

Buffalo Bill's

Buffalo Bill's
defunct
        who used to
        ride a watersmooth-silver
                                        stallion
and break onetwothreefourfive pigeonsjustlikethat
                                                                Jesus
he was a handsome man
                                    and what i want to know is
how do you like your blueeyed boy
Mister Death

—e. e. cummings (1923)

Other modern writers contributed to the redefinition of poetry by insisting that it need not be confined to "romantic" subjects and that the range of human experience treated by poetry should be broadened to include "restless nights in one-night cheap hotels" and all the other trivial, humiliating, or inane aspects of modern life. In "The Love Song of J. Alfred Prufrock" (1917), from which we have just quoted, T. S. Eliot took the position that poets, like all the rest of us, must live in a world made trivial by "a hundred indecisions" and that the romantic poet's visions of hearing "mermaids singing, each to each," are only *dreams*. The romantic poet, Eliot insists, is more like Polonius than Prince Hamlet:

> Full of high sentence, but a bit obtuse;
> At times, indeed, almost ridiculous—
> Almost, at times, the Fool.

Eliot's use of mundane, realistic events in this poem had been foreshadowed in the nineteenth century by realism and naturalism in fiction and by the work of George Meredith in verse. Meredith's *Modern Love* (1862) was the first attempt in poetry to treat love, an inherently "romantic" subject, in a strictly realistic and antiromantic fashion by laying bare the emotional and psychological implications of ordinary and sometimes trivial interactions between a husband and wife. One stanza from the fifty that comprise the poem may serve to illustrate the modern temper:

> By this he knew she wept with waking eyes:
> That, at his hand's light quiver by her head,
> The strange low sobs that shook their common bed,
> Were called into her with a sharp surprise,
> And strangle mute, like little gaping snakes,
> Dreadfully venemous to him. She lay
> Stone-still, and the long darkness flowed away
> With muffled pulses. Then, as midnight makes
> Her giant heart of Memory and Tears
> Drink the pale drug of silence, and so beat
> Sleep's heavy measure, they from head to feet
> Were moveless, looking through their dead black years
> By vain regret scrawled over the blank wall.
> Like sculptured effigies they might be seen
> Upon their marriage-tomb, the sword between;
> Each wishing for the sword that severs all.
>
> —from *Modern Love,* George Meredith (1862)

The situation here is quite unlike anything written before in English verse. There is no love, just as there is no conversation, between the two unhappy people—the scant distance between them in bed cannot be spanned because of an immense, and as yet unspoken, distance in spirit. This stanza records the husband's realization that their marriage is dying. His wife has been weeping silently in bed, and when he reaches over to comfort her, she stiffens, betraying her repugnance. On the surface, the incident appears ordinary and perhaps even insignificant, but Meredith analyzes the meaning of the action through a poetic rhetoric that is terse, difficult, and occasionally obscure. The husband's attitude is revealed in imagery dominated by death. Snakes, venoms, midnight drugs, dead years, sculptured effigies, and marriage-tombs all play a part in transforming the narrator's discovery of his wife's tears into an acute death-wish. The significance of the wife's sobbing is to be found almost entirely in the poisonous thoughts that those tears seed and water in her husband's mind.

The difficulties we may experience on our first quick reading of *Modern Love* are the results of another general characteristic of modern poetry: its terse language and tight structure. An analogy can be drawn between the construction of the poem and organic growth; each word in the poem, like each cell in a plant, should perform a specific function in the life of the whole. The poem itself is the natural outgrowth of the idea that gave it birth. Although such a view of poetry was vigorously expressed by Coleridge in his *Biographia Literaria* (1817) and later by Ralph Waldo Emerson, only in the twentieth century has it been greeted with general acceptance. Archibald MacLeish, speaking for his contemporaries, has written that

> A poem should be palpable and mute
> As a globed fruit
>
> . . .
>
> A poem should not mean
> But be.
>
> —from "Ars Poetica,"
> Archibald MacLeish (1926)

The increased emphasis on imagery and symbolism implied by this view adds to each line of poetry a greater richness and density; however, it also complicates the critic's task of understanding the author's purpose and clarifying his achievement.

Taken as a whole, then, the poetry of the twentieth century demands more of its readers than it has in the past. According to Allan Tate, an important contemporary poet and critic, the reader must give to the poem "the fullest cooperation of his intellectual resources, all his knowledge of the world, and all the persistence and alertness that he now thinks of giving to scientific studies."[6] Tate encourages us "to look upon language as a field of study, not as an impressionistic debauch."[7] The analytical approach to literary criticism, which we adopt in this text, is an outgrowth of this modern attitude that language and literature are academic disciplines and that poetry can be both read and studied.

In the preceding pages we have surveyed the changing historical consensus about the nature and purpose of poetry. Each generation of poets has contributed something to our understanding of the genre, but no generation has had the whole answer; and it is unrealistic to expect that such an answer will ever be forthcoming. If we stand outside the historical spectrum, we can see how one view dominates an age only to give way to another. So long as poetry remains a vital form of human expression, we can expect that its techniques and purposes will continue to change.

What *is* poetry? We ask again. Although we may be unable to answer this question for all time, we *can* summarize those elements in the definition of poetry that have remained nearly constant throughout the ages.

Poetry, like all literature, attempts to communicate an author's emotional and philosophical responses to his or her own existence and to the surrounding world. It is an expression of what is thought and felt, rather than what is known as fact. It depends on observation, just as science does, but poetry draws comparisons between phenomena that science might find distant and unrelated. When Keats wishes to share his emotions upon first reading Chapman's translation of Homer's poetry, he finds an apt metaphor in the conquistador's silent wonder at the vast Pacific Ocean. When Meredith wishes to describe the emotional impact of a wife's stifled sobs, he conjures up venemous snakes. Such comparisons require a bold leap of the imagination in both the poet and his audience. When they are

[6] Allen Tate, "Understanding Modern Poetry," *Essays of Four Decades* (Chicago: Swallow Press, 1968), p. 163.

[7] Ibid., p. 168.

effective, they reproduce emotions in the reader similar to those actually experienced by the author. Thus, poetry is fundamentally metaphoric and is capable of communicating in very few words thoughts and emotions of great complexity.

Prose literature, of course, is capable of achieving everything suggested in the preceding paragraph. As a result of modern experiments with free verse and the increasing literary artistry of short-story writers and novelists, the distinctions between poetry and prose are often slight. Hence, all of the techniques of poety can, on occasion, be properly considered in the critical explication of fiction and drama. However, poetry ordinarily does differ from prose in several significant regards. First, it provides an accepted format (in ballads, odes, and sonnets) for the publication of short but independent pieces of narration, description, or reflection. Second, "poetic license" permits verse to depart on occasion from the standard rules of logic and grammar governing ordinary prose. Third, poetry tends to make more use than prose of symbolism, imagery, and figures of speech. And finally, poetry relies more heavily than prose on the sound and rhythm of speech and hence usually employs both rhyme and meter.

The formal patterns of meter and rhyme, which continue to dominate poetry despite modern experiments with free verse, place obvious restrictions on the poet's choice of words. He must write carefully and reflectively in order to find words that not only fulfill the demands of meter and rhyme, but also express the meaning in a manner that complements the imagery and tone of the rest of the poem. This careful use of language is the most significant difference between ordinary prose and poetry. The ordinary prose writer neatly builds an argument using words the way a mason builds a house using bricks; the poet is a craftsman who creates a fieldstone hearth—each stone or each word is turned over, examined, and often laid aside until it can be placed where its shape, weight, and color will contribute to the strength and beauty of the whole. Prose, according to Samuel Taylor Coleridge, is "words in their best order," and poetry is "the best words in their best order."

Very little of the verse of any age comes up to the high standards set in the previous paragraph. Even great poets write relatively few great poems, and our disappointment in the inferior works of notable poets is greater than it is in the secondary works of great novelists. This, too, points out a difference between prose and poetry. Mediocre prose is often enjoyable in much the same way that a walk in the city can be enjoyable even though it is not so fresh and invigorating as a hike through the wilderness. But prose is still linguistic walking, and poetry is linguistic riding. Either the rider *or* his mount will have control over the rhythm, the pace, and the direction of the journey. When the horse is in command—that is, when the meter and rhyme govern and control the poet—the ride will be uneven, misdirected, unintelligible, and sometimes fearsome. When the rider is in control—that is, when the poet fully controls the meter and rhyme—the ride will be swift, smooth, graceful, and elegant, like Buffalo Bill astride his "watersmooth-silver stallion."

In the preceding paragraphs we have compared the poet with an artisan and an equestrian. Both comparisons convey something about the essential quality of poetry, but perhaps they emphasize too strongly the skill of the poet and not strongly enough the skills that are necessary in an appreciative reader. Poetry shares with all other forms of literature the fact that it is a form of communication between the author and the reader. It depends as much on the good will, intelligence, and experience of the latter as on the genius of the former. Robert Frost once said that writing free verse is like playing tennis with the net down. Regardless of whether we agree with Frost's implied criticism of free verse, his remark underscores the fact that poetry is a game played according to established rules between poet and form and also between poet and reader. In order to play the game, in order to understand poetry, one must first learn the rules.

4

Poetic Diction

THE MEANING OF WORDS

Words are the building blocks of poetry. By the time students enter college, they have heard at least 100 million words in school; spoken 30 million words in school and out; and read, in spite of television, some 10 million words.[1] During the years of formal schooling language is so ingrained in us that we cannot imagine an existence without words; our most private thoughts often take the form of an inner dialogue and even our dreams incorporate words. In short, we become so sophisticated in language, and at such an early age, that we seldom realize the complexity of the language we read, speak, and hear.

Our understanding of language, whether as auditors or as readers, depends almost entirely on two factors: our knowledge of the meaning of individual words and our recognition of various cues (syntax, punctuation, and structure in reading; syntax, emphasis, and vocal pauses in listening) directing our attention to the relationships among

[1] The precise numbers are unimportant so long as the order of magnitude is correct. Readers are welcome to make their own estimates, which, we trust, will not differ greatly from ours.

the words.[2] Our first concern is with the meaning of individual words, but it will soon become clear that meaning is largely determined by context and by the interrelationships of words in a sentence. Several of the elements of poetry, however, are occasionally independent of context: specifically, denotation, connotation, and allusion. Each word in a language is distinguished from every other word by its unique combination of denotations and connotations; there are no perfect synonyms. Poetry is the form of writing that takes greatest advantage of the personalities of words; it welcomes their eccentricities. Therefore, no word in great poetry can be moved or replaced without changing and perhaps harming the whole. An understanding of the meaning of individual words, therefore, is the first step in understanding poetry.

Denotation

"When I use a word," Humpty Dumpty said in rather a scornful tone, "it means just what I choose it to mean—neither more nor less."

"The question is," said Alice, "whether you *can* make words mean so many different things."

"The question is," said Humpty Dumpty, "which is to be Master—that's all."

Alice was too much puzzled to say anything, so after a minute Humpty Dumpty began again. "They've a temper, some of them—particularly verbs, they're the proudest—adjectives you can do anything with, but not verbs—however, *I* can manage the whole lot of them! Impenetrability! That's what *I* say!"

—from *Through the Looking Glass,* Lewis Carroll (1871)

As is often the case, Lewis Carroll's humor is far from absurd. In fact, the quotation points to an interesting paradox about words. A word is only an accurate tool of communication if it conveys the same idea to both the speaker and the listener; yet the meanings of words continually change and, despite the existence of dictionaries, can only be said to mean what people *think* they mean. New words are continually entering the language and old words dropping out or

[2] Literary critics have not sufficiently emphasized the fact that poetry gives—through rhythm, rhyme, and verse form—more cues about meaning than prose. This was even more obvious in the Middle Ages than it is now. Our elaborate gradations of punctuation are relatively recent inventions; medieval scribes used only the slash and the period. Consequently, medieval manuscripts are much easier to read in verse than in prose and, perhaps as a result, verse was often preferred for any composition of lasting value.

changing their implications. Furthermore, the same word can mean different things to different people or different things in different contexts. If, for example, we say of someone, "He's a bit red," we may mean that he is embarrassed, sunburned, or attracted to Communism, depending on the context. If an Englishman escorting an American woman through London suggests going to a local "dive," she will undoubtedly be put off by the thought of entering a disreputable bar, while he may have in mind a fashionable pub that is located below street level. Similarly, if a man living in the fifteenth century introduced a woman as John Smith's "mistress," he would have been praising her as an honest wife of noble blood; today, he might be disparaging her lack of a marriage license. (The word *mistress* is derived from the same root as *master* and was long represented by the abbreviation *Mrs.* Paradoxically, the abbreviation now has a meaning incompatible with that of the word it represents.) And if we object to using words that carry the clutter of variant definitions based on history, location, and context . . . well, we can turn to *new* words, freshly minted to meet their creators' needs. Lewis Carroll was remarkably adept at coining such words. We are indebted to him for the *boojum* (which is now the name of a species of tree found in southern California), the *snark* (now used as the trade name of a small sailboat), and the Cheshire cat's smile. To Joseph Heller, we owe the expression *Catch-22,* and to Harriet Beecher Stowe, we owe *Uncle Tom.* The military's fondness for acronyms has produced *radar* (radio detection and ranging) and *snafu* (situation normal, all fouled up).[3] The list goes on.

The various meanings of the words we have been discussing so far are all denotative—that is, they are listed as definitions in nearly any good dictionary. Most of us, when asked the meaning of any particular word, reply with a single, rather loose, definition. But we know that nearly every word has many definitions and that its denotation in a particular instance will depend largely on the context. These multiple meanings make the whole issue of a word's denotation much more complex and much less clear-cut than it may seem at first. It is an indication of the complexity of this issue that the most authoritative dictionary in the language, *The Oxford English Dic-*

[3] Not all acronyms are felicitous or dignified. Richard Nixon's ill-fated Committee to Re-elect the President was known as CREEP, and the device used by NASA to blow up misguided missiles is called EGADS (Electronic Ground Automatic Destruct System.)

tionary (1933), is 16,464 pages long. In it one finds, for example, more than eighteen pages, with three columns of print to the page, defining the verb *set,* which is capable of taking on 154 separate senses with nearly a thousand minor subdivisions of meaning.

The first task in understanding a poem is to understand thoroughly each word in it. Often, the best clues to the meaning of an unfamiliar word are to be found within the poem itself. Suppose, for example, that one wishes to know the meaning of "heal-all" in the following sonnet by Robert Frost:

DESIGN

I found a dimpled spider, fat and white,
On a white heal-all, holding up a moth
Like a piece of rigid satin cloth—
Assorted characters of death and blight
Mixed ready to begin the morning right,
Like the ingredients of a witches' broth—
A snow-drop spider, a flower like a froth,
And dead wings carried like a paper kite.
What had that flower to do with being white,
The wayside blue and innocent heal-all?
What brought the kindred spider to that height,
Then steered the white moth thither in the night?
What but the design of darkness to appall?—
If design govern in a thing so small.

—Robert Frost (1936)

A dictionary only tells us that a "heal-all" is either a panacea of some kind or one of a number of plants (*Rhodiola rosea, Valeriana officinalis, Prunella vulgaris,* and *Collinsonia canadensis*) that are thought to have medicinal value. This, although accurate, is no real help. If we don't know what a "heal-all" is in the first place, we certainly aren't going to know anything about a *Rhodiola rosea* or any of the other species listed. If we turn to a book on horticulture for help, we will learn where these plants grow, how large they get, how many stamens and pistills the flower have, and so on. We may even find pictures of each of the four plants, but without referring to the poem we won't learn anything telling us which of the four Frost meant or what emotions he hoped to evoke in the reader through the name. In comparison, look at the mass of information about the word contained in the poem itself. We know that a heal-all is a blue flower (lines nine and ten) of substantial height and size (large enough to support a fat spider and tall enough so that Frost is surprised to see the spider on it). We know that it grows by the wayside and that it is innocent; if it doesn't heal everything, as its name suggests, it is not ordinarily poisonous either. But the particular heal-all in the poem is unusual and almost an object of horror. It is blighted and white, a deformed member of its species. Thus, Frost sees its frothlike flowers as a fitting element in a witches' brew—and a fitting element in a poem that raises the possibility of malevolent destiny.

In the course of the poem, Frost has defined what he means by a heal-all. He has told us about the flower and, more importantly, he has told us about himself and the destiny he thinks governs existence. We learn what the word means and also what it symbolizes for Frost. The risk involved in defining a word from its context is, of course, that we are often unable to differentiate between the general denotative meaning of the word and its special symbolism for the poet. For this reason it is wise to check any definitions derived from context with those given in the dictionary.

Any ample dictionary will answer most of the needs of the student-critic; but one should keep in mind that the meaning of words changes with time, and dictionaries of only one volume seldom trace historical change. As a result of the civil rights movement of the 1960s, for example, the verb *discriminate* has come to mean "to make a decision based on prejudice." In the *Oxford English Dictionary,* however, the history of the word reveals that prior to about 1880 the verb meant only "to distinguish, differentiate, or exercise discernment." According to these early meanings of the word, an intelligent person should always be discriminating; today, we hope to avoid discriminating. Such changes in language are so common that we can expect to find some archaism in virtually every poem written before the beginning of the eighteenth century.

Connotation

As we have seen, denotation refers to the dictionary meaning of a word. Connotation, on the other hand, is determined by the ideas associated with or suggested by the word. Denotation is the meaning a word gives *to* a sentence; connotation is the verbal coloring a word takes on *from* those sentences in which it is commonly used. When a word like *discriminate* is uniformly employed in a narrow set of circumstances (in this case, involving some form of prejudice), its connotations may eventually be incorporated into the definition of the word itself. This is the principle process by which the definitions of words change. Thus, a word's connotations may be compared to the living, growing bark of a tree, and its denotations, like the rings in the tree's core, are the permanent record of its past growth. To change the simile slightly, the denotations of a word are visible, like a tree's branches and leaves; the connotations are the roots, which go deeply into the subsoil of our experience creating invisible ties between contexts and associations and drawing up nourishment for a continuing growth above ground.

Many words have multiple and even conflicting connotations. In the sonnet by Frost on page 114 the spider, the moth, and the flower are all white. Most of the time we associate the adjective *white* with innocence, purity, and cleanliness. A young bride is customarily married in a white gown and angels are depicted wearing white robes. In other contexts, however, this color can also signify pallor, illness, blight, or even death. Frost is probably drawing on both sets of connotations in his poem. The white moth fluttering toward its destruction in the darkness is harmless and innocent; the white flower that attracts it is blighted and unusual; and the fat white spider is a ghastly object of poison and death. Frost expects us to react—perhaps even shudder—at this departure from the normal and expected. Indeed, Frost's own attitude changes. In the last six lines he moves from questioning to despair—("What had . . . ? What brought . . . ? What but . . . ?")—as his conviction grows that such an evil distortion of "whiteness" can only be brought about by "the design of darkness to appall."

A word's connotations, like its denotations, may change over time; indeed, even the connotations of an *idea* may change with time. In "A Valediction: Forbidding Mourning" (1633), John Donne compares the separation of lovers with death:

As virtuous men pass mildly away,
   And whisper to their souls, to go,
Whilst some of their sad friends do say,
   The breath goes now, and some say, no:

So let us melt, and make no noise,
   No tear-floods, nor sigh-tempests move,
T'were profanation of our joys
   To tell the laity our love.

To a modern reader, love would seem least of all like death, but Donne sees the separation of lovers and the death of a saintly man as similar changes in state, from earthly to spiritual. At the same time, Donne is also playing with the connotations of *dying*. He is, no doubt, well aware that the verb *to die,* when used by Renaissance poets in discussing sexual love, inevitably refers to sexual exhaustion. He immediately reinforces these erotic implications in the fifth line, when he chooses the verb *melt* instead of *part,* because the former may suggest the "melting looks" of lovers and the "melting ecstasies" of passion. Thus, Donne's superficial piety in referring to the passing of virtuous men is undercut by erotic connotations. Most modern readers become aware of such connotations only through the labors of literary historians.

Perhaps a more dramatic example of change in a word's connotations occurs in Samuel Taylor Coleridge's "Sonnet to the Reverend W. L. Bowles" (1796). Coleridge claims that the verses of Reverend Bowles were capable of soothing a tumultuous mind:

> As the great Spirit erst with plastic sweep
> Mov'd on the darkness of the unform'd deep.

Coleridge here uses "plastic" to mean "having the power of molding or shaping formless material"—a meaning of the word that the dictionary still lists. He is not referring to the ubiquitous plastic that we associate with cheap merchandise and that was then still an alchemist's dream. Instead of implying artificiality, "plastic" then connoted superhuman power.

The connotations of "white," "melt," "die," and "plastic" all result from the common uses of the words, but all words have different sounds and the connotations associated with these sounds may also influence poetic meaning. Thus, when Donne writes, "As virtuous men pass mildly away, . . . So let us melt, and make no noise," part of the emotional effect is caused by the soft sounds of "mild," "melt," and the implied background of murmurs. Similarly, in *Don Juan* Byron exaggerates the sappy tra-la-la of lovely *l* sounds before satirically blasting the effect with the summarizing word "bland" in the following lines:

> When amatory poets sing their loves
>   In liquid lines mellifluously bland,
> . . . .
>   They little think what mischief is in hand.

As these examples indicate, our sensitivity to connotations of sound is generally reinforced by alliteration, consonance, or assonance—musical devices that will be discussed more fully later.

Allusion

When the English peasants marched against London in their ill-fated revolt of 1381, it is said that they rallied their spirits by chanting this brief ditty:

When Adam dalf° — °*delved, farmed*
And Eve span° — °*spun (yarn)*
Who was then the gentleman?

The peasants wanted to throw off their serfdom and assume the rights of free-born citizens. Their argument, at least in the chant, depended on a Biblical allusion: in Genesis, when God created mankind, he made Adam and Eve, not nobles and serfs—how then is serfdom justified?

A literary allusion is a brief reference to a person, place, phrase, or event drawn from history or literature. Allusions are effective not because of the meaning of the words themselves but because of the associations or connotations that allusive words carry for the intelligent reader. The use of allusion allows poets to reinforce an argument by illustration, to compress complex ideas into brief phrases, and to suggest thoughts they may not wish to state directly. In the case at hand, the peasants' allusive chant allowed them to request their freedom without putting it in the form of rebellious demand and to support their position with the authority of the Bible.

Names are the most common forms of allusion and the easiest to identify. As another example of names used allusively, let us look again at the stanza from Lord Byron's *Don Juan* that we started to quote earlier:

When amatory poets sing their loves
  In liquid lines mellifluously bland,
And pair their rhymes as Venus yokes her doves,
  They little think what mischief is in hand;
The greater their success the worse it proves,
  As Ovid's verse may give to understand;
Even Petrarch's self, if judged with due severity,
  Is the Platonic pimp of all posterity.

—from *Don Juan,* Lord Byron (1821)

Byron uses four allusions in eight lines. The first is almost self-explanatory: a poet's rhymes are paired in the same way as the doves that draw Venus's chariot through the heavens are yoked into pairs. The allusion is intended less to send the reader stumbling off to consult his copy of Ovid's *Metamorphoses* than to imitate the similes of love poetry. Byron then goes on to argue that the more successful poets are in writing about love, the worse it is for public morality, "As Ovid's verse may give to understand." Although Byron only expects from his reader the general knowledge that Ovid is renowned as the most seductive of all love poets, he may also be alluding to the rumor that Ovid was banished from Rome because his verse had tempted the daughter of Emperor Caesar Augustus to turn from the path of virtue. The reference to Petrarch in line seven assumes that the reader will know that this fourteenth-century Italian poet (who wrote 227 sonnets about his unrequited love for Laura living and another 90 about his love for Laura dead) inspired the amorous Elizabethan sonnet cycles by his own example. Elizabethan poets like Wyatt and Surrey used Petrarch's sonnets as models in their own attempts to seduce the maidens of their day. A final allusion is contained in the expression *Platonic love,* but this term is so commonly used for "spiritual love" that it is now less allusive than denotative and serves to emphasize that allusion, like denotation and connotation, is one of the factors in determining the meaning of words.

Allusion through literary name dropping is generally less effective than allusion through quotation or imitation of an author's works. Historically important and well-stated words have an emotional impact that transcends their denotative meaning. A literary allusion that is created through quotation draws on our reaction to the quoted work, the circumstances under which the work was written, and the whole range of our attitudes toward the author. We respond with patriotism to the idealism of the *Declaration of Independence* ("We hold these truths to be self-evident . . ."); with mystical piety to the gospel according to St. John ("In the beginning was the Word, and the Word was with God, and the Word was God"); and with a shiver to the opening of Edgar Allan Poe's "The Raven" ("Once upon a midnight dreary . . ."). When Keats wrote of "deep-browed Homer" (see p. 103), he was imitating Homer's penchant for such epithets as his often repeated "rosy-fingered Dawn." When Coleridge, in his sonnet to Reverend Bowles, compared the calming of his mind to the calming of waves after the great Spirit "Mov'd on the darkness of the unform'd deep," he was alluding to Genesis, Chapter 1, verse 2:

> And the earth was without form, and void; and darkness was upon the face of the deep. And the Spirit of God moved upon the face of the waters.

Such examples of allusion all refer to *famous* people, events, or words, because an allusion is only effective if it is understood and appreciated by the reader. But poets themselves often gain considerable notoriety as public figures, so that allusions to events in their personal lives come to be widely understood. For instance, when Byron writes in the first canto of *Don Juan,*

> 'Tis pity learned virgins ever wed
>   With persons of no sort of education.
> Or gentlemen, who, though well born and bred,
>   Grow tired of scientific conversation:
> I don't choose to say much on this head.
>   I'm a plain man, and in a single station,
> But—Oh! ye lords of ladies intellectual,
> Inform us truly, have they not hen-peck'd you all?
>
> —from *Don Juan,* Lord Byron (1819)

the irony in the stanza may elude us if we fail to recognize that Byron's wife Annabella had been a "learned virgin," that he often called her the "Princess of Parallelograms" and "a walking calculation," and that their separation proceedings provided scandal enough to delight gossips throughout England *and* Europe. Similarly, when Laurence Sterne, the eighteenth-century novelist and clergyman, was married, he wryly made reference to this event in his personal life by taking as his keynote for the following day's sermon this passage from Luke 5:5: "We have toiled all the night and taken nothing."

Repetition

Thus far, we have been examining elements in the meaning of words that are nearly independent of their context in a poem. It is the poetic context, however, that now requires attention because context alone allows us to distinguish among the competing possibilities offered by a word's denotations and connotations. A word will rarely mean exactly the same thing in two different contexts, even within the same poem.

The repetition of a word or phrase in itself tends to change the emphasis and to make prominent what otherwise might be overlooked. This is Robert Frost's intention in repeating the last line in the final stanza of the well-known poem "Stopping by Woods on a Snowy Evening":

> The woods are lovely, dark, and deep,
> But I have promises to keep,
> And miles to go before I sleep,
> And miles to go before I sleep.
> —from "Stopping by Woods on a Snowy Evening," Robert Frost (1923)

At first we are inclined to take the last line literally: the narrator must not linger because his trip home is a long one, and presumably he is already late. But, when repeated, the line attains an emphasis that makes this literal interpretation unsatisfactory. We may then ask ourselves a number of questions: How are the clauses in this one long sentence interrelated? What "promises" might go unkept because of this sojourn in the woods? What has the dark woods to do with "sleep?" And, finally, what kind of sleep is the poet talking about? The literal interpretation of the lines seems too mundane to accept the emphasis that Frost's repetition creates, and we are tempted to look for additional meaning. The "promises to keep" may be the whole burden of life's obligations, while the dark woods may be a bittersweet symbol of escape from these responsibilities into fantasy, fairyland, or premature death. And the final word "sleep," when repeated, assumes a greater finality, for death *is* an eternal sleep. In this case, therefore, the simple repetition of a line may encourage us to change our interpretation of the entire poem, affecting both its denotation and symbolism.

Frost achieves a different transformation of meaning by repeating the word "white" in the first three lines of his sonnet "Design":

> I found a dimpled spider, fat and white,
> On a white heal-all, holding up a moth
> Like a white piece of rigid satin cloth—

By repeating the word "white" he focuses our attention on it. Nothing obliged Frost to repeat himself; adjectives like *pallid, bleached, sallow, wan, hoary,* and *pale* are roughly synonymous and could have introduced the variety in style and imagery that ordinarily is desirable in a poem. But each of these alternatives suggests a slightly different shade of white and each carries a slightly different connotation. Only by repeating the *same* word can Frost make the point that the colors are identical. The blighted flower has perfectly concealed the hideous albino spider, and the single white flower in a field of blue has, presumably, enticed the moth into the trap. The incident is remarkable because of its improbability and suggests to the poet that this eerie nighttime rendezvous may have been foreordained. The repetition of "white," a color associated with both innocence and death, builds in the reader a foreboding of evil design, a bleak and blighted destiny in which even the purest of colors can serve the purposes of darkness.

In stanzaic poetry and ballads, repetition is often introduced in the form of a *refrain,* or chorus. The refrain generally occurs at the close of a stanza, where it helps to establish meter, influence mood, or add emphasis. A refrain may be identical in each stanza or it may vary in subtle but important ways during the course of the poem. An example of the effective use of a refrain is found in Rudyard Kipling's "Recessional":

Recessional

God of our fathers, known of old,
  Lord of our far-flung battle-line,
Beneath whose awful Hand we hold
  Dominion over palm and pine—
Lord God of Hosts, be with us yet,
Lest we forget—lest we forget!

The tumult and the shouting dies;
  The captains and the kings depart:
Still stands Thine ancient sacrifice,
  An humble and a contrite heart.
Lord God of Hosts, be with us yet,
Lest we forget—lest we forget!

Far-called, our navies melt away;
  On dune and headland sinks the fire:
Lo, all our pomp of yesterday
  Is one with Nineveh and Tyre![4]
Judge of nations, spare us yet,
Lest we forget—lest we forget!

[4] Nineveh and Tyre: Prosperous Old Testament cities destroyed by God because of their impiety.

If, drunk with sight of power, we loose
Wild tongues that have not Thee in awe,
Such boastings as the Gentiles[5] use,
Or lesser breeds without the Law—
Lord God of Hosts, be with us yet,
Lest we forget—lest we forget!

For heathen heart that puts her trust
In reeking tube and iron shard,
All valiant dust that builds on dust,
And guarding, calls not Thee to guard,
For frantic boast and foolish word—
Thy mercy on Thy people, Lord!
—Rudyard Kipling (1897)

A recessional is a hymn sung at the end of a religious service to signal the stately withdrawal of the clergy and choir from the altar to the vestry. Kipling's "Recessional," however, was not intended as a contribution to Anglican liturgy. It was written at the end of the festivities commemorating Queen Victoria's Diamond Jubilee, in her sixtieth year on the throne of England, and it reflects Kipling's emotions as he contemplates the end of an era. In 1897 Great Britain still governed an extensive empire, but her colonial power had already been challenged by the Sepoy rebellion in India and the Boer War in South Africa. Kipling was born in India and had sympathy for the native population, even though he endorsed the ideals of English colonial government. As we will see in this section and the next (Ambiguity), Kipling's poem expresses the complexity of his attitudes and, in doing so, draws on many of the literary devices we have discussed here. Behind the celebration of the Diamond Jubilee—behind even Kipling's expression of faith in God—we sense in the poem a prophetic lament for the decline of a once glorious empire.

Three of the poem's five stanzas contain an identical two-line refrain:

Lord God of Hosts, be with us yet,
Lest we forget—lest we forget!

The contribution of this refrain to the meaning of the poem depends in part on its literary allusions, in part on the meaning of the words themselves, and in part on repetition. The phrase "Lord God of

[5] Gentiles: Any persons who are not Jewish. Here used to mean anyone who does not believe in the true faith as, for example, the inhabitants of Nineveh and Tyre.

Hosts" or "Lord of Hosts" occurs frequently in the Bible, especially in the passages describing the destruction of Nineveh by heathen hordes and God's subsequent warnings against impiety. Apart from these Biblical allusions, Kipling's two-line refrain combines both a prayer and a warning: a prayer for God's continuing presence in the hearts of Englishmen and an implicit warning about the consequences of neglecting Him. The repetition of "lest we forget" in the second line of the refrain makes this warning all the more solemn; and by repeating the entire refrain three times, Kipling increases the religious implications (three is a number with mystical overtones). Thus, the refrain and the repetition within it not only add an air of solemnity and piety to the mood of the poem, but also underscore the slight differences in the refrain of the third stanza and the radical differences in the last stanza. As it happens, these stanzas present us with important clues to the meaning of the poem, clues best discussed under the heading of *ambiguity*.

Ambiguity

The use of a word or phrase in such a way as to give it two or more competing meanings is called ambiguity. In many instances, ambiguity is both a stylistic flaw and an annoyance because it creates confusion. In fact, the famous "Charge of the Light Brigade," immortalized in verse by Alfred Lord Tennyson, would never have taken place were it not for an ambiguity in Lord Raglan's orders to the commander in the field, Lord Lucan: "Lord Raglan wishes the cavalry to advance rapidly to the front, and try to prevent the enemy carrying away the guns." Unfortunately, as Tennyson pointed out, there were cannon to the right of them, cannon to the left of them, and cannon straight ahead. When the baffled Lord Lucan asked *which* guns were meant, the officer who had delivered the order frowned, pointed vaguely into the valley, and said sharply, "There, my Lord, is your enemy. There are your guns." With more courage than common sense, the Light Brigade charged the most distant guns—into the pages of history. As a result of ambiguity in the initial orders, of the 673 horsemen who entered the valley, only 195 returned.

The ambiguity in Lord Raglan's order was a result of imprecise wording. Other forms of ambiguity involve a play on the dual meanings of a particular word or a particular syntactic structure. As an example of the former, let us say that you are driving a friend home for the first time. As you approach an intersection, you ask, "Which way? Left?"

"Right!" your companion replies.

No exercise of logic can tell you whether the word *Right* here means "That is correct, turn left!" or "No! Turn right!" Only more information can clarify your friend's meaning.

Most cases of ambiguity involve a similar play on the meanings of a particular word, but it is also possible to have syntactic ambiguity—that is, ambiguity caused by the ordering of words. For example, there is a story that when Pyrrhus, the king of Epirus, consulted the oracle at Delphi before going into battle, he was encouraged by the prophesy that "Pyrrhus the Romans shall conquer," which he interpreted as meaning that he, Pyrrhus, would prove victorious. The Romans, however, were also encouraged because the sentence seemed to them equivalent to "The Romans shall conquer Pyrrhus." The actual battle demonstrated that the ambiguity of the oracle was appropriate. Although Pyrrhus won the field, he did so at such a cost that he was recorded as saying, "Another such victory, and we are lost." This battle, by the way, gave rise to the phrase *Pyrrhic victory,* which in itself incorporates the paradox (a form of ambiguity) of an undesirable victory.

As the preceding example illustrates, ambiguity can be used by a careful writer to increase the subtlety, impact, and concision of an expression. It can conceal truths that are only superficially contradictory (as in the oracle's prophesy), display an honest ambivalence, expand poetic meaning, or create humor or shock.

Ambivalence and expanded meaning are both revealed in Kipling's "Recessional." Here the ambiguity is not created by a single word with contradictory meanings, but rather by the dual interpretations that the poem as a whole invites. Each stanza is appropriate to the occasion of Victoria's Diamond Jubilee, at the end of which the captains and the kings depart, the naval vessels return to their normal duties, the celebratory bonfires die into embers, and the satisfied masses boast of the national might. But at the same time each stanza can also be interpreted as a comment on the future of the empire, and it is this prophetic element that makes the poem so memorable.

This duality of meaning is not forced on us until the third stanza. If by the lines, "Far-called, our navies melt away;/ On dune and headland sinks the fire," Kipling is referring to the dispersal of ships after the naval display on the Thames and to the fading of bonfires, then surely he is exaggerating when he says, "Lo, all our pomp of yesterday / Is one with Nineveh and Tyre." The end of a celebration is scarcely like the annihilation of two cities and their civilizations. And surely his prayer, "Judge of Nations, spare us yet,/ Lest we forget—lest we forget!" is nonsensical because nothing about the close of the Jubilee directly suggests the fall of the British empire.

In order to make sense of the stanza we must interpret it *figuratively,* paying as much attention to connotation as to denotation. It is true that England is an island encircled by "dune and headland," but these words are equally applicable to the extremities of the empire—Egypt, India, and Africa. In discussions of empires a "fire" or conflagration may be used to describe a minor uprising, such as the Indian mutiny of 1857, the first Boer war in 1881, or the British defeat at Khartoum in 1885. All of these well-publicized "fires" along the outskirts of the British empire occurred during the years preceeding Victoria's Diamond Jubilee. Furthermore, in primitive regions, the campfire is the symbol of civilization, which staves off an encroaching savagery. The sinking fire, when accompanied by allusions to the fall of Nineveh and Tyre, thus suggests unrest and upheaval along the fringes of the empire. The same suggestion is included in the preceding line, "Far-called, our navies melt away"—especially because melting (as with ice) is ordinarily an irreversible process. By implication, the strength of a navy that melts away is permanently diminished. Furthermore, "far-called" is not quite the same as "widely deployed." Kipling's term suggests that the navy has been called into action rather than merely reassigned to simple peace-keeping missions.

After Kipling has drawn our attention to his intentional ambiguity in this third stanza, we may turn with renewed interest to the earlier stanzas. If we pursue Kipling's allusions to Nineveh and Tyre by reading in the Bible Chapters 26–28 of Ezekiel and Chapters 1–3 of Nahum, we discover that Nineveh, like England, had "multiplied [her] merchants above the stars of heaven" and that her "crowned are as the locusts, and [her] captains as the great grasshoppers, which camp in the hedges in the cold day, but when the sun ariseth they flee away." Suddenly Kipling's simple statement that "the captains and the kings depart" takes on ominous connotations. No longer is this just a reference to their return to other duties after the Diamond

Jubilee; now it has become a prophesy of their unreliability during future upheavals in the empire.

Similarly, the expression "Lord God of Hosts" becomes ambiguous as the poem progresses and as we begin to track down Kipling's Biblical allusions. In the first stanza it seems obvious that God is on England's side. He is, after all, "Lord of our far-flung battle-line." His "Hosts" are the hordes of British "tommies" and loyal Indian sepoys who have long and successfully defended the empire. But again, after reading the Bible, we discover that the "Lord of Hosts" destroys Tyre by raising up in revolt "the terrible of nations." Like England, Tyre had been a great sea power but eventually had begun to boast, "I am a God, and I sit in the midst of the seas." These boasts, like those Kipling reprehends in the fourth and fifth stanzas, were made by men "drunk with sight of power" who put their trust in "reeking tube and iron shard" (guns and bullets) instead of in God. Their fate was to be swallowed up by the "lesser breeds without the law" and this is exactly what Kipling fears will happen to England. Thus, in commemorating Queen Victoria's Diamond Jubilee, Kipling has written what he fears might prove to be the empire's dirge. He is obviously ambivalent—torn between his pride in the "far-flung battle-line" and his shame in the "reeking tube and iron shard" that maintain it. This ambivalence laps at his consciousness like the waves of a rising tide through the repetitions of the word "lest," meaning "for fear that . . . for fear that!" Eventually his fears predominate and he bursts out with the concluding prayer:

> For frantic boast and foolish word—
> Thy mercy on thy people, Lord!

Puns and Paradoxes

An ambiguous statement that is intended to be humorous is called a *pun*. Puns almost invariably attain their effect by using one of the thousands of word pairs in English (called homonyms) that are identical in sound and spelling but different in meaning. If, for example, a woman tells us that she knows nothing of labor, either she has never borne children or never held down a job, depending on whether she is using *labor* to mean "the pains and efforts of childbirth" or "employment." When such word play is risqué or sexually suggestive, it is called double entendre (a French phrase meaning "to understand in two ways").

Shakespeare uses double entendre with exuberance in the final couplet of Sonnet CXLIII:

CXLIII

Lo, as a careful housewife runs to catch
One of her feathered creatures broke away,
Sets down her babe, and makes all swift dispatch
In pursuit of the thing she would have stay;
Whilst her neglected child holds her in chase,
Cries to catch her whose busy care is bent
To follow that which flies before her face,
Not prizing her poor infant's discontent:
So runn'st thou after that which flies from thee,
Whilst I thy babe chase thee afar behind;
But if thou catch thy hope, turn back to me,
And play the mother's part, kiss me, be kind;
So will I pray that thou mayst have thy "Will,"
If thou turn back and my loud crying still.

—William Shakespeare (ca. 1600)

If we have read Shakespeare's other sonnets (particularly, numbers CXXXIII, CXXXIV, CXLII, and CXLIV), we know that this one is addressed to the famous "woman colour'd ill," with whom he is in love; we also know that she is in love with Shakespeare's friend, "a man right fair." The first twelve lines of the poem carefully prepare us for the concluding couplet. The dark lady is compared with a housewife who chases after a "feathered" creature (presumably a cock or hen; but Shakespeare's use of synechdoche—in which a part of an object or animal signifies the whole—makes it possible for us to think of this creature as a fashionable, "feathered" courtier),[6] while her "neglected child" (Shakespeare) chases after her. Thus, the phrase "have thy 'Will' " may mean:

So I will pray that thou mayst catch thy cock,
If thou turn back and my loud crying still.

But the original phrase "have thy will," when applied to relations between the sexes, may also mean to "satisfy one's lust"; and finally, to

[6]The phrase *"feathered creatures"* is, therefore, *ambiguous* and can serve as one more example of that rhetorical device.

"have thy 'Will'" may mean—rather shockingly—that "Will" Shakespeare is prepared to tolerate his mistress's sexual infidelities so long as she returns to him afterward. In effect, Shakespeare has created a *triple entendre!*

Just as a pun is a form of ambiguity that plays on words, a *paradox* plays on *ideas*. When Mark Twain wrote, for example, that soap and education are less sudden than a massacre but more deadly in the long run, he was using a paradox. He expected his readers to recognize that, although the analogy is literally untrue, it would pass for truth with anyone who has seen the anguish of a schoolboy forced to wash or sit still. The paradox turns on the difference between physical death and the "deadly fear" of soap or the "deadly boredom" of school. Thus, a paradox is a statement that is true in some sense, even though at first it appears self-contradictory and absurd. When a paradox is expressed in only two words (living death, wise fool, etc.) it is called an *oxymoron*.

Paradoxes are used in poetry for at least three reasons. First, they invariably startle the reader. They are unexpected and, initially, inexplicable. Next, paradoxes involve the reader in an effort at understanding. And finally, if that effort is successful, each paradox delights the reader with a personal sense of discovery. Like allegory and metaphor, a paradox requires the reader to participate intellectually in the creation of literary meaning. Without this active participation, the paradoxes are simply incomprehensible.

In the sonnet "Design" (p. 114) Frost builds toward a paradox by lulling us into complacency with his fluid and unanswerable rhetorical questions:

> What had that flower to do with being white,
> The wayside blue and innocent heal-all?
> What brought the kindred spider to that height,
> Then steered the white moth thither in the night?

Then, just as we are beginning to reassure ourselves that such incidents are the result of pure happenstance, Frost startles us by suggesting a paradoxical solution:

> What but design of darkness to appall?—
> If design govern in a thing so small.

According to Frost, the odd congruence of whites in the poem is the "design of darkness." At first, perhaps, our intellects rebel against the paradox that darkness controls these three white objects—it is, after all, a little nonsensical. But Frost's intention is to hint at the possibility that malevolence lurks beneath the otherwise orderly surface of the natural world. By creating the paradox of a darkness that transforms the purest of whites into "assorted characters of death and blight," he makes us question our faith in the eventual triumph of good over evil.

In general, a paradox involves a contradiction between the physical or material meaning of words and their spiritual, emotional, or supernatural connotation, as in the case of Frost's poem. Such contradictory connotations also govern the lighthearted paradox by Twain, for soap and education are emotionally, but not physically, painful. Because paradoxes are capable of playing on the contrasts between earthly and spiritual truths, they are particularly common in religious revelations. In the ancient *Upanishads* of India (the chief theological documents of Hinduism), we learn, for instance, that "the gods love the obscure and hate the obvious." And the *Katha Upanishad* contains a number of paradoxes that raise questions about the interrelationship among mind, matter, and reality:

> If the slayer thinks he slays,
> If the slain thinks he is slain,
> Both these do not understand:
> He slays not, is not slain.
>
> —from the *Katha Upanishad* (700–600 B.C.)

Similarly, Taoism, a Chinese religion that dates back more than 2,000 years, teaches that

> One may know the world without going out of doors.
> One may see the Way of Heaven without looking through the windows.
> The further one goes, the less one knows.
> Therefore the sage knows without going about,
> Understands without seeing,
> And accomplishes without any action.
>
> —from *The Way of Lao-tzu* (800–300 B.C.)

Later, in the gospel according to St. John, 11:25–6, we find Jesus saying,

> I am the resurrection, and the life: he that believeth in me, though he were dead, yet shall he live:
> And whosoever liveth and believeth in me shall never die.
> —from *The New Testament* (first century A.D.)

In each case the paradox is initially disconcerting, or at least difficult to understand; however, each ultimately extends to us the principal consolation of religion: the faith in an existence that is more permanent and more attractive than the nasty, brutish, and short life allotted to ordinary man.

Pure paradoxes, involving wholly contradictory ideas, are relatively uncommon in poetry. However, *incongruity,* a similar rhetorical device, is plentiful. A word, a phrase, or an idea is said to be incongruous when it is out of keeping, inconsistent, or inappropriate in its particular surroundings. As was the case with ambiguity, incongruity is sometimes a stylistic flaw—a sign of sloppy thinking or imprecise writing—but when used carefully, it can subtly change the meaning of the surrounding words. When Byron wrote about amatory poets who "sing their loves/ In liquid lines mellifluously bland," he relied on the incongruity of the word "bland" to indicate his satiric disapproval of most love poetry. Byron knew very well that bland writing, like bland food, is usually dull or tasteless—the very opposite of the spicy passion one would expect to find in love poetry. This startling word choice hits us like a slap in the face when we have been expecting a gentle goodnight kiss. It creates a paradox in tone.

Irony

The term *irony* refers to a contrast or discrepancy between appearance and reality. This discrepancy can take on a number of different forms.

In *dramatic irony* the state of affairs known to the audience (or reader) is the reverse of what its participants suppose it to be. This is the form of irony used in *Oedipus Rex.* When the action of the play begins, Oedipus believes that, by fleeing his homeland as a youth, he has evaded the prophesy that he will murder his father and marry his mother. The audience knows, however, that he has already committed these crimes. (The audience's knowledge derives in part from the fact that Sophocles was writing about a widely known Theban legend and in part from the prophecies made by the oracle Teiresias early in the play.) Thus, the tragic impact of *Oedipus Rex* depends largely on our fascination with the plight of a man who is unaware of his own past, unable to avoid his own destiny, and driven remorselessly toward his fate by his very efforts to avoid it.

In *situational irony* a set of circumstances turns out to be the reverse of what is appropriate or expected. Richard Cory, the "hero" of Edwin Arlington Robinson's poem of 1897 by that name, is widely envied and admired because of his wealth, his charm, and his apparently agreeable life. Everything about him leads the "people on the pavement"—and the reader as well—to assume that he must be happy. He is "a gentleman from sole to crown," "clean favored," "quietly arrayed," and "richer than a king." In a world polarized between rich and poor, beautiful and plain, dignified and common, "them" and "us," Richard Cory seems without question to be "one of them," until the last lines of the poem shows us otherwise:

> And Richard Cory, one calm summer night,
> Went home and put a bullet through his head.

Henry David Thoreau once wrote that "the mass of men lead lives of quiet desperation." Ironically, Richard Cory's suicide proves that he was "one of us."

The most common form of irony, *verbal irony,* involves a contrast between what is literally said and what is actually meant. Lord Byron wittily uses this figure of speech to satirize religion in explaining that a series of consumptive attacks have made him pious—presumably because of the usual fear of dying unrepentant:

> The first attack at once proved the Divinity
>   (But that I never doubted, nor the Devil);
> The next, the Virgin's mystical virginity
>   The third, the usual Origin of Evil;
> The fourth at once established the whole Trinity
>   On so uncontrovertible a level
> That I devoutly wished the three were four,
> On purpose to believe so much the more.
>
> —from *Don Juan,* Lord Byron (1823)

Verbal irony always requires the reader to detect the discrepancy between the denotative meaning of the words and the author's intention in using them—in this case, between Byron's *claim* that he wished the three persons of the Trinity were four and his *purpose* in satirizing death-bed piety and Christian credulity in general. Thus, verbal irony is the riskiest of all poetic devices because there is always the possibility that the author's intentions will go unrecognized. In 1702 Daniel Defoe, who was himself a Puritan "dissenter," anonymously wrote an essay called "The Shortest Way with the Dissenters," in which he tried to satirize the excessive zeal of his Anglican opponents by ironically contending that Puritan ministers should be hung and all members of their congregations banished. To his surprise, no one perceived the irony: the Anglican establishment fully endorsed his proposals. Public unrest followed, the government intervened, and Defoe was fined, pilloried, and imprisoned—all because his irony was misunderstood.

Jonathan Swift, Defoe's contemporary, escaped a similar misunderstanding by making his ironic exaggerations so extreme that no one could take them seriously. In 1729, when he wanted to draw the attention of the Anglican government to the plight of starving Catholic children, he published *A Modest Proposal for Preventing the Children of Poor People in Ireland from Being a Burden to Their Parents or Country, and for Making Them Beneficial to the Public.* In this pamphlet he suggested that they be fattened, slaughtered, and sold as a delicacy like veal:

> A child will make two dishes at an entertainment for friends; and when the family dines alone, the fore or hind quarter will make a reasonable dish, and seasoned with a little pepper or salt will be very good boiled on the fourth day, especially in winter.
>
> —from *A Modest Proposal,* Jonathan Swift (1729)

In using such overstatement to ridicule the government's disregard of the sufferings of the Irish Catholics, Swift hoped to force a change in policy. Just as a surgeon's blade cuts so that it may cure, Swift's language is corrosive so that it may be corrective. Writing such as this, which holds up persons, ideas, or things to varying degrees of ridicule or contempt in order to bring about some desirable change, is known as *satire.*

Swift, Defoe, and Byron all sought to underscore and identify their ironies through comic *overstatement* (sometimes called hyperbole). Each hoped that the reader would perceive the exaggeration and therefore interpret the text as meaning the opposite of what it appeared to say. Swift really recommended Christian charity, not infanticide; Defoe really endorsed Christian tolerance, not narrow bigotry; and Byron really advocated Deism or agnosticism, not Christian credulity. The risk of misunderstanding an author's irony is particularly great when we ourselves have strong prejudices. Byron was so well aware of the potential ambiguity of irony that he probably considered it a form of protection. If accused of atheism and heresy for his comments on the Trinity, he could always claim he was merely satirizing death-bed repentances.

The other principal means by which poets signal irony is *understatement*—as when J. Alfred Prufrock, the protagonist of T. S. Eliot's famous poem, sadly reflects in a moment of self-disparagement that he has "measured out [his] life with coffee spoons." Just as overstatement is too emphatic, too exuberant, or too harsh, an understatement is too mild or too reserved. In both cases the reader's attention is arrested and his sensitivity to potential irony heightened because the poet's words are inappropriate and literally unbelievable.

Understated irony is often sarcastic. Unlike satire, *sarcasm* (from the Greek word *sarkazein* meaning "to tear flesh") is intended to hurt, not heal. Prufrock's bitter reflections about his life are often sarcastic. For a more modern and clearer example of sarcasm, consider Sir Winston Churchill's characterization of his political rival, Clement Atlee (England's Prime Minister between 1949 and 1951): "a very modest man—and with reason." Sarcasm, however, is not always so understated. Oscar Wilde, the nineteenth-century English novelist and dramatist, for example, was obviously exaggerating when he sarcastically claimed that "there are two ways of disliking poetry: one way is to dislike it, the other is to read Pope."

Although we have suggested that both overstatement and understatement often signal irony, it is wise to remember that they are not invariably ironic. Overstatement is especially susceptible to use and abuse in everyday speech by those who hope to be vivacious and enthusiastic. It is the linguistic equivalent of a facile smile. Thus, we sometimes exclaim, "How time flies!" when we mean, "it's getting late"; or, when we meet someone for the first time, we may say, "I'm delighted to meet you!" when we mean only, "Hello." Sometimes poets also overstate the truth as a means of showing enthusiasm; but, they, of course, find fresh and original ways of revitalizing tired hyperbolic formulas. Andrew Marvell expresses the idea of time flying by writing in "To His Coy Mistress" (1681),

But ever at my back I hear
Time's winged chariot hurrying near.

And Dr. Faustus, in Christopher Marlowe's play of that name, greets Helen of Troy, not with a lame "pleased to meet you," but with a rhetorical question that combines metonymy and overstatement in an expression of sheer rapture:

Was this the face that launched a thousand ships,
And burnt the topless towers of Illium?

Indeed, it may be that exuberance and a delight in words are the fundamental qualities of poetry. Poetry, it has been said, is what is lost in translation. The poet's use of ambiguity, irony, puns, and paradoxes depends almost entirely on the fact that certain words have multiple meanings. A skilled poet is almost by definition sensitive to the specific denotations and connotations of each word at his or her command. A poet knows that any change in word choice is a change in poetic meaning; that any attempt to translate, paraphrase, or summarize a poem is also an attempt to rewrite it—an act that inevitably damages its essence. Even the gentlest touch can be destructive. One cannot, even in admiration, stretch out the wings of the monarch butterfly without brushing the gold from their tips.

But if, in criticism as in entomology, we murder to dissect, what we murder through literary criticism is imperishable. After we have learned all we can from dissection, we have only to turn away from the battered specimen on the critic's pages—we have only to turn back to the poem itself—in order to find our monarch butterfly both alive and made more beautiful by understanding.

IMAGERY

Every word which is used to express a moral or intellectual fact, if traced to its root, is found to be borrowed from some material appearance. "Right" means "straight"; "wrong" means "twisted." "Spirit" primarily means "wind"; "transgression," the "crossing of a line"; "supercilious," the "raising of an eyebrow."

—from "Nature," Ralph Waldo Emerson (1836)

Words that describe a "material appearance" are referred to as *images*. Of course images may take a variety of forms. We see our reflected image in a mirror, and we find a representational image of Liberty in New York harbor. But when we speak of images in literature we mean primarily mental images—words that evoke our memories of events and objects. Poetic language pours out to us, like the plenteous and varied fruits of a cornucopia, a rich, sweet, and nourishing series of mental images that recall sensory experiences. We commonly think of an image as something seen, and indeed most imagery *is* visual. Thus, Emerson traces the words "right" and "wrong" to their visual roots in objects that are either "straight" or "twisted;" similarly, an offense against the law, a "transgression" (from the Latin *trans,* meaning "across," plus *gradi,* meaning "to step"), recalls the observable action of "crossing a line"; and a haughty or "supercilious" attitude describes the facial expression of someone—perhaps an aristocrat—"raising an eyebrow" in scorn.

Yet Emerson also shows us that not all imagery is primarily visual. We cannot *see* the wind, although we may see its results as it scatters dead leaves along the ground. The wind is more often felt than seen. The word "spirit," like most other words for emotional, intellectual, or philosophic concepts, probably evolved out of a comparison between a sensory experience and an abstract concept (wind/breath/vitality). This effort to make an abstract concept understandable through the use of sensory imagery is characteristic of nearly all poetic comparisons; but before examining the many uses of imagery, we ought to understand why imagery is essential to poetry and what forms it may take.

As Emerson's examples indicate, even the most abstract words often contain a tacit appeal to the senses. Everything we know about the world and about life is a result of what we have seen, heard, smelled, tasted, touched, and felt internally. Our senses provide the link between our minds and external reality. Sensations alone create for us the familiar world of men and women, mountains and valleys, lakes and rivers, physical pleasure and physical pain. So, too, with poetry. Poems without imagery are like a people without vision or hearing. Both exist in darkness and in silence, struggling for understanding in a world of inexpressible abstractions.

One of the achievements of mankind, of course, is the development of languages and systems of thought that allow us to intellectualize our experiences. When we read a poem we are actually declaring ourselves independent of the sensations of the moment. We call forth from our memories various sensual experiences or images. We rearrange those memories in the patterns suggested by the poet—patterns that often do not correspond with any of our actual experiences. In so doing, we participate in vicarious experiences. Images, therefore, are the windows through which we see (or imagine) how other men and women live, and love, and die. They enable us to make discoveries about ourselves and about the world in which we live.

To some extent, as Emerson reminds us, all words create images. The most abstract terms, as well as the most precise verbal pictures, require us to find meaning *in the words* by recollecting, however vaguely, experiences of our own in which we have read, heard, or used those words. Words such as *dragonfly, hollow,* and *heft* summon up fairly specific sensual responses based on sight, sound, and muscular exertion. We see mentally the bulbous eyes, the quivering wings, and the slim, hovering body of the dragonfly. We hear mentally the "hollow" sound of a voice in an empty room. We feel mentally a muscular play in the forearm and shoulder at the "heft" of a nine-iron, a favorite tennis racquet, or a crammed suitcase. But if we replace these imagistic words with scientific or generic terms—if, that is, *dragonfly* becomes *insect, hollow* becomes *void,* and *heft* becomes *specific gravity*—suddenly our mental images are deflated, like limp balloons, because the new terms are mere abstractions divorced from physical sensation.

A good poet always uses an exact image—an image with its own spicy taste, aroma, and appearance—in preference to the trite and overly general words or combinations of words served up like a tasteless pasta in sentimental verse. The difference between concrete, original imagery and imprecise, overworked banality can be illustrated by comparing the first stanza of George Meredith's *Modern Love* with three stanzas on the same subject (the discovery of infidelity) in "Lady Byron's Reply to Lord Byron's 'Fare Thee Well' ":

By this he knew she wept with waking eyes:
That, at his hand's light quiver by her head,
The strange low sobs that shook their common bed,
Were called into her with a sharp surprise,
And strangled mute, like little gaping snakes,
Dreadfully venemous to him. She lay
Stone-still, and the long darkness flowed away
With muffled pulses. Then, as midnight makes

Her giant heart of Memory and Tears
Drink the pale drug of silence, and so beat
Sleep's heavy measure, they from head to feet
Were moveless, looking through their dead black years,
By vain regret scrawled over the blank wall.
Like sculptured effigies, they might be seen
Upon their marriage-tomb, the sword between;
Each wishing for the sword that severs all.
—from *Modern Love,* George Meredith (1862)

Yes, farewell, farewell forever,
Thou thyself hast fix'd our doom,
Bade hope's sweetest blossoms wither,
Never more for me to bloom.
. . .
Wrapt in dreams of joy abiding
On thy breast my head hath lain,
In thy love and truth confiding,
Bliss I cannot know again.

When thy heart by me "glanc'd over"
First displayed the guilty stain,
Would these eyes had closed forever,
Ne'er to weep thy crimes again.
—from "Lady Byron's Reply,"
Anonymous

Both poets describe their feelings of betrayal, but "Lady Byron's" hack work is entirely devoid of real action and imagery. It is made up of sentimental commonplaces. Each line from "Yes, farewell, farewell forever" to "Ne'er to weep thy crimes again" deserves, and most likely gets, nothing more than an exasperated groan from readers who recognize that this "poet" has nothing to say, nothing to describe, no actions to represent, no knowledge of the world, and no understanding of poetic style beyond that which allows her to pull at the "throbbing heart-strings" of the most lachrymose and imperceptive readers.

In contrast, Meredith's poetry is packed with specific sense experiences. It is true that throughout the stanza the unhappy marriage partners lie almost motionless. But Meredith allows us to see the wife as she weeps with "waking eyes," to watch her reaction at "his hand's light quiver by her head," to hear and feel "the strange low sobs that shook their common bed," and perhaps even to taste the bitterness of "the pale drug of silence." Furthermore, a series of vivid phrases builds a sense of muscular tension: the wife's sobs were "*strangled mute;*" she "*lay stone still;*" together they looked back on "dead black years,/ By vain regret *scrawled* over the blank wall."

Even the greatest poets rarely find ways to call into play as many different senses as Meredith has in this stanza. Only the sense of smell is missing; and, as if to make up for the deficiency, Meredith manages to work an image of smell into his second stanza, where the wife's beauty sickens the husband, "as at breath of poison flowers." No doubt this exhaustive catalogue of sensuous imagery is intentional. Meredith's purpose is to show that the subtle change in the relationship between the former lovers has uprooted their lives and left them unable to engage in any human experience without seeing it anew and finding in it signs of their own emotional decay.

Thus, Meredith makes a thematic point by showing that every sensation the couple feels is altered by their present unhappiness. The use of poetic imagery does far more than simply add vigor to his writing; and what is true of Meredith's poem is true of poetry in general. Poets often choose their imagery according to some *principle of selection* and develop it with some meaningful pattern in mind. In Meredith's case, the principle of selection is an attempt to register the fact that all of the husband's senses have been altered by the discovery of his wife's infidelity. A second principle of selection is at work in Meredith's preoccupation throughout the poem with images of death. The first stanza alone makes reference to snakes, venoms, pale drugs, dead black years, sculptured effigies, and marriage tombs. At no point in the stanza does Meredith *tell* us that he is describing the death of love; however, his images allow us to determine that this must be his theme—that the wife's slight stiffening at her husband's touch is a sign of marital *rigor mortis*.

We should also be aware of the *pattern of development* in the imagery of the stanza. Initially, the focus is on the woman's waking eyes and the quivering hand beside her head. Then Meredith expands our vision to take in the bed, the surrounding darkness, and finally midnight's "giant heart of Memory and Tears." The effect is like that achieved by "zooming out" while filming a movie. It puts the marriage partners at the center of a universe that resonates "with muffled pulses" to their sufferings. Having established this broad perspective, Meredith uses imagery that closes in again—first to the memories scrawled across the blank walls and then to the marriage-tomb and the imaginary sword between the man and wife. This cyclical pattern in the development of the imagery is one of several devices Meredith uses to make each stanza a self-contained and satisfying "sonnet."[7] It contributes to our impression that *Modern Love* is an autobiographical series of journal entries written at discrete and circumspect moments as a real marriage decays. This poetic illusion, derived in large part from the pattern in the development of Meredith's imagery, makes *Modern Love* seem contemporary and realistic to each new generation of readers. It is one of the major stylistic features of the poem.

On rare occasions the principle of selection or pattern of development in imagery is more than simply a stylistic feature. It may provide a key to the entire poem or even to the poet's entire personality. In the poetry of Percy Bysshe Shelley, for example, we find repeated images involving sunsets, the wind and waves, moonlight, fountains, veiled women, and shadows. The very fact that Shelley returns so frequently to the same images suggests that he is giving voice to a philosophical preoccupation—namely, that the reality of life lies beneath its surface features and that everything we think to be real is the product of unseen forces. As a result, Shelley's images are all indirect: the colors of the sunset proceed from the unseen sun; the waves are driven by the unseen wind, and the wind itself is caused by unknown forces; moonlight is reflected indirectly from the sun; fountains pulse as a result of unseen pressures; veils conceal feminine beauty; and shadows are indirect images. In each image there is a veil of some kind that conceals the true source of beauty, for Shelley was a strong believer in Platonic idealism.[8]

We have seen that images make writing tangible, and we have seen that the manipulation of imagery is implicit in creative thought. The more exact and evocative the imagery in a poem, the more interested and entertained the reader will remain. Imagery is as indispensable to an exciting poem as action and emotion are to an exciting life. Furthermore, the poet's choice and arrangement of images may provide important clues to thematic and artistic purposes in philosophical poetry. Shelley's belief in the Platonic ideal of intellectual beauty was

[7] The stanza is not technically a sonnet because it is formed entirely of quatrains and contains sixteen lines to the sonnet's fourteen. Nevertheless, critics from Swinburne to Trevelyan have recognized the independence of each stanza by using the term *sonnet*.

[8] In Plato's allegory of the cave in *The Republic,* human beings are chained in such a way that they see only shadows cast on the wall of the cave and hear voices echoing from that wall. Naturally, they mistake the shadows and voices for reality.

abstract in the extreme, and it was a continual challenge to his poetic capabilities to find a way to write about the themes that interested him without allowing his poetry to degenerate into images the reader would be unable to comprehend intellectually or emotionally.

Even themes less abstract than Shelley's are necessarily difficult to express imagistically. Although Meredith examines the effect on the human spirit of disappointments in love, he finds no direct way to tell us it is his theme. Indeed, the human spirit is itself an abstraction, and Emerson's brief indication that the word *spirit* originated as a metaphor is enough to remind us that comparison is the principle technique used by poets to render the abstract in images. Poetic comparisons—more often than any other devices in the arsenal of figurative language—are the keys to a work's philosophical or ethical implications. They allow abstract ideas to be expressed in terms of sensory images that, in turn, find counterparts in the reader's imagination.

COMPARISONS

Prominent among the twelve "good rules" by which King Charles I of England sought to live was his proscription, "Make no comparisons!" It is suspected that his disdain for comparisons grew out of his belief in the divine and *incomparable* status of kings; this egotism so grated on his subjects that Oliver Cromwell, after comparing the king with other "traitors," ordered him executed in 1649. Since then, the right to draw comparisons—even invidious ones—has been one of the most cherished prerogatives of a free people, for it allows us to acquire new information, helps us to reach rational decisions, enables us to express abstract ideas imagistically, and provides us with endless opportunities for entertainment and the exercise of imagination.

We compare politicians before voting and products before purchasing as a means of collecting information and arriving at a decision. Poetic comparisons (*simile, metaphor, implied comparison, metonymy, personification, apostrophe, animism,* and *juxtaposition*) are more entertaining than those of everyday life, but the usefulness of comparison in influencing decisions remains virtually unchanged. John Donne, for example, in wooing a young woman compares the act of love with the predations of a flea:

Mark but this flea, and mark in this,
How little that which thou deniest me is;
It sucked me first, and now sucks thee,
And in this flea our two bloods mingled be;
Thou know'st that this cannot be said
A sin, nor shame, nor loss of maidenhead,
    Yet this enjoys before it woo,
    And pampered swells with one blood made of two,
    And this, alas, is more than we would do.
—from "The Flea," John Donne (1633)

In developing this analogy at such length—and it actually continues for another two stanzas—Donne is creating an *extended comparison.* He uses the flea as one argument to illustrate that the physical relationship he desires is not in itself a significant event: a very similar union has already taken place within the flea without "sin, nor shame, nor loss of maidenhead." Thus, in "The Flea," as in shopping or voting, a comparison identifies and illustrates some of the issues involved in making a decision.

Most poetry, however, is not directly intended to influence conduct or decisions. John Donne's comparison of true lovers to the twin legs of a geometric compass (see p. 99) is a good example of an illuminating comparison that has few implications for conduct; that analogy merely allows Donne to reassure his wife that distance can do nothing to separate them for, as Donne observes, "Thy firmness [as the fixed foot] makes my circle just,/ And makes me end, where I begun."

Whether used to influence conduct or to define abstract ideas through specific images, poetic comparisons may take on a variety of forms. This variety is well represented by the five comparisons in the first two stanzas of Donne's "Valediction: Forbidding Mourning":

As virtuous men pass mildly away,
    And whisper to their souls, to go,
Whilst some of their sad friends do say,
    The breath goes now, and some say, no:

So let us melt, and make no noise,
    No tear-floods, nor sigh-tempests move,
'Twere profanation of our joys
    To tell the laity our love.

The first of the comparisons runs through four and one-half lines and says, in essence, "Let us be just as calm in separating as a virtuous man is in dying." Comparisons such as this, which formally develop similarity between two things using *as, as when, like, than,* or other uivalent constructions, are known as *similes* (similes assert simi-arity). However, when a poet insists that two terms are identical instead of merely similar he creates a *metaphor.* In Donne's lines here, the hyphenated terms ("tear-floods" and "sigh-tempests"), although exaggerations, are good examples of metaphors; it is, however, more common to find a slightly fuller statement of the metaphor, using a form of the verb "to be," as in Shakespeare's assertion that "All the world's a stage." Both similes and metaphors are common in everyday speech. We say somebody is "sharp as a tack" or "as slow as molasses"; a brand-new car may be either a "lemon" or a "peach." Such similes and metaphors may once have been original and exciting, but they have become overused. Indeed, a shiny new comparison, like the latest model from Detroit, may emerge from the factory with a built-in obsolescence. Even though the comparison may originally have been a very good one, constant repetition may eventually cause us to react with insensitivity, indifference, or even hostility. The better the metaphor is, the more miles are put on it and the more rapidly it is worn out. Good poets, like all good writers, know this and as a result seek constantly to manufacture new analogies.

All similes and metaphors contain two parts, or terms. The *principle* or *primary term* is the one that conveys the literal statement made in the poem. In Donne's metaphors of "tear-floods" and "sigh-tempests," the literal statement concerns tears and sighs—hence, these are his principle terms. The *secondary term* in a metaphor is used figuratively to add color, connotations, and specificity to the more abstract primary term. Thus, Donne's "floods" and "tempests" are his secondary terms. Some literary critics call the primary term in a metaphor its tenor and the secondary term its vehicle.

An analogy in which one or both of these terms is implied but not stated may properly be called a metaphor, but we prefer the term *implied comparison* as being clearer and more accurate. When, for example, Donne writes, " 'Twere profanation of our joys/ To tell the laity our love," he is using one form of implied comparison. What he means is that their love is holy and spiritual like a secret religious ceremony, but only the primary term of the simile ("our love") is actually expressed. The idea that this love is analogous to a religious rite is implicit in the connotations of "profanation" and "laity," but this is left unstated.

On rare occasions, both terms in a comparison may be implied, as in Donne's phrase, "So let us melt." Here he is comparing the separation of spiritual lovers with the gentle natural process that transforms ice to water; however, he relies on the reader to reconstruct mentally this comparison from the single clue he provides in the verb "melt."

While metaphors, similes, and implied comparisons are useful to poets primarily because they offer a mechanism for stating abstract truths through specific images, they also contribute intellectual stimulation, emotional connotations, and conciseness. In the two stanzas just examined, Donne has been struggling to put into words his conception of the relationship between himself and his lover and of how their separation can best reveal the depth of their love. Donne wisely avoids any generalized statement of his intentions, choosing instead to express himself entirely through images of a dying man, of melting, of floods and tempests, and of clergy and laity. In addition to making his writing vivid and concrete, these images are intellectually stimulating, imaginative, and even a little audacious. The gist of Donne's argument is that true love is not wholly physical. It is capable of going through a change in state from physical to spiritual (as the soul does in death), or from fixed to formless (as hard ice becomes fluid water). By confronting, in the beginning, the hyperbolic fear that separation forebodes death, Donne is able to transform that foreboding into a religious consolation in which the secret joys of the lovers become sacramental experiences. In one bold and inherently sacrilegious sentence, Donne manages to tie together an awesome image of human mortality, a fundamental law of physics, the stormy forces of nature, and the powerful attraction of love. All of this imagery is permeated with emotional overtones (sorrow, resignation, fear, piety) that might have been lost in any direct statement about spiritual love, self-restraint, and patience. Finally, Donne's comparisons allow him to express all of this in only fifty-five words. Comparisons, in short, give to poetry both concision and density. They link the human senses and the human psychology without acknowledging the stages in logic and analysis that underlie this union.

Several other forms of implied comparison may occasionally be encountered in poetry. In *synecdoche,* a part of something is used to suggest the *whole* thing. George Meredith includes synecdoche when he uses the phrase "she wept with waking eyes" (p. 137). Obviously the woman is awake—not just her "waking eyes." In *metonymy* (meaning "change of name"), something associated with an object or idea replaces what is actually meant. Shakespeare uses metonymy when he writes that "the poet's pen/ . . . gives to airy nothing/ A local habitation and a name," since the poet, and not his pen, is clearly responsible for imaginative creation. Both synecdoche and metonymy are frequently found in slang. A "redneck" is a working man whose neck has been toughened by years in the wind and sun; an "old hand" means an experienced workman; and the "heavy" in a movie is a villain whose enormous size and aggressive behavior have become conventional.

The distinction between metonymy and synecdoche is not always clear, as we can see by reconsidering the first stanza of Rudyard Kipling's "Recessional":

> God of our fathers, known of old,
>   Lord of our far-flung battle-line,
> Beneath whose awful Hand we hold
>   Dominion over palm and pine—
> Lord God of Hosts, be with us yet,
> Lest we forget—lest we forget!

Is the "far-flung battle-line" to be taken as a part of the British empire (and is it, therefore, synecdoche), or is it a product of that empire (and thus metonymy)? Are the "palm and pine," which suggest the huge expanse of an empire ranging from the Middle East to Canada, the partial elements of the empire or are they allied and suggestive objects? Obviously, metonymy and synecdoche overlap in these images, and the most sensible decision is to use one word, metonymy, for both rhetorical devices.

An idea, object, or animal that is portrayed as having human traits is said to be personified. Storms, for example, have been traditionally personified by being given women's names. *Personification,* then, constitutes a form of implied comparison and allows the poet to describe with energy and vitality what might otherwise have remained inanimate or lackluster. Thus, John Milton in "Lycidas" uses personification in writing, "Under the opening eyelids of the Morn/ We drove a-field," when he really means that they drove out at daybreak. Similarly, Chaucer personifies the sunset in writing, "the brighte sonne lost his hewe;/ For th' orisonte hath reft the sonne his lyght," when he actually means what he says in the next line, "This is as muche to seye as it was night!" And George Meredith in the stanza quoted on p. 137, personifies midnight when he writes, "midnight makes/ Her giant heart of Memory and Tears/ Drink the pale drug of silence."

Personification is not always effective, as the third of these examples illustrates. The crucial test here, as with other rhetorical devices, is whether concision, specificity, meaning, and clarity are increased or decreased by the personification. In each of our examples, what is gained in vividness through personification is threatened by verbosity or exaggeration. Chaucer, however, makes fun of his own rhetorical excesses, while Milton's image of "the opening eyelids of Morn" effectively unites the emotional associations of daybreak, physical awakening, and dawning understanding. Chaucer's rhetoric is neither defensible nor intended to be so; it is comic. Milton's comparison, on the other hand, is appealing because it is imagistic and thoughtful. Meredith's imagery in this instance is simply baffling, however. We cannot be certain whether "Her giant heart" refers to Meredith's wife's heart or to midnight's heart. If it is midnight's, in what sense does midnight have a heart? Why should this heart be composed of "Memory and Tears"? Why should these nouns be capitalized? How can midnight be said to "beat/ Sleep's heavy measure"? And, finally, how can a "heart" be said to "drink"? But if it is the wife who is sleeping, does she wake up again when she looks back through her dead black years, wishing "for the sword that severs all"? Such ambiguities weaken Meredith's verse and demonstrate that personification is often facile and ridiculous.

Apostrophe, a limited form of personification, occurs when a poet or one of his characters addresses a speech to a person, animal, idea, or object. Although apostrophe is often ineffective in poetry, Geoffrey Chaucer uses it throughout his humorous "Complaint to His Empty Purse" (1399), which begins:

> To you, my purse, and to non other wight
> Complayne I, for ye be my lady dere!

and Shakespeare uses apostrophe during King Lear's ragings on the heath:

> Blow, winds, and crack your cheeks! Rage! Blow!
> You cataracts and hurricanoes, spout
> Till you have drench'd our steeples, drown'd the cocks!° °*weathervanes*

You sulph'rous and thought-executing fires,
Vaunt-couriers° of oak-cleaving thunderbolts, °*fore-runners*
Singe my white head! And thou, all-shaking thunder,
Strike flat the thick rotundity o' th' world!
Crack nature's mold, all germens° spill at once °*germs, seeds*
That makes ingrateful man!
—from *King Lear,* William Shakespeare (1605)

However, Chaucer's address to his purse is but a playful piece of foolishness and Lear's address to the storm is but a symptom of his madness. In neither case does the poet expect us to abandon our belief in the futility of talking to the walls and the winds. If apostrophe were *always* used ironically, as in both of these examples, or comically, as in Robert Burn's poems "To a Mouse" and "To a Louse," then inept poets would undoubtedly have developed some other means of debauching the English language. As things are, however, too many second-rate poems are packed with silly and sentimental apostrophes to Truth, Beauty, Love, and a host of other capitalized abstractions. Weak poets, having worked themselves or their characters up to a stage of violent emotions, often degenerate into what John Ruskin called the "pathetic fallacy" of facile and unimaginative personification. The trite and insipid tribute of Anna Laetitia Barbauld to "Life" is a typical example of the worst form of apostrophe:

Life! We've been long together,
Through pleasant and through cloudy weather;
'Tis hard to part when friends are dear—
Perhaps 'twill cost a sigh, a tear.
—from "Life," Anna Laetitia Barbauld (1811)

Excessive personification or apostrophe is not the only way to ruin a poem, but it may be the most reliable.

A poet may also describe an idea or inanimate object as though it were living, without attributing human traits to it. Before the development of the motion picture, this device could be called animation, but because that term is now best confined to cartoons, we will use the term *animism* for poetic comparisons that give life to inanimate objects. Carl Sandburg employs animism to good effect in his brief poem "Fog":

Fog

The fog comes
on little cat feet

It sits looking
over harbor and city
on silent haunches
and then moves on.
—Carl Sandburg
(1916)

Similarly, Robert Burns uses animism when he compares the high spirits of love with the appearance of a newly sprung rose:

O, my luve is like a red red rose
That's newly sprung in June
O, my luve is like the melodie
That's sweetly played in tune.
—from "A Red, Red Rose,"
Robert Burns (1796)

Of course, Burns is also comparing the woman he loves (as well as the emotion of love) with a red rose—young, fresh, fragrant, and beautiful. All depends on whether "my luve" is taken as meaning "my feeling when in love" or "my loved one." In the former, a feeling or idea is animated by comparison with the rose; in the later, the appearance and personality of the maiden are described. Because both interpretations are compatible, this pleasant ambiguity is best left unresolved; however, we should at least mention that the second reading suggests yet another form of comparison. This technique of speaking about a person in terms that are more applicable to a plant, animal, or machine is just the opposite of personification, and yet, oddly, it has no commonly accepted name other than metaphor. T. S. Eliot used this form of comparison in "The Love Song of J. Alfred Prufrock" (1917) to add to the narrator's scorn for his own insignificance:

I should have been a pair of ragged claws
Scuttling across the floors of silent seas.

Theodore Roethke, in his "Elegy to Jane," described the "sidelong pickerel smile" of one of his former students, whom he also compared to a wren, a sparrow, and a skittery pigeon. And early blues musicians, whose roots were in the soil of the Mississippi Delta, compared themselves to a variety of country creatures in such songs as "The Bull Frog Blues" (Willie Harris), "The Crawling Kingsnake Blues" (John Lee Hooker), and "The Milk Cow's Calf Blues" (Robert Johnson) in describing their passions and sorrows.

One final form of implied comparison is created through *juxtaposition.* In juxtaposition, two items are merely placed side by side. The author makes no overt comparison between these items and draws no inferences. The reader is free to make of them what he or she will. An impressive example of juxtaposition occurs in Henry Reed's post-World War II poem entitled "Lessons of the War: Naming of Parts." Each of the five stanzas in the poem describes some stage in the military exercise of breaking down and naming the parts of an army rifle; and then, in juxtaposition to this, Reed "names" some of the parts of springtime. The first stanza is representative of the technique followed throughout the poem:

> Today we have naming of parts. Yesterday,
> We had daily cleaning. And tomorrow morning,
> We shall have what to do after firing. But today,
> Today we have naming of the parts. Japonica
> Glistens like coral in all of the neighboring gardens,
> And today we have naming of parts.
>
> —from "Lessons of War: Naming of Parts,"
> Henry Reed (1947)

The first four sentences of the stanza are mechanical, denotative, and dull, whereas the first clause in the next sentence ("Japonica/ Glistens like coral in all of the neighboring gardens") is naturalistic, figurative, imagistic, and appreciative. We see the author's mind at play just as it had been at rather dull work in the preceding lines. We see him transform himself from a military automaton to a sensually aware human. We see him in an act of mental rebellion against a numbing, mechanical, and inhumane routine. At the same time that his hands and arms go through the rituals of slaughter, his eyes and intellect follow the processes of natural rebirth. From a strictly logical point of view, the two parts of Reed's stanza are incompatible, but he unites them by his repetition of the final phrase, "today we have naming of parts." And in that repetition Reed is implicitly asserting his ability to metamorphize his army experiences in a triumph of human feeling over inhumane behavior.

Juxtaposition is rarely used with as great a dramatic effect as in "Naming of Parts," but it is frequently important in creating the impression of fate or inevitability. When Edwin Arlington Robinson wrote that "Richard Cory, one calm summer night,/ Went home and put a bullet through his head," he was juxtaposing the calm, warm weather and the cold, irrational action in order to prod us into pondering possible reasons for Richard Cory's death. And when Robert Frost found "a dimpled spider, fat and white,/ On a white heal-all, holding up a moth," the juxtaposition of those symbols of death and blight became ominous and potentially fateful.

SYMBOL AND ALLEGORY

As we noted in our earlier discussion of fiction, a symbol is something that stands for something else, and an allegory is a narrative that uses a system of implied comparisons—often including symbols—to develop two or more simultaneous levels of meaning. Both devices occur naturally in literature to expand the suggestiveness and significance of writing.

A symbol may be *private* (its meaning known only to one person), *original* (its meaning defined by its context in a particular work), or *traditional* (its meaning defined by our common culture and heritage). At its most complex, a symbol may be all three as, for example, in this extract from "The Whale," a poem that occurs in the ninth chapter of Herman Melville's *Moby-Dick:*

The ribs and terrors in the whale
　Arched over me a dismal gloom,
While all God's sun-lit waves rolled by,
　And left me deepening down to doom.

I saw the opening maw of hell
　With endless pains and sorrows there;
Which none but they that feel can tell—
　Oh, I was plunging to despair.

—from "The Whale," Herman Melville (1851)

Here, and throughout *Moby-Dick,* the whale is a private symbol, in the sense that it emerges from Melville's own whaling experiences. Melville once wrote, "If, at my death my executors (or more properly, my creditors) find any precious manuscripts in my desk, then I prospectively ascribe all the honor and glory to whaling; for a whale-ship was my Yale and Harvard." But actual experience with whales may have been responsible for only part of the private symbolism in the poem. The battle with the whale may also have served as a metaphor for confrontation with Melville's own despair and reflect the "dismal gloom" of his failure to make a living as a bank clerk, a teacher, a surveyor, a seaman, and finally an author. At the time that he completed *Moby-Dick,* Melville was in debt to his publisher and to his friends, and he saw little hope of attaining solvency.

No one, of course, can truly gauge the extent to which a poem symbolizes an author's personal turmoil, but there can be no doubt that the whale in *Moby-Dick* is an original, powerful, and fully developed symbol within the novel. Even in the eight lines of poetry quoted here, it is clear that the whale is an object of horror, a force of evil, and an embodiment of the darkest spiritual despair. These symbolic associations arise out of the poem itself and require of the reader only a sensitivity to the meaning of words.

The eight lines, however, also suggest the traditional *parable* (an instructive moral story) of Jonah and the Whale. In fact, Melville's poem, when read in its entirety, exactly parallels the story of Jonah, who was thrown to the whale because of a lack of faith in God, confined to the whale's belly in black distress, and finally resurrected after calling upon God for assistance. In this sense, the whale is an *archetype* (a basic and repeated element of plot, character, or theme) that symbolizes separation from God and even death; its symbolic associations are traditional—that is, common to all readers who share the Judeo-Christian heritage.

Symbols are not, however, always this complex. In one sense, symbolism is the most common of all linguistic devices. After all, a word is nothing but a sound that symbolizes a particular image or concept. No word has meaning unless our human ability to symbolize makes it so. There is no necessary connection, for example, between the word *dog* and the familiar four-legged animal we associate with that word; after all, people of other nations have developed the same symbolic associations with other sounds: *chien* in French, *hund* in German, *canis* in Latin, and so on.

Even literary symbols are often quite simple. Winter, for example, often is a symbol of old age, spring of youth, summer of maturity, and autumn of decline. Similarly, a lamb may be a symbol of innocence, a lion of courage, a fire of vitality, and a rock of firmness. In each case, an implied comparison is drawn between a vivid image and an abstract quality.

The one-to-one correspondences set up by these symbols are akin to those established in simple *allegories* like the medieval morality play, *Everyman.* The hero, Everyman, is accompanied on his journey to the grave by characters whose actions and even names symbolize his Good-Deeds, Five Wits, Strength, Discretion, Beauty, and Knowledge. *Everyman* is known as an allegory because its simple symbols are systematically used to emphasize the moral point that only our good deeds are of lasting value both in life and after death. The systems of symbols used in allegories often tend toward didacticism and overt moral instruction. Such blatancy is a major reason why allegory is no longer a popular literary mode.

It is incorrect, however, to say that allegory no longer has a place in literature. Just as symbolism is a universal element of language, allegory is a universal element of fictional narration. Any literary (as opposed to journalistic) presentation of characters or events invariably prompts the reader to inquire, "What does it mean? What is the author's point?" And such questions represent the first step toward uncovering an allegorical purpose. Graham Hough, an important contemporary scholar, has developed a useful example of the process:

> We read some report of, say, treachery, sexual misadventure, and violence in the newspapers, and it is there only to record the fact that such events took place. We read of the same sequence of events in a novel or a short story, and we can hardly escape the feeling that it is there to say something to us about human passions and motives in general. From there it is only a step to seeing the characters as types of Treachery, Violence and Lust. . . .[9]

If the actions of fictional characters are highly idiosyncratic and suggest no universal traits of humanity, we will probably be reluctant to identify them as allegorical "types"; but if the thematic element in the story is strong—that is, if the story seems to be making a general comment about humanity—it must to some extent suggest allegorical possibilities.

[9] *An Essay on Criticism* (London: Duckworth, 1966), p. 121.

The problem facing the student of literature is not, then, whether a given story, poem, or play includes symbolism and allegory, but whether these nearly universal elements of literature are so important in the specific work that they need to be isolated, discussed, and evaluated. We can best resolve this problem by answering two questions. First, does the author put unusual emphasis on a particular image or series of images? Second, does the poem or story fail to make literal sense *unless* we interpret the images symbolically or allegorically? An affirmative answer to either or both questions should make us suspect that the author may be using images as symbols—perhaps, but not necessarily, in an allegory.

Discussions of symbolic or allegorical meanings in literature should always be very cautious. Because all words are in some sense symbolic and because every theme is in some sense allegorical, inexperienced critics (and even some experienced ones) are too easily tempted to "read things into" the works they study. Even at its best, symbol hunting is an attempt at mind reading. We can all easily identify the images an author uses, but we often get into trouble when we begin to speculate about what the author intended in choosing them. Unless we can find strong evidence in the poem to support our symbolic interpretations, there is a very high probability that the only mind we are capable of reading is our own. When an author thinks his use of symbols is important, we can be quite confident that he will hint at their meaning in one or more places. When no authorial interpretation (or even acknowledgment) of the symbols can be found, the wise critic will think carefully before insisting on a symbolic interpretation. Like Hawthorne's Ethan Brand, who looked throughout the world for signs of the Unpardonable Sin—before finding it in himself—we may find that the symbolic meanings we seek in the works of others exist only in the smithy of our own souls.

Perhaps the best known of all forced symbolic interpretations is the one once given by religious authorities to the "Song of Solomon" in the Old Testament. For centuries ecclesiastical scholars saw the entire poem as an allegory in which the Lord is portrayed as a lovestricken shepherd and His church as a beautiful Shulamite maiden. Thus, the following four verses are alleged, in the gloss of the King James version of the Bible, to be "a further description of the graces of the church":

1. How beautiful are thy feet with shoes, O prince's daughter! the joints of thy thighs are like jewels, the work of the hands of a cunning workman.

2. Thy navel is like a round goblet, which wanteth not liquor: thy belly is like a heap of wheat set about with lillies.

3. Thy two breasts are like two young roes that are twins.

4. Thy neck is as a tower of ivory; thine eyes like the fishpools in Heshbon, by the gate of Bath-rabbim: thy nose is as the tower of Lebanon which looketh toward Damascus.

—from "The Song of Solomon," Chapter 7

Clearly, this passage creates difficulties for very straight-laced and pious readers. If the entire Bible is a direct revelation of the word of God, what is the purpose of this tantalizing description of how a maiden's thighs, navel, and breasts have proven her to be most "fair and pleasant . . . for delights"? Why should God want to take up our time with what on the surface appears to build toward censurable heavy breathing? To many religious readers, a symbolic interpretation seemed like the only escape from biblical pornography. To them, the first verse was not really about the juncture of a maiden's thighs, but rather about the beauties of holy mother church. In truth, even an atheistic reader might find some comfort in an interpretation that allows an escape from the apparent fact that in the fourth verse the shepherd compliments his lover upon having a nose like the tower of Lebanon. But nothing in the poem itself gives much support to a symbolic or an allegorical reading. Evidently the "Song of Solomon" is just what it appears to be, a beautiful and imagistic love poem. And it is reassuring to note that, after nearly two millennia of distorted allegorical approaches, Biblical scholars now hold that "the poem may be interpreted literally," while they cautiously and ambiguously observe that it is yet another question "whether the allegorical interpretation . . . is admissible."[10]

If we are to draw any lessons from the "Song of Solomon," they should certainly include the following points: (1) That vivid imagery in poetry is an end in itself and need not imply a symbolic purpose; (2) that symbolic and allegorical interpretations of imagery are always possible but not always defensible; and (3) that it is better to say nothing about a few true symbols than to find false ones every-

[10] George J. Spurrell and Rev. Charles H. H. Wright, "Books of the Bible and the Apocrypha," in *The Holy Bible: Authorized King James Version* (Philadelphia: The Judson Press, 1936), Part III, p. 35.

where. Many stones are best left unturned. While one in a million may conceal a glittering treasure, the rest are homes for vipers.

THE PLAIN SENSE OF POETRY

As I. A. Richards noted almost half a century ago in his seminal book *Practical Criticism* (1929), the chief problem faced by the student of poetry is "the difficulty of making out [the poem's] plain sense." In the preceding pages we have identified some of the sources of this difficulty by demonstrating that poets often use unfamiliar denotations, connotations, or allusions and may change the meaning of words through repetition, ambiguity, puns, paradoxes, and irony. Furthermore, poetic comparisons, although often vivid and delightful, may also be suggestive, symbolic, or ambiguous. Finally, poetry is, as a general rule, much more densely packed with meaning than prose. The author of a sonnet has, after all, only fourteen lines in which to make a point—a restriction that requires him either to confine himself to a very minor point or to make every word count. A sonnetlike density is traditionally expected in poetry, even when the actual length of the poem is not limited by any formal strictures. In spite of these difficulties, the simple prose meaning of most poetry can be determined by using common sense and our accumulated knowledge of how poetry works. By following seven relatively simple steps, the risk of misapprehending the plain sense of poetry can be reduced.

LIST DENOTATIONS AND CONNOTATIONS. As we have already shown, many words have multiple meanings, and poets often intentionally play on this multiplicity. We need to be cautious, of course, about assuming that an author is always—or even generally—toying with multiple denotations. In poetry, as in prose, an author normally intends to make a clear and forceful point, and ambiguity, by its very nature, must always interfere with the clarity of a statement. But even if the poet avoids ambiguity, he or she is almost certainly cognizant of the connotations of each word and may use them to modify the meaning. Thus, in studying a poem for the first time, the reader should look up in the dictionary any difficult or unfamiliar words and jot down their connotations and alternate definitions. Let us see how we can apply this first recommendation to the analysis of the following well-known lyric:

UPON JULIA'S CLOTHES

Whenas in silks my Julia goes
Then, then (methinks) how sweetly flows
That liquefaction of her clothes.

Next, when I cast mine eyes and see
That brave vibration each way free;
O how that glittering taketh me!
—Robert Herrick (1648)

Like most poetry written in an age and in circumstances quite distant from our own, these six lines present several problems in denotation. After more than three hundred years, we have naturally changed some of the ways in which we use words, and Herrick's vocabulary, although not archaic, is uncommon and distinctive. To be on the safe side, we might look up a half-dozen words with the following results:

whenas: whenever
methinks: it seems to me
cast: turn, direct, throw
goes: moves about, leaves
liquefaction: fluidity
brave: strong, finely dressed, courageous

In moving from denotation to connotation, we find more to interest a literary critic:

silks: Silken clothing is thin, expensive, lustrous, and sensuous. Although Herrick is presumably referring to a silken dress, "silks" may also connote silk stockings or a silk nightgown. Thus, the connotations of the word are luxuriant and slightly sensual.

my Julia: The use of the possessive adjective "my" suggests that Julia may be Herrick's possession, his mistress—both confirming and compounding the sensuous connotations of "silks."

goes: This is a curious word choice. Clearly, when Julia "goes," she is walking. Perhaps Herrick thought that walking was too common an activity and perhaps, too, he was trying to be precise, for a woman in a long, full skirt may seem to glide about—or "go"—without seeming to walk at all. Possibly Herrick wanted to suggest that Julia was leaving, "going away." If so, "whenas" reminds us that this is something that she does frequently, and we may be tempted to assume that Herrick is describing her as she leaves after a lovers' tryst. Certainly, "goes" was in part dictated by Herrick's need for a word to rhyme with "flows" and "clothes."

liquefaction: Here sound connotations come into play. The word itself is equivalent to "liquid action," but it rolls off the tongue more smoothly and thus is most appropriate.

cast mine eyes: The phrase is vigorous and active. Because Herrick had been watching Julia in the first three lines, these words must mean something more than that he simply continued to look at her. If indeed Julia had been leaving in the first sentence, then in "casting" his eyes, Herrick is probably turning his head to watch her receding figure. The phrase shows Herrick's strong attraction to Julia.

brave: We have already had something to say about the denotations of the adjective "brave." Undoubtedly, Herrick is using the archaic definition, "finely attired"; however, that was a secondary definition even in Herrick's day, and therefore the connotations of "boldness" and "courage" cannot be escaped.

vibration: In the twentieth century we are apt to associate this word with very rapid oscillations—especially with the vibrations of automobiles, trains, and planes moving at high speed. In the seventeenth century, however, the word was most often used to describe the slow swing of a pendulum. In this poem, therefore, "that brave vibration each way free" suggests the gentle side-to-side swishing of a woman's skirts. And, in fact, the bravado and freedom of these oscillations may indicate that Julia's swaying motion is a trifle wanton.

ANALYZE SYNTAX. If the meaning of a particular sentence is unclear, analyze its syntax by identifying the subject, the verb, the object, and the function of the major clauses. We have just as much right to expect syntactic clarity in verse as in prose, and no poet who habitually disregards the rules of English grammar can attain the respect of literate readers unless his or her verse has remarkable compensatory elements. Of course, good poets sometimes, by design, use syntax ambiguously to suggest competing interpretations (Remember the Delphic oracle's, "Pyrrhus the Romans shall conquer"?); however, this possibility merely underscores the need to understand fully the syntactic relationships among words.

Herrick's brief poem "Upon Julia's Clothes" is constructed of two parallel sentences. Each consists of a subordinate clause followed by an exclamation. Because the two sentences are similar in so many respects, the slight differences between them are all the more pronounced. The first sentence is introspective ("methinks") and intransitive ("how sweetly flows/That liquefaction of her clothes"). In contrast, the second sentence is active ("I cast mine eyes") and transitive ("O how that glittering taketh me"). In the first sentence, Herrick is a reflective observer; in the second, he is acting and being acted upon. The two sentences combine to show that he is prey to a passion that intensifies as he watches the rustling of his mistress's clothing. Even in the choice of his syntactic subjects, we find him moving from water ("liquefaction") to fire ("glittering") and thus from tranquility to excitement.

IDENTIFY THE FIGURES OF SPEECH. By definition, figurative language is not meant to be taken literally. Poetic language deviates from ordinary language to point the way toward meaningful emotional truths. When Herrick exclaims, "Then, then (methinks) how sweetly flows/That liquefaction of her clothes," he certainly does not mean that Julia's dress dribbles down into a soggy pool at her feet—although that is the image we may get if we try to interpret his lines literally. Actually, Herrick is drawing an implied comparison between the soft, shiny movements of Julia's silken dress and the gentle, rippling flow of a stream.

This is the only figure of speech used in Herrick's brief poem, and we should not ordinarily expect to find more in such short poetic passages. Figures of speech are like distilled liquors: the first dram or two elevates the spirits, but successive draughts befuddle and bewilder the brain. (They may also leave an unfortunate aftertaste.) Whenever an author *does* use numerous figures of speech, it becomes absolutely essential to identify the various types being used (whether allusion, ambiguity, irony, paradox, pun, or one of the various forms of comparison), and it is often useful as well to recast those figures, at least temporarily, into language that is not poetic. Allusions, ironies, paradoxes, and puns should be explained; metaphors and implied comparisons should be rewritten as similes; and symbols should be identified. To do so without greatly distorting the poem, we must be sensitive to the connotations of words and to the uses of ambiguity.

PARAPHRASE THE POEM. The purpose of a paraphrase is to help us understand the prose sense of a poem by changing the poetic language of difficult passages into language that we can easily comprehend. This process is the most direct means of making sure that we understand what a poet is saying—quite apart from how well it is said.

Having enumerated denotations and connotations, analyzed syntax, and identified figures of speech, it should not be difficult to write down a full prose statement of the poem's content. Thus, "Upon Julia's Clothes" might be paraphrased in the following manner:

> Whenever my Julia walks in silks, then (it seems to me) that the sounds made by the movement of her clothing are as lovely as the rippling of a stream. Next, when I look at the glamorous vibrations of her skirts, O how their glittering attracts me!

Any paraphrase, as long as it is reasonable, helps us to check our understanding of a poem's literal meaning by expressing it in slightly different words. The process itself, however, is fraught with risks. We may be tempted to substitute our own prose statement for the poem itself, which may obscure our appreciation of the poem's style and feeling. Or, we may persuade ourselves that the poem means exactly what we say it means and nothing else—a conclusion that glosses over the questionable decisions about denotation and connotation that must be made in attempting to paraphrase any poem. We might, for example, be tempted to change a few words in our paraphrase of "Upon Julia's Clothes" and as a result come to interpret the poem more sensuously:

> Whenever my mistress Julia comes toward me dressed in silks, then (it seems to me) that her clothes flow about her body as smoothly and beautifully as water in a stream. Next, when I turn my eyes and see the saucy and free swing in her walk as she passes, O how the glittering of her skirts enamours me!

It would be difficult to determine a rational reason for preferring one of these paraphrases over the other. The first moves from the *sound* of Julia's dress to the *sight* of it, whereas the second implies that Herrick watches Julia as she walks by—admiring her figure from front and rear. The first paraphrase is a little too staid; the second a little too steamy. The poem itself contains something of both; it manages to be suggestive without the slightest trace of immorality. This elusiveness is, of course, exactly what makes poetry more interesting than common prose. Stripping the nuances from a poem is like skimming the cream from milk: it takes away the richness and taste. In each case, all that remains is a thin, watery, and almost denatured product. The language of poetry is *not* static or technical or purely denotative; it is rich and complex, and no paraphrase can fully do it justice. Yet, the risks of leaving the poem's prose meaning unstated are even greater, for then the ambiguities of poetic diction may entice the reader into believing that his or her own preoccupations and fantasies are somehow mirrored in each line. If anything, the temptation to read something into the poem that its actual content will not justify implies a greater disrespect for the written word than the opposite risk of relying too heavily on the paraphrase. The latter may be nothing more than a shadow of the true poetic substance, but the former is too often the product of an overstimulated imagination, having no relationship whatsoever to the poem.

VISUALIZE AND SUMMARIZE THE IMAGERY AND ACTIONS. The preceding steps have all been analytical. They require us to look up definitions, to examine verbal structures, to reword sentences: to act, to think, and to write. In doing so, however, we have omitted what is certainly the most important process of all: to enjoy. When we relax and allow the poet's imagery to carry us into the world of imagination, we are most in harmony with the true poetic impulse. But more than that, visualizing the events in the poem and attempting to recreate imaginatively everything that the poet describes can often be indispensable to careful critical judgment. Careless writers sometimes juxtapose incongruous and even ludicrous images because they themselves fail to see clearly what they ask their readers to envision: for example, "March roared in like a lion and crawled out like a baby." Here the conventional analogies have been preserved—probably without any expectation that we will actually visualize this lion transformed into a puling infant. The use of such incongruous comparisons is called *mixed metaphor*.

Once we have tried to visualize everything that the poet describes for us, we will find it easier to summarize the action and circumstances in the poem. In so doing, we will generally wish to identify the speaker (who may or may not be the poet himself), the setting, and the circumstances. A summary of "Upon Julia's Clothes" will not add much to our understanding of the poem because the poem itself is so short and uncomplicated. However, Frost's sonnet "Design," which is only slightly longer, can snap into focus if we first visualize it and then summarize our vision in something like the following manner:

> The poet, on a morning walk along a roadside, sees a white moth within the grasp of a white spider perched on a white and blighted wildflower.

> This strange and incongruous combination leads him to reflect about the role of fate in the events of the world.

A line-by-line paraphrase of "Design" might isolate and clarify problems in the interpretation of specific words and phrases, but it would also equal or exceed the length of the original fourteen-line poem. A simple four-line summary, such as the one proposed here, has an advantage: it allows us to think of the poem as a totality—to get a single image of it—and that image, if well formed, can serve as a starting point for further explanation, analysis, and understanding.

EVALUATE THE POEM'S TONE. The tone of a poem is created by the author's overall attitude toward his subject or audience. It helps to determine the choice of words and rhetorical devices. Thus, when we wish to evaluate a poem's tone, we do so by examining the emotional effects of its words, images, and figures of speech (particularly overstatement, understatement, irony, paradox, and ambiguity). In any collection of poetry, we will find some poems in which the tone is obvious; others in which it is complex; and still others in which it changes as the poet develops his or her thoughts.

In many cases, the author's tone is unmistakable. "Upon Julia's Clothes," for example, clearly reflects Herrick's passionate preoccupation with Julia. His attitude is expressed directly by his exclamations, "how sweetly flows/That liquefaction of her clothes" and "O how that glittering taketh me!" And it is expressed indirectly by the fact that the poet's excitement is stimulated so easily. We recognize that he must indeed be deeply in love if so small a thing as the rustle of Julia's skirts drives him to poetic expression. Herrick's tone, then, is enraptured, loving, and excited.

The analysis of tone becomes more difficult when the author uses irony, paradox, or ambiguity because conflicting meanings and, hence, conflicting attitudes toward the subject are implied by those devices. When, for example, Byron writes that a serious illness made him so devoutly religious that he wished the three persons of the Trinity were four "On purpose to believe so much the more," we will wholly misunderstand his tone and meaning unless we recognize that he is being ironic. The literal sense of the words is at odds with their real intention, and Byron's tone is sceptical, instead of pious, and playful, instead of serious.

The determination of tone becomes even more complex when, as in the case of Frost's "Design," the poet's attitude seems to change as he reflects more and more deeply on the significance of the events he describes. The first eight lines of Frost's poem are largely descriptive. The tone is observing, meticulous, and perhaps a little eerie. We see the flower, the moth, and the spider close up, as if through a magnifying glass; and the preoccupation with death and blight, along with the analogy to a witches' broth, is chilling. The next six lines present three rhetorical questions and a final conditional clause. Here Frost begins to inquire into the meaning of what he has just described. The first two questions merely underscore the unusual combination of events that brought together the blighted flower, the albino spider, and the innocent white moth. Frost's tone is inquisitive and concerned, but still fairly neutral and objective. In the last question, the tone suddenly becomes fearful. What else, Frost asks, can this incident be "but the design of darkness to appall?" Then Frost moves in a direction that at first appears reassuring when he doubts, almost as an afterthought, "If design govern in a thing so small." Yet the line also opens up the unsettling possibility that there is no design at all and the world is governed by chance. If there is any reassurance in these thoughts, that reassurance ought to be thoroughly undermined by the fearful realization that the scene *has* seemed fated. The designs of darkness *have* seemed to operate—even at the insignificant level of the moth, the spider, and the innocent heal-all! This sobering and somewhat horrifying possibility ultimately summarizes the direction toward which the poem—both in tone and in meaning—has been driving all along.

IDENTIFY THE THEME. A literary *theme,* as we use the term in this text, is the central idea or insight that unifies and controls the total work. It is the main point an author wishes to make about his subject. As such, identifying a poem's theme involves two steps: finding the poem's subject and formulating the poet's main statement about that subject.

It is easy to determine the subject of most poems: often it is named or suggested by the title, and, of course, it is the focus of the whole poem. Herrick's title, "Upon Julia's Clothes," clearly names his subject—although we might add that the only significance of the clothes is that Julia is wearing them. At heart, the poem is an expression of Herrick's love for Julia. And this more general statement of the subject carries us far toward understanding the poem's theme, which—

broadly stated—is that everything associated with the woman one loves becomes as beautiful and enchanting as she is.

The title of Frost's sonnet, "Design," reflects both the poem's subject and its theme. The subject is the possibility of design in the convergence of the white flower, the white moth, and the white spider. The theme—as nearly as one can state what Frost leaves only as a question—is that perhaps the designs of darkness control even the trivial and insignificant events in nature.

Stating a poem's theme in one sentence can be useful in summarizing its purpose and importance, but it is also a coarse and misleading approach to poetry. If Herrick or Frost had wished to develop only those themes that we have assigned to their poems, then they could easily have stated their purposes more directly. In the case of Herrick's poem, we have probably looked too hard for the significance of his simple imagistic description. Herrick himself probably realized that a poem of six lines cannot state abstract truths without sounding pompous and grandiose. A brief description may suggest those truths, but it ought not insist on them. The scope of Herrick's poem is wisely confined to the movement of Julia's clothes; it does not actually describe her clothing nor does it describe her person, for these subjects, presumably, would require a much more lavish treatment. The poem does not mention Herrick's love for Julia, nor does it assert Julia's beauty—everything, therefore, that we have said about the poem's theme is deduced without any direct support from a text that is imagistic rather than judgmental or argumentative.

5

Versification

RHYTHM AND METER

If you hold a conch shell to your ear, you will seem to hear within it the rhythmic rush and retreat of the sea surf. Although children find deep fascination and mystery in this audible reminder of the ocean, science explains away that magic meter as an echo of the blood throbbing in the listener's inner ear. But in this case, as indeed in many others, the scientific explanation does less to erase our wonder than to transpose it and intellectualize it. The rhythm of the conch—the crashing of the sea—is also in the beat of our blood, the core of our very being. We are, it seems, rhythm-making creatures. When we listen to the monotone ticking of a wristwatch, we hear it as a rhythmic tic-tock. The rattle of a moving train is heard as a rhythmic clickety-clack. We hear the drumming of a horse's hooves as clip-clop. We make something rhythmic out of even the most dull and invariable experiences.

This affection for rhythm has never been fully explained, but it is probably the result of the natural rhythms of human life. In addition to the systolic and diastolic beat of the heart, there are similar rhythms in our breathing, in our movements as bipeds, and in a great variety of our habitual activities. Generations of farmers, pressing one ear to a cow's churning and drum-tight belly, have rhythmically squeezed her milk into a pail. Generations of farm men have raised and dropped a hoe or slung and recoiled a scythe. Generations of farm women have rhythmically kneaded dough or scrubbed at a washboard. Generations of children have grown up loving chants, nursery rhymes, and jingles.

It should come as no surprise then that both prose and poetry are rhythmic. According to the nineteenth-century French poet Charles Baudelaire, "rhythm and rhyme answer in man to the immortal needs of monotony, symmetry, and surprise." Furthermore, strong emotions tend to find memorable expression through strong rhythms. This is obviously true of music, dance, and poetry; but it can also be true of prose. Julius Caesar's pride in conquering Gaul shone through the rhythms of his message to the Roman senate, "Veni, vidi, vici!" ("I *came,* I *saw,* I *conquered!*") Patrick Henry's belief in the cause of American independence was passionately expressed through the strong patterns in his speech to the Virginia Convention on March 23, 1775:

> The gentlemen may cry, Peace, Peace! but there is no peace. The war is actually begun! The next gale that sweeps from the north shall bring to our ears the clash of resounding arms! . . . Is life so dear or peace so sweet as to be purchased at the price of chains and slavery? Forbid it, Almighty God. I know not what course others may take, but as for me, give me liberty or give me death!

Abraham Lincoln's firm belief in the need for reconciliation following the Civil War was beautifully embodied in the cadence of his second inaugural address of 1865:

> With malice toward none, with charity for all, with firmness in the right as God gives us to see the right, let us bind up the Nation's wounds.

As we have just seen, poets have no monopoly on meter; it is also true that the correct use of meter does not make a poet, any more than the correct use of grammar makes a novelist or the correct use of chewing tobacco makes a baseball player. As Ralph Waldo Emerson observed in 1844, "it is not meters, but a meter-making argument that makes a poem—a thought so passionate and alive that like the spirit of a plant or an animal it has an architecture of its own and adorns nature with a new thing." Just as our hearts beat vigorously at moments of violent emotion, so, too, our words begin to beat more forcefully while we express those emotions—and the rhythms of poetic words often re-create in a careful reader the same sense of breathless excitement that possessed the poet.

Although we respond as readily to the rhythms of prose as poetry and although, to quote Shelley, "the distinction between poets and prose writers is a vulgar error," the fact remains that most poetry (and little prose) is cast into formal metrical patterns. Perhaps the reason for this, as we have already suggested, is that the metrical patterns of verse help to create a more direct relationship to natural human rhythms than is possible in prose. When the alternating accents of iambic verse are read aloud, they almost inevitably match the 72 beats per minute of our pulse. Moreover, when we speak aloud, our words are naturally grouped in response to our breathing. After giving voice to eight or ten syllables, most speakers must pause for another breath. English verse makes the speaker's breathing easier by being written in lines of roughly equal length. The two most common measures in our language, tetrameter and pentameter, normally contain eight and ten syllables, respectively. Lines longer than pentameter are uncommon because they can be difficult to recite. Shorter lines, like trimeter which has six syllables, by encouraging rapid breathing, give the illusion of haste or excitement. Thus, verse itself is both a response to human physiology and an influence on it. Like a natural force, verse sets up a pattern of expectations that we recognize intuitively and to which we respond both physically and emotionally. The study of metrics allows us to name and to analyze the prevailing rhythms of most poems.

Meter is basically a system for helping the reader reproduce the rhythm intended by the author. The word *meter* comes from the Greek "metron," meaning "measure." These words, *meter* and *measure,* are used interchangeably in describing poetic rhythms. The units with which we measure verse are the syllable, the foot, the line, and sometimes the stanza and the canto. A syllable, which is the smallest unit in metrics, is any word or part of a word produced in speech by a single pulse of breath. It is a simple link in the chain of sounds. Between sixty and eighty percent of the words in English poetry are monosyllables—words like *root, tree, leaf, fruit, man, child, boy, girl, a, an,* and *the.* The remaining words are polysyllabic and are divided by dictionaries into their individual links of sound: *re-main-ing, pol-y-syl-lab-ic, di-vi-ded,* etc. The basic rhythmic unit in verse is called a *foot* and is composed of an established number of stressed (emphasized) and unstressed syllables. An established number of feet makes up a *line* and an established number of lines often makes up a *stanza*. The number of lines or stanzas in a *canto* is rarely fixed in advance.

Scansion

The process by which we discover the dominant rhythm in a poem is called scansion. The basic steps in scanning a poem are quite simple and entail (1) finding the average number of syllables in a typical line, (2) marking the stressed or accented syllables in each line and (3) identifying the prevailing foot and the number of feet per line. It should be noted that the entire process focuses on the number of syllables and stresses in a given line of poetry. For this reason, English verse is said to be written in syllabic-stress meters.

Now let us go through each step in scansion for a representative poem, "On First Looking into Chapman's Homer" by John Keats:

On First Looking Into Chapman's Homer

Much have I travell'd in the realms of gold
And many goodly states and kingdoms seen,
Round many western islands have I been
Which bards in fealty to Apollo hold.
Oft of one wide expanse had I been told
That deep-browed Homer ruled as his demesne:
Yet did I never breathe its pure serene
Till I heard Chapman speak out loud and bold.
Then felt I like some watcher of the skies
When a new planet swims into his ken;
Or like stout Cortez when with eagle eyes
He stared at the Pacific—and all his men
Look'd at each other with a wild surmise—
Silent upon a peak in Darien.

—John Keats (1816)

1. Inspection of the poem shows that the average line contains ten syllables, but lines 4, 6, 12, and 14 present minor problems in syllabification. The word "fealty" in line four is usually divided into three syllables, "fe/al/ty," but because this would give the line a total of eleven, we may feel more comfortable eliding "fe/al" into one syllable which sounds like the word *feel.* There are, in fact, an unusual number of words in our language that are divided differently on dif-

ferent occasions: for example, *unusual* (un-use-yul, un-use-u-al), *our* (are, ow-er), *different* (diff-er-ent, diff-rent), *occasions* (o-cay-zhuns, o-cay-zhi-ens). Moreover, the syllabification of certain words has changed over the centuries—notably in the pronunciation of the *ed* form of verbs: *bathed* was once *bath-ed, in-spired* was once *in-spi-red, changed* was once *chang-ed,* and even now *aged* may be pronounced *age-ed.* Archaic forms are, of course, common in medieval verse, but they are sometimes deliberately used in more contemporary poetry where the unanticipated accents are generally marked (*changéd*). Keats, however, so often required his readers to pronounce the final *ed* of verbs that in the first line of "On First Looking into Chapman's Homer," he used the contraction "travell'd" to show that the end of the verb was *not* to be sounded.

Alternate pronunciations and archaisms are only two of the problems of syllabification. Many of us are unfamiliar with the pronunciation of some words used in poetry. In line six, for example, the word "demesne" appears to have three syllables, but we learn from the dictionary that it may be pronounced to rhyme with "serene", in line seven:

> *de.mesne* (di-mān′,-mēn′), n....3.any territory or domain.

Thus, line six, like most of the others, contains the expected ten syllables. In line 14 we might again turn to a dictionary to reassure ourselves that "Darien" does indeed have the three syllables (Da/ri/en) required by the meter.

No reading of line 12, however, can produce any fewer than eleven syllables, and therefore we are forced to describe that one line as slightly irregular. The expectation of ten syllables should be *only* an expectation. Slight variations are normal and even desirable when they serve some rhythmic function. But in order to discuss a poem's rhythm, we must learn to identify the pattern of stressed and unstressed syllables.

2. The problem of determining where the stresses fall in poetry is more complex than counting the syllables, but with a good ear and the guidance of a few simple rules, most readers can produce satisfactory results.

The first rule is that a poem's meter cannot change the normal pronunciation of a polysyllabic word. In all words of two syllables or more, the permissible accentuation is defined by the dictionary.

Thus, in lines three and four, for example, we can immediately mark several stressed syllables. The dictionary tells us that the accent falls on the middle syllable of "A·pól·lo" and on the first syllables of "mán·y," "wés·tern," "iś·lands," and "feál·ty." If we place a straight line over the accented syllables, the preliminary scansion of the lines looks like this:

> Round māny wēstern īslands have I been
> Which bards in fēalty to Apōllo hold.

The second rule is that monosyllabic words have no inherent stress; they take on stresses to fit the metrical pattern of the poem and the rhetorical rhythm of a particular sentence. In other words, monosyllables may be either stressed or unstressed. In general, however, the emphasis should fall where it would in a normal prose reading of the lines; and in normal English prose, stressed and unstressed syllables tend to alternate. When we read Keats's lines aloud we find that weak, but still noticeable, stresses fall on "have" and "been," while more pronounced emphasis is placed on "bards" and "hold." If we now mark each of these as an accented syllable and mark the remaining unaccented syllables with a cup (˘), we will have produced a complete metrical picture of the lines:

> Rŏund māny̆ wēstĕrn īslănds hāve Ĭ bēen
> Whĭch bārds ĭn fēaltў tō Ăpōllŏ hōld.

3. Having scanned the lines, we now need only name the specific meter being used. In the syllabic-stress system there are only five commonly used feet: iambic, anapestic, trochaic, dactylic, and spondaic.

Table of Metrical Feet

Name	*Example*
Dactyl	"Mūch hăve Ĭ
Trochee	trāvĕll'd
Anapest	ĭn thĕ rēalms
iamb	ŏf gōld."
Spondee	Jōhn Kēats.

Of these, the iamb is by far the most popular and versatile. It is the principle foot used in such narrative and dramatic verse as Chaucer's *Canterbury Tales,* Shakespeare's plays, Milton's *Paradise Lost,* Wordsworth's *Prelude,* Byron's *Don Juan,* and most other substantial poems written in English. The iambic foot is equally popular in lyric verse and is predominant in ballads and obligatory in sonnets. It is, therefore, used in Keats's sonnet, "On First Looking into Chapman's Homer," and the two lines that we have just scanned can be shown to have five iambic feet to the line:

> Rŏund mān/y̆ wēs/tĕrn īs/lănds hāve/ Ĭ bēen
> Whĭch bārds/ ĭn fēal/tў tō/ Ăpōl/lŏ hōld.

We use a vertical slash (/) to mark the divisions between the feet. These divisions are helpful in counting the feet, but they do not signal pauses in speech; they may fall either between words or between the syllables of a word.

In critical analysis we generally replace the wordy and awkward phrase "five feet to the line" with the term *pentameter.* The technical term for each of the possible lines in English poetry is provided in the following table:

monometer: one foot per line
dimeter: two feet per line
trimeter: three feet per line
tetrameter: four feet per line
pentameter: five feet per line
hexameter: six feet per line
heptameter: seven feet per line
octameter: eight feet per line

Of these, pentameter and tetrameter are the most commonly used.

Once chosen, the dominant metrical foot normally remains fixed throughout a given poem. Thus, for example, iambic rhythm prevails in Donne's "A Valediction: Forbidding Mourning" (p. 99), whereas trochaic rhythm prevails in Poe's "The Raven" (p. 178) and anapestic rhythm dominates his "Annabel Lee" (p. 177). Although the principal metrical foot almost invariably remains unchanged throughout a poem, the length of the lines often varies according to a preestablished pattern. "A Valediction: Forbidding Mourning" is tetrameter throughout, but the odd-numbered lines in "The Raven" are trochaic octameter, and the even-numbered lines lack one syllable in the final foot (*catalectic* trochaic octameter). In "Annabel Lee" tetrameter alternates with trimeter.

Thus, in choosing iambic pentameter for "Chapman's Homer," Keats commits himself to creating the possibility of a scansion that includes five metrical feet in each line, and he has to work within the expectation that each line will follow an iambic rhythm. We use the words *possibility* and *expectation* because the metrical pattern of a poem is not intended to be a straitjacket that restricts all movement and permits scant room to breathe. Rather, the pattern should be cut like a well-tailored dress that, like Julia's silks, complements both the shape and movement of the human form it adorns. Deviations from the expected metrical pattern create surprise, emphasis, and often delight.

Anapestic, dactylic, trochaic, and spondaic feet are all used more frequently to provide variety in iambic verse than to set the rhythm of an entire poem. As the examples in our Table of Metrical Feet show, each of these (except the spondee) is used in the first line of Keats's sonnet:

dactyl *trochee* *anapest* *iamb*
Much have I/ travell'd/ in the realms/ of gold . . .

Keats's first line is, therefore, highly irregular, and two questions now confront us: What purposes are served by variations from an established meter? And how do different rhythms affect our emotional response to poetry?

A partial answer to the first question was proposed by Samuel Johnson when he wrote, in his "Life of Dryden" (1781), that "the essence of verse is regularity and its ornament is variety." This implies that a poem should be regular enough to establish a pattern and varied enough to banish monotony. It is a corollary to the familiar rule endorsing moderation in all things, and in recent years it has become almost commonplace to condemn poets whose meters are too regular. In a fine example of logical inconsistency, however, Johnson went on to defend Alexander Pope from detractors who charged that the monotonous regularity of his heroic couplets (pairs of rhymed iambic pentameter lines) diminished their power by "glutting the ear with unvaried sweetness." To this Johnson replied, "I suspect this objection to be the cant of those who judge by principles rather than perception: and who would even themselves have less pleasure in his words, if he had tried to relieve attention by studied discords, or affected to break his lines and vary his pauses."

There is, then, little value in any attempt to state a general principle about regularity and variety in meter. Such esthetic judgments can only be made within the context of a particular poem's meaning. What *can* be said, however, is that rhythm and any deviations from rhythm should contribute to the overall effect sought in the poem. "What is wanted is neither a dead mechanical beat nor a jumble of patternless incoherence, but the rich expressiveness of a verse that is alive with the tension of living speech."[1]

"The tension of living speech" is an apt expression for the effect of metrical variation in "On First Looking into Chapman's Homer." If we look again at its first line, we see that, although it has ten syllables and can conceivably be read as iambic pentameter,

Mŭch HĀVE/ Ĭ TRĀ/vĕll'd ĪN/ thĕ RĒALMS/ ŏf GŌLD,

such a reading distorts the rhythms of living speech. But if we read the line naturally,

MŪCH hăve Ĭ/ TRĀvĕll'd/ ĭn thĕ RĒALMS/ ŏf GŌLD,

we find neither a metrical pattern—indeed, each foot is different—nor the five feet we expect in pentameter. Clearly, Keats is creating a tension between living speech and our expectations of a sonnet. The line has fewer accents and more unstressed syllables than we expect; and because unstressed syllables roll rapidly from the tongue, the pace of the line is more rapid than in standard iambic pentameter.[2] Furthermore, Keats has arranged the unstressed syllables so that nearly all of them pour forth in two rolling clusters. Thus, the poem begins with a sense of surprise and breathless excitement. As we continue reading, we learn that this tone is exactly right for the story Keats has to tell. Reading Chapman's translation of Homer was a new and exciting experience for Keats. It showed him that poetry could unexpectedly "speak out loud and bold"; it did not need to be an effeminate concoction of unvaried sweetness. The rhythm in the

[1] Cleanth Brooks and Robert Penn Warren, *Understanding Poetry,* 4th ed. (New York: Holt, Rhinehart, and Winston, 1976), p. 503.

[2] This can be stated as a general principle of metrics: unaccented syllables in anapests and dactyls accelerate the pace of narration; heavily accented syllables in spondees slow the pace.

first line of the sonnet helps to capture and communicate Keats's emotions.

One line in a sonnet is, of course, insufficient to set the tone for the rest of the poem, but the rhythm of this first line is repeated again and again. The dactyl-trochee combination, which helps to make these first syllables forceful and rugged, occurs at the beginning of lines 5, 7, 9, 13, and 14:

1 Much have I/ travell'd/ . . .
5 Oft of one/ wide ex/panse . . .
7 Yet did I/ never/ . . .
9 Then felt I/ like some/ . . .
13 Look'd at each/ other/ . . .
14 Silent up/on a/ . . .

The tension between regular iambic pentameter and Keats's startling irregularity is especially noticeable in the final verses, both because these lines occur at the poem's climax and because two irregular patterns occur in immediate succession. Keats achieves a perfect blending of sound and sense when he says of Cortez:

12 He stared/ at the Pa/cific//—and all/ his men
13 Look'd at each/ other// with a wild/ surmise—
14 Silent// upon/ a peak/ in Da/rien.

In describing the metrical effects in this combination of lines, we will find it useful to define three more terms: *end-stopped verse, enjambment,* and the *caesura.* An end-stopped line, like line 13 in Keats's sonnet, is simply one that concludes with a pause. A strongly end-stopped verse ends with some mark of punctuation—a comma, semicolon, colon, dash, question mark, exclamation point, or period. The punctuation tells the reader to pause for breath and emphasis. Although a lightly end-stopped verse may have no formal punctuation, it must still mark a pause between phrases or clauses. Lines one, three, five, seven, and eleven are all lightly end-stopped. *Enjambment* (or "striding over"), as in line 12 of Keats's sonnet, is the running on of one line into the next without a grammatical pause. End–stopping tends to reinforce the metrical structure of a poem, whereas enjambment tends to minimize the difference between the sound of verse and that of prose. A *caesura* (marked with a double slash, //) is a pause that occurs near the middle of most verses. This pause may be indicated by punctuation, as in line 12; or it may fall between phrases, as in line 13. If a line has an even number of feet, the caesura tends to bisect it, as in line 13. One advantage of iambic pentameter is that its five accents can never be divided evenly. This ensures a certain amount of variety in even the most regular pentameters and opens up the possibility of a caesural pause as late as the fourth foot or as early as the first (line 14).

How do end-stopping, enjambment, and the caesural pause contribute to the impact of Keats's poem? It is quite apparent that a dramatic pause is signaled by the dash at the end of line 13. The effect of this pause is to emphasize the "wild surmise" and to encourage us to determine *what* is surmised. These men have discovered an entirely new ocean and are briefly struck dumb with wonder. They pause, just as Keats's punctuation forces us to pause. The content of these lines is in absolute harmony with their end-stopped rhythm.

The contribution of the enjambment from line 12 to 13 is also important, but it is atypical of the general effect of that device. If we examine Keats's poem as a whole, we find that exactly half of the lines are run-on or very lightly end-stopped. Thus, the poem has the typographical appearance of verse, but because strongly end-stopped lines are avoided, it has a fluid movement resembling that of melodious prose. In this respect, Keats's style is unusually mature for a poet who had not yet reached the age of legal majority. Most other great poets from Chaucer and Shakespeare to Byron and Wordsworth passed through a period of strong end-stopping before evolving at last to a more flexible style. But the enjambment at line 12 is grammatical only. In prose we do not ordinarily pause between a subject and verb. We use but one breath to say, "and all his men looked at each other." But when these words are put into a sonnet and scanned as on page 173, a substantial pause before "Look'd" is almost obligatory for several reasons. In the first place most readers of poetry inevitably pause slightly at the end of a line of verse—even when such a pause is not syntactic. The end-line pause is one of our expectations in verse. Furthermore, in this particular case, the last syllable of line 12 ("mēn") is accented, as is the first syllable of line 13 ("Lo͞ok'd"). As we mentioned before, strong accents in juxtaposition always slow the pace of poetry, here augmenting the natural end-line pause. And finally, it makes dramatic sense to pause before "Look'd." The pause helps to create suspense and emphasis. It informs us that this is a penetrating look, a look of rapture and astonishment. Hence, the grammatical enjambment between lines 12 and 13 is offset by a combination of poetic effects, and once again we have "verse that is alive with the tension of living speech."

The caesural pauses in lines 12 and 13 merit no special analysis—the one in line 12 is plainly grammatical and the one in line 13 falls at the exact midpoint of the line and between two prepositional phrases, each of which independently modifies the verb. We might, however, be tempted to omit the caesura we placed after the first foot in line 14,

Silent// upon/ a peak/ in Da/rien.

It certainly could not be placed later in the line because it would then either divide words within a prepositional phrase or separate two phrases closely linked both in logic and in grammar. And in placing a caesura after "Silent," we disrupt the rhythm of the dactyl-trochee combination that has characterized the poem. But if we wish to protect that rhythm, we must omit the caesura altogether and scan the line in a way that produces an unusual monosyllabic foot:

Silent up/on a/ peak/ in Da/rien.[3]

Of the two options, the former is clearly preferable. It is closer to regular iambic pentameter; it includes the expected caesura at a grammatically acceptable place; and, most importantly, it helps the sound of the poem to echo its sense. A momentary silence *should* follow the word—as if in recognition of its meaning.

In summary, the goal of a metrical analysis is to clarify how the rhythm of language contributes to its poetic meaning. In order to assist in this process, the full scansion of a poem or passage should identify the underlying metrical pattern; analyze the important deviations from that pattern; and consider the effects of end–stopping, en-

[3] Note that the placement of the caesura marks the only audible difference in the two possibilities in scansion. It makes no difference in the rhythm whether the feet are scanned as a trochee and four iambs or as a dactyl, a trochee, a monosyllable, and two iambs. Both scansions should be read in precisely the same manner.

jambment, and placement of the caesura. An analysis of rhythmic effects that is not based on scansion is likely to be imprecise and unintelligible; however, scansion that does not include analysis and interpretation is mechanical and meaningless.

The iambic pentameter of Keats's sonnet on "Chapman's Homer," although the most common of English meters, is by no means the only possible rhythm. Nor is the syllabic-stress system the only possible approach to writing and scanning verse. Before closing our discussion of rhythm and meter, it is, therefore, expedient to survey the variety of poetic meters, the limitations of syllabic-stress scansion, and the other possible systems of scanning English verse.

VARIETY OF METERS. While trochees, anapests, and dactyls are most frequently used to provide variety within an iambic rhythm, each can also establish the underlying meter of a poem, and each creates a very different rhythmic effect. The rhythm of a poem does not, of course, dictate its tone. Rhythm is at best a contributing factor that can be used by able poets to complement the mood created through the denotations and connotations of words. There are, however, differences among the four basic meters of English poetry, and these differences can easily be heard, even though their effects cannot be perfectly described.

The *trochee* (trāvĕll'd) is the mirror image of the iamb and is perhaps even more common than the iamb in everyday speech. The plurals of many monosyllabic words become trochaic (*fīshĕs, hōusĕs, āxĕs,* etc.) and a great many two-syllable words are natural trochees (*pōĕt, wātĕr, āblĕ,* etc.).

Trochaic and iambic meters do not differ greatly in their effects. In fact, trochaic pentameter can be described as iambic pentameter with a defective first foot and an extra syllable at the end.

trochaic – | ˘ – | ˘ – | ˘ – | ˘ – | ˘ – ˘
iambic ˘ – | ˘ – | ˘ – | ˘ – | ˘ – ˘ –

Because the first syllable in a trochaic line is accented, poems in this meter often sound assertive and vigorous. But the use of trochees makes end rhyme difficult because rhyme words are usually stressed. Thus, some poems that start out with a trochaic rhythm end up iambic, as in the catalectic (meaning "incomplete") trochaic octameter of Swinburne's "The Sunbows":

Spray of/ song that/ sings in/ April,// light of/ love that/ laughs through/ May
Live and/ die and/ live for/ever:// nought of/ all things/ far less/ fair
Keeps a/ surer/ life than/ these that//seem to/ pass like/ fire a/way.

—from "The Sunbows," Algernon Charles Swinburne (1884)

Incantations are often trochaic, possibly because the strong accents that begin each trochaic line complement a chanting rhythm:

Double/, double// toil and/ trouble;
Fire/ burn and// cauldron/ bubble.

—from *Macbeth,*
William Shapespeare (ca. 1607)

Very probably, this affinity for the supernatural in trochaic rhythms guided Edgar Allan Poe in choosing the meter for "The Raven" (1845):

Once up/on a/ midnight/ dreary,// while I/ pondered/ weak and/ weary,
Over/ many a/ quaint and/ curious// volume/ of for/gotten/ lore—

A *dactyl* (Much have I) is a trochee with an extra unstressed syllable. Because unstressed syllables are pronounced easily, poems in dactylic meter move with a rapid, waltzing beat (dum-dee-dee, dum-dee-dee). The dactylic dimeter of the following stanza from Ralph Hodgson's "Eve" provides a good example of the lyrical but unsettling possibilities in the rhythm:

Picture that/ orchard sprite;
Eve, with her/ body white,
Supple and/ smooth to her
Thin finger/ tips;
Wondering,/ listening
Listening,/ wondering,
Eve with a/ berry
Half-way/ to her lips.

—from "Eve,"
Ralph Hodgson (1913)

Alfred Tennyson took advantage of the strength and speed of dactyls to imitate the drumming of galloping horses in his famous "Charge of the Light Brigade":

Half a league,/ half a league
  Half a league/ onward,
All in the/ Valley of/ Death
  Rode the six/ hundred
"Forward the/ Light Brigade!
Charge for the/ guns!" he said:
Into the/ Valley of Death
  Rode the six/ hundred.

—from "The Charge of the Light Brigade,"
Alfred, Lord Tennyson (1854)

And Longfellow used the unfamiliar sound of the dactylic line to accentuate the primitive, pagan mood at the beginning of "Evangeline" (1847):

This is the/ forest prim/eval.// The/ murmuring/ pines and the/ hemlocks/ . . .
Stand like/ Druids of/ old.

The *anapest* (in the realms), like the dactyl, is a rapid meter, but in proceeding from unstressed syllables to stressed ones, it also parallels the iamb. Hence, it has none of the strangeness of the dactyl or trochee. It works well in rapidly paced poems:

The Assyr/i–an came/ down// like the wolf/ on the fold,
And his co/horts were gleam/ing in pur/ple and gold;
And the sheen/ of their spears// was like stars/ on the sea,
When the Blue/ wave rolls night/ly on deep/ Galilee.

—from, "The Destruction of Sennacherib," Lord Byron (1815)

And it also pleases in very mellifluous ones:

It was man/y and man/y a year/ ago,
  In a king/dom by/ the sea,
That a maid/en there lived// whom you/ may know
  By the name// of An/nabel Lee;

—from "Annabel Lee," Edgar Allan Poe (1849)

Someone once argued that a long poem in anapests, like a long ride on a roller coaster, is apt to cause nausea, but there can be little doubt that this rolling meter is exquisitely suited to many brief pieces.

The *spondee* (John Keats) is never the dominant meter in a whole poem, but one or two spondees will tend to dominate a line. This is well illustrated in Alexander Pope's lines on the role of sound and rhythm in poetry:

> True ease in writing comes from art, not chance,
> As those move easiest who have learned to dance.
> 'Tis not enough no harshness gives offense,
> The sound must seem an echo to the sense:
> Soft is the strain when Zepher gently blows,
> And the smooth stream in smoother numbers flows;
> But when/ loud sur/ges lash// the sound/ing shore,
> The hoarse,/ rough verse// should like/ the tor/rent roar;
> When A/jax strives// some rock's/ vast weight/ to throw,
> The line/ too/ labors,/ and the words/ move slow.
>
> —from "An Essay on Criticism," Alexander Pope (1711)

There is at least one spondee in each of the last four lines, and each time a spondee occurs three stressed syllables line up in front of us like hard blocks of granite that our voices must surmount. Stressed syllables require more effort from the speaker and they take longer to pronounce than unstressed syllables. As a result, spondees always slow down the pace of a poem. They can be especially useful when an author wishes to express anger or violence, as in King Lear's line:

> Blow, winds,/ and crack/ your cheeks!// Rage! Blow!

In addition to the four principle rhythms (iambic, trochaic, anapestic, and dactylic) and that of the slow spondee, there are a great many feet with unpronounceable Greek names that pop up occasionally to vary the dominant rhythm of a poem: *pyrrhic* (˘ ˘), *bacchius* (˘ – –), *antibacchius* (– – ˘), *amphimacer* (– ˘ –), *amphibrach* (˘ – ˘), and so on. Although there is no need to remember these names, their existence demonstrates that, within the framework of a dominant rhythm, a poet may proceed almost as he pleases. He has what is called the "poetic license" to take liberties with meter, syntax, and even diction, *providing* the result is a more forceful, unified, and distinctive poem.

THE LIMITATIONS OF SYLLABIC STRESS SCANSION. The rules of scansion are loose, and nearly every line of verse can be marked in a number of ways. We have, for example, scanned King Lear's line as two spondees and two iambs:

Blow, winds,/ and crack/ your cheeks!// Rage! Blow!

But because the line occurs in a passage that is predominantly iambic pentameter, we might chose to give it the required five feet by marking with a carat (^) the pauses that would naturally fall at the exclamation points:

Blow, winds,/ and crack/ your cheeks!// Rage!^/ Blow!^

Similarly, we have scanned the first line of "On First Looking into Chapman's Homer" as a dactyl, trochee, anapest, and iamb,

Much have I/ travell'd// in the realms/ of gold.

It could also be a trochee, iamb, pyrrhic, and two iambs:

Much have/ I tra/vell'd in/ the realms/ of gold.

Such changes in scansion are cosmetic only and indicate no significant difference in the way each line *should be* read.

There is, however, considerable room for actual changes in the way a line *can* be read. Different readers rarely use stresses and pauses in precisely the same places, as anyone can testify after hearing one of Hamlet's soliloquies spoken by actors so different as Laurence Olivier, Richard Burton, and Richard Chamberlain. Sometimes we do not agree on the syllables that should be stressed or on the relative amount of stress on each. Scansion is, after all, a system of simplifying and visually presenting the complex rhythm in a line. It is not an exact science. Even if a precise system were possible, it would be too complicated to be useful in pointing out the simple, recurring rhythms of poetry. There must be a certain amount of ambiguity in the scansion of any poem.

Although we must accept the limitations of our system and recognize that there will rarely be only one "right" way of scanning a poem, yet we must also recognize that this loosely constructed system is of considerable usefulness to both poets and readers. Because syllabic-stress meters are common in English poetry and their scansion is well understood, poets can confidently expect that readers will pick up most of the clues to rhythm that the meter conveys and therefore will read the lines with an emphasis closely approximating what was intended. Conversely, readers can easily determine a poem's underlying meter and then decide how they wish to read each line. The decisions made should be based, where possible, on the poem's content, its prose emphases, and its basic meter. The commonly accepted terminology of scansion allows us to explain more easily the decisions about the rhythm that we have made and how these decisions reflect and reinforce the meaning of the poem. Finally, the prevalence of syllabic-stress meters allows great poets to create a tension between the rhythm of ordinary speech and the heartbeat of the poetic line. The discovery of new possibilities in poetic rhythm in a poem like "Chapman's Homer" is one of the pleasures of travel in the realms of gold.

ALTERNATE SYSTEMS OF SCANSION. The syllabic stress system of metrics slowly came to dominate English poetry between the twelfth and sixteenth centuries because it proved better suited to the evolving English language than any of the competing systems: *accentual-alliterative meters, purely syllabic meters, quantitative meters,* and *free verse.* Nonetheless, each of these has left its mark on English poetry.

Alliterative, accentual, or *strong-stress* verse was the metrical system native to our Anglo-Saxon forbears. An impressive amount of alliterative poetry survived the Middle Ages, but only two poems in this meter are encountered frequently enough to be mentioned here. *Beowulf,* the earliest surviving poem in a European language, was composed about A.D. 725; it describes the epic adventures of Beowulf in defeating the male monster Grendel and then Grendel's dam before Beowulf himself succumbs to a fire-breathing dragon. The poem is written in Old English, which is so different from modern English that it must be learned just like a foreign language. Each line in the poem has a variable number of unaccented syllables and four strong stresses, three of which are usually emphasized by alliteration. The line is bisected by a caesural pause.

The same alliterative meter is used in the Middle English Arthurian romance, *Sir Gawain and the Green Knight.* The following lines, which describe Gawain's sufferings during his winter quest for the Green Knight, provide an example of the original appearance of the meter. Note where the accents are in the following lines:

For wērre wrāthed hym not so much,// that wȳnter was wōrs,
When the cōlde clēr water// from the clōuds schādde,
And frīes er hit fālle mygth// to the fāle ērthe.
Ner slāyn wyth the slēte// he slēped in his ȳrnes
Mo nȳghtes then innōghe// in nāked rōkkes,
Ther as clāterande fro the crēst// the cōlde bōrne rennes,
And hēnged hēghe// over his hēde in hārd ysse-ikkles.[4]

—from *Sir Gawain and the Green Knight,* anonymous (ca. 1375)

Of the poems considered in this text, "Eve" (p. 177) is perhaps more easily classified as strong-stress dimeter than as dactylic dimeter. Each line has only two strong stresses, while the number of unstressed syllables varies from two to four. "Fog," by Carl Sandburg, is also best classified as strong-stress dimeter. Each line has two major stresses that are surrounded, in no particular pattern, by weakly stressed or unstressed syllables. In general, the strong-stress system requires alliteration if it is to sound poetic, and the required alliteration is too limiting and too repetitive to appeal to most modern poets. When strong-stress verse is used without alliteration, as in Sandburg's "Fog," it has the appearance and sound of free verse.

Purely *syllabic meters* represent another alternative to the syllabic-stress system. Some modern languages, notably French, make little use of stress in speech. Each syllable is given roughly the same weight. As a result, French poetry is based almost entirely on syllable count.

After the French-speaking Normans conquered the Saxons at Hastings in 1066, our modern English language began to emerge as a hybrid between Old English and Old French; at the same time, mod-

[4] Translation: For fighting troubled him not so much, that winter was worse,/ When the cold clear water from the clouds fell,/ And froze ere it might fall to the faded earth./ Near slain with sleet he slept in his irons (armor)/ More nights than enough in naked rocks,/ There where clattering from the crest the cold stream ran,/ And hung high over his head in hard icicles.

ern syllabic-stress meters began to emerge, as the alliterative tradition of Old English poetry met with the syllabic tradition of French verse.

In the absence of other musical devices (rhyme, alliteration, etc.), syllabic verse is often indistinguishable from prose, as we see in the following "stanza" from Thom Gunn's "Vox Humana":

> Being without quality
> I appear to you at first
> as an unkempt smudge, a blur,
> an indefinite haze, mere-
> ly pricking the eyes, almost
> nothing. Yet you perceive me.
>
> —from "Vox Humana," Thom Gunn (1957)

Although these lines can be defended on the basis that their formlessness is in harmony with the poem's theme that our own human spirit is difficult to define, they are still open to the criticism that anyone with the mental capacity to count on his fingers can write as poetically as this. Under the circumstances, it is no surprise that few English poems are written in purely syllabic verse.

A third alternative to syllabic-stress verse is made possible by the differences in the amount of time it takes to pronounce various syllables. The word *truths,* for example, takes longer to say than *lies*—even though each is monosyllabic. *Quantitative meter* is based on the length (in units of time) of various syllables, instead of on the relative degree of their stress.

Greek and Latin poetry was based on quantitative metrics, and therefore the few English poems in quantitative verse have usually been written by poets who were heavily influenced by the classics. During the late sixteenth century, at the height of the English revival of Greek and Latin learning, such poets as Spenser and Sidney experimented briefly with quantity in verse before concluding that most English syllables take up about the same amount of time in pronunciation and that few readers are able to perceive the slight differences that do exist.

It is, however, possible to demonstrate some quantitative differences in English pronunciation. The first line of the following couplet reads much more rapidly than the second, even though both have an identical number of syllables:

> By slight syllables we show
> Those truths whose worth you now know.

But there is a great difference between this theoretical possibility and its application in fluent poetry. The most that can be said is that quantitative factors sometimes play a secondary role in the impact of normal syllabic-stress verse. When, for example, Alexander Pope wrote about the effects of sound in poetry, he skillfully used lengthy vowel sounds (ow, oar, ough, ur) to slow down the movement of his lines:

> But when loud surges lash the sounding shore,
> The hoarse, rough verse should like the torrent roar.

Free verse, the final alternative to syllabic-stress meter, is not a meter at all. In free verse, no formal patterns of metrical feet, quantitative feet, or syllable count are sought, and the verse is "free" to develop in any manner that fits the poem and contributes to the overall rhythm of the words. The only real distinctions between free verse and the rhythmical prose of Thomas Paine or Abraham Lincoln are that (1) free verse uses variable line length as a unit in rhythm, (2) free verse may use rhyme more frequently than would be acceptable in prose, and (3) free verse is less restrained than prose by the rules of logic and grammar.

In Elizabeth Bishop's "Sandpiper," for example, the number of syllables per line ranges from 6 to 13, the number of stresses ranges from three to six, and the metrical pattern remains irregular throughout the poem:

Sandpiper

The roaring alongside he takes for granted,
and that every so often the world is bound to shake.
He runs, he runs to the south, finical, awkward,
in a state of controlled panic, a student of Blake.

The beach hisses like fat. On his left, a sheet
of interrupting water comes and goes
and glazes over his dark and brittle feet.
He runs, he runs straight through it, watching his toes.

—Watching, rather, the spaces of sand between them,
where (no detail too small) the Atlantic drains
rapidly backwards and downwards. As he runs,
he stares at the dragging grains.

The world is a mist. And then the world is
minute and vast and clear. The tide

is higher or lower. He couldn't tell you which.
His beak is focussed; he is preoccupied,

looking for something, something, something.
Poor bird, he is obsessed!
The millions of grains are black, white, tan, and gray,
mixed with quartz grains, rose and amethyst.
—Elizabeth Bishop (1947)

It would be inaccurate, however, to say that Bishop's free verse lacks form. The poem is broken up into four-line units, or stanzas, in which the second line always rhymes with the fourth. Thus, the poem has the visual appearance and sound of verse, while its rhythm remains as hectic and irregular as the darting motion of the sandpiper itself. The poem begins with two flowing and forceful lines describing the surf; then it continues with brief, erratic, and repetitious phrases that help to characterize the bird's mindless panic: "He runs, he runs . . . watching . . . watching . . . he runs, he stares . . . focussed . . . preoccupied,/ looking for something, something, something./ Poor bird, he is obsessed!" The central portion of the poem is a descriptive tour de force, but it shows only the bleak and monotonous aspects of the sandpiper's existence. In the final lines, however, the point of view shifts. After being told *about* a bird "looking for something, something, something," we now see *with* him that the millions of grains of sand that slip through his toes are "black, white, tan, and gray,/ mixed with quartz grains, rose and amethyst." The existence that had seemed so futile and repetitious a moment earlier is now varied, and even beautiful. The endless patterns of sliding sand, like those in a child's kaleidoscope, offer their own delightful rewards. And suddenly, too, the poem achieves an unexpected unity. We may at first have chuckled at Bishop's description of the sandpiper as "finical, awkward,/ in a state of controlled panic, a student of Blake." The implied comparison makes fun of the often fanatical followers of the famous romantic poet, William Blake, whose preoccupation with his own visionary experiences was so great that his wife once complained, "I have very little of Mr. Blake's company. He is always in Paradise." But by the end of the poem we learn to view the sandpiper and all "students of Blake" more sympathetically. Certainly they see something the rest of us do not; and perhaps in their preoccupation they see many things more closely, more clearly, and more perceptively than we.

Free verse is no longer experimental or even new. Although it is an established and popular alternative to syllabic-stress meters, it does not appear that free verse will ever entirely supplant conventional metrics, for there are many advantages to meter. In the first place, poets use meter because it is traditional. It allies them with Chaucer, Shakespeare, Milton, Wordsworth, Byron, Tennyson, Frost, and scores of other distinguished literary men and women. A poem that breaks with this long tradition risks an unsympathetic response from an audience that is accustomed to meter in poetry. Second, the use of meter demonstrates that the author took at least some care in writing, and this implies that he or she considered the content of the poem important. Few authors are likely to bother versifying ideas they think are trivial. (It is true, of course, that prose and free verse may be every bit as carefully crafted as metrical poetry, but the latter signals its importance through its form.) Third, a regular rhythm is inherently musical. It lays down a beat that appeals to us not only in poetry, but also in the sonatas of Beethoven and the songs of The Beach Boys. Fourth, regular rhythms arise out of strong emotions and enhance them in an auditor. They seem to be tied in with the rhythms of our human body. And fifth, meter creates an opportunity for interaction between the sound and sense of language. The tension between the expected and the actual rhythm of a particular line makes it easier for a poet to establish a tone—to speed up the rhythm where the illusion of speed, excitement, or fluidity is wanted, and to slow it down where the content demands emphasis and sobriety. Meter, then, is useful, but it cannot make an otherwise weak poem strong. Meter is only one of many ingredients in verse, although it is a catalytic ingredient, as Coleridge noted in comparing it to yeast, "worthless or disagreeable by itself, but giving vivacity and spirit to the liquor with which it is proportionally combined." Dame Edith Sitwell may have been even closer to the truth, however, when she argued that rhythm is "to the world of sound, what light is to the world of sight."[5] It is, finally, the rhythm of a poem, and not its meter, that should be the focus of commentary.

RHYME AND OTHER MANIPULATIONS OF SOUND

Two words rhyme when they end with the same sound. In *perfect rhyme,* the final vowel and any succeeding consonant sounds are

[5] *Taken Care Of* (London: Hutchinson, 1965), p. 123.

identical, and the preceding consonant sounds are different. Although rhyme words may be similar in spelling, they need not be. Thus, *ripe* and *tripe* rhyme to the eye and to the ear, but *rhyme* and *sublime* or *enough* and *snuff* rely entirely on aural similarity.

Rhyme is the most unnatural, the most noticeable, the most controversial, and possibly the most common of all poetic devices. Almost as soon as critics began to examine the elements of poetry, they also began to bicker about the merits of rhyme. Milton, for example, claimed, in 1668, that rhyme is "the invention of a barbarous age" and appeals only to "vulgar readers," to which Edward Young added the observation, a century later (1759), that rhyme "in epic poetry is a sore disease, in the tragic absolute death. . . . but our lesser poetry stands in need of a toleration for it; it raises that, but sinks the great, as spangles adorn children, but expose men." Interestingly enough, it is harder to find defenders of rhyme, although John Dryden, writing in 1664, felt that the device has so many advantages "that it were lost time to name them," and in 1702, Edward Bysshe called rhyme "the chief ornament of versification in any of the modern languages." On the whole, rhyme's detractors seem to make a more vigorous and impassioned argument; yet the great majority of all anthologized poetry in every period (including our own) is rhymed. Evidently, rhyme adds something to exceptional poetry. The question is, what?

Rhyme contributes to the effect of poetry in several ways. (1) It rings an audible end to each line. This is important because the rhythm of iambic verse is so similar to that of prose that without the aid of rhyme the sense of hearing poetry can easily be lost. Rhyme helps us to recognize aurally where one line ends and the next begins and thus reinforces the rhythmic pattern of the poem. (2) Rhyme makes words memorable. Of course, it cannot in itself make words *worthy* of being remembered; the content of the poem must do that. But rhyme has always been used to make things *easier* to remember. Wandering medieval minstrels, whose livelihood depended on their ability to delight a crowd with the lengthy adventures of Sir Gawain or King Arthur, used a tale's rhyming pattern as a prod to memory in the same way that we still use rhyming chants in daily life ("Thirty days hath September"). (3) Rhyme is pleasing because it is inherently musical. Verse appeals to small children long before they understand the full meaning of the words they chant, and rhyme is almost always used in popular songs. (4) Rhyme can be used to affect the pace and tone of poetry, as well. In the following stanza from "The Rime of the Ancient Mariner," for example, Coleridge uses the first four rhyme words ("prow," "blow," "shadow," and "foe") at the eighth, sixteenth, twenty-first, and twenty-fourth syllables to enhance the illusion of a chasing (and gaining!) storm:

With sloping masts and dipping prow,
As who pursued with yell and blow
Still treads the shadow of his foe,
And forward bends his head,
The ship drove fast, loud roared the blast,
And southward aye we fled.
—from "The Rime of the Ancient Mariner,"
Samuel Taylor Coleridge (1798)

(5) Well-managed rhymes are a sign of skill. Much of the fun in reading a poem like Byron's *Don Juan* is to observe how the poet wriggles out of the tight spots created by words that seem impossible to rhyme. When, for example, he ends the first line of the following quatrain with "annuities," we may think him trapped, only to find him scamper gleefully through the rhyme without the slightest apparent strain:

'Tis said that persons living on annuities
Are longer lived than others,—God knows why,
Unless to plague the grantors,—yet so true it is,
That some, I really think, do never die.
—from *Don Juan,* Lord Byron (1819)

Conversely, poorly managed rhymes are a sign of clumsiness, as Pope made clear in his "Essay on Criticism":

Where'er you find 'the cooling western breeze,'
In the next line it 'whispers through the trees';
If crystal streams 'with pleasing murmurs creep,'
The reader's threatened (not in vain) with 'sleep.'
—from "Essay on Criticism,"
Alexander Pope (1711)

(6) Because worn rhymes are so tiring and because interesting ones are difficult to find, a good rhyme facilitates witticism. Rhyme used in comic or satiric poetry tends to sharpen a well-honed phrase, as, for example, in the "Epitaph Intended for his Wife," attributed to John Dryden:

Here lies my wife: here let her lie!
Now she's at rest, and so am I.

and in Hilaire Belloc's sardonic "Lines for a Christmas Card":

May all my enemies go to Hell.
Noel, Noel, Noel, Noel.

One has only to rewrite these lines without rhyme (substituting *dwell* for Dryden's "lie" and *Amen* for Belloc's "Noel") to recognize that, with the change of words, the humor is lost.

In summary, rhyme in poetry is like salt in cooking. It adds almost nothing to nutrition, but it appeals to our taste. A poem that is unseasoned by rhyme may be as dull as a saltless diet, whereas too much rhyme, like too much salt, may spoil the dish.

Rhyme ordinarily falls on an accented syllable at the end of a line, in which case it is called *masculine end rhyme.* In *feminine (or double) rhyme,* the final two syllables in a line rhyme, and the final syllable is unaccented. In *triple rhyme,* three syllables rhyme. Both double and triple rhyme are generally used to create a comic effect. In the following stanza, lines one, three, and five are masculine end rhymes, lines four and six are feminine end rhymes, and lines seven and eight are triple rhymes.

'Tis pity learned virgins ever wed
  With persons of no sort of education,
Or gentlemen, who, though well born and bred,
  Grow tired of scientific conversation:
I don't choose to say much on this head,
  I'm a plain man, and in a simple station,
But—Oh! ye lords of ladies intellectual,
Inform us truly have they not hen-peck'd you all?
  —from *Don Juan,* Lord Byron (1819)

Not all rhymes fall at the end of a line. *Internal rhyme* occurs within a line of poetry. Often the word preceding the caesura rhymes with the last word in the line, as in Poe's "The Raven":

Once upon a midnight *dreary,* while I pondered weak and *weary.*

But internal rhyme may occur anywhere within a line or even between lines:

And the silken, sad, *uncertain* rustling of each purple *curtain*
  Thrilled me—*filled* me with fantastic terrors never felt before
So that now, to still the *beating* of my heart I stood *repeating*
  " 'Tis some visiter *entreating* entrance at my chamber door."
    —from "The Raven," Edgar Allan Poe (1845)

In *imperfect rhyme* the sound of two words is similar but it is not as close as is required in *true* or *perfect rhyme.* In the lines just quoted, "silken" and "uncertain" are imperfect rhymes, as are "filled," "felt," and "still." Ogden Nash combines imperfect rhyme with an ingenious play on words in the following anecdote on a happy marriage:

> I believe a little incompatibility is
> the spice of life, particularly if he has
> income and she is pattable.

Imperfectly rhymed words generally contain identical vowels or identical consonants, but not both. Imperfect rhyme is also referred to as approximate rhyme, or as half-rhyme, near rhyme, oblique rhyme, off-rhyme, or slant rhyme.

False rhyme pairs the sounds of accented with unaccented syllables. In the lines we quoted from "The Rime of the Ancient Mariner," "shādŏw" is a false internal rhyme with "hĭs fōe:"

> With sloping masts and dipping prow,
> As who pursued with yell and blow
> Still treads the *shadow* of *his foe* . . .

And at the same time, "prow" and "blow" are known as *visual rhymes*. These words—and such others as "rough-bough" and "love-prove"—rhyme to the eye, but not to the ear. Their spellings are similar, but their pronunciations are different.

Finally, repetition is occasionally used as an alternative to true rhyme. It provides the recurrence of sound expected in rhyme, but not the difference in meaning and initial consonants that makes rhyme delightful.

Modern poets have, on the whole, set themselves apart from much traditional poetry by replacing true rhymes with one or more of the alternatives, and so retaining some sense of music without rhyme's characteristic chime. Let us examine how W. H. Auden uses rhyme in describing the surf-washed shore of an island:

Look, Stranger

> Look, stranger, at this island now
> The leaping light for your delight discovers,
> Stand stable here
> And silent be,
> That through the channels of the ear
> May wander like a river
> The swaying sound of the sea.

Here at the small field's ending pause
Where the chalk wall falls to the foam, and its tall ledges
Oppose the pluck
And knock of the tide,
And the shingle scrambles after the suck-
ing surf, and the gull lodges
A moment on its sheer side.

Far off like floating seeds the ships
Diverge on urgent voluntary errands;
And the full view
Indeed may enter
And move in memory as now these clouds do,
That pass the harbor mirror
And all the summer through the water saunter.
—W. H. Auden (1936)

Although the words are musical, the poem is not arranged in any of the easily recognizable patterns of verse. The meter is loosely based on the strong-stress system, and the rhyme scheme is unconventional. The first line in each stanza is unrhymed. The second and sixth lines are imperfect rhymes. The third line rhymes perfectly with the fifth, as does the fourth line with the seventh. We can simplify our description of the rhyme scheme in "Look, Stranger" (or any other poem) by representing each new rhyme sound by a different letter of the alphabet, with capital letters reserved for perfect rhymes and lowercase letters for imperfect, false, or visual rhymes, and by representing unrhymed lines with an X. Thus, each of Auden's stanzas rhymes according to the scheme XaBCBaC. Identifying the *rhyme scheme* in this way is an important stage in cataloguing the manipulations of rhythm and rhyme within a specific poem. Although some critics prefer to ignore the various forms of partial rhyme, the system we have outlined allows us to indicate the subtle presence of imperfect, false, and visual rhymes without unduly complicating our representation of the total rhyme pattern. The rhyme schemes of most poems, of course, can be fully described using only the capital letters and the X for unrhymed lines.

Schematizing the rhyme in this way leads us to two important observations about the effect of Auden's verse. First, although six out of these seven lines rhyme, each of the first four lines ends with a different and unrelated sound. (In the first stanza the actual words are "now," "discovers," "here," and "be.") This means that each stanza is more than half complete before Auden begins to give it the sound of rhyming verse. Second, Auden never establishes a strong and repeated interval between rhymes. In most poetry, the rhymes recur predictably—every ten syllables in Pope's iambic pentameter couplets (p. 179), every twelve syllables in the anapestic tetrameter couplets of Byron's "The Destruction of Sennacherib" (p. 178), and so on. Almost immediately, we subconsciously pick up the rhyme pattern and begin to *expect* rhymes at the proper intervals. Auden makes it difficult for us to have any such expectations because he varies the interval between his rhymes. "Here" (line three) is separated by 12 syllables from its rhyming partner "ear" (line five), while "be" (line four) is separated by 22 syllables from "sea" (line seven) and "discovers" (line two) is separated by 23 syllables from its approximate rhyme with "river" (line six). Although the second and third stanzas follow the same rhyme scheme, the number of syllables separating the rhyme words may vary because lines of strong-stress meter often differ in number of syllables. "Look, Stranger" is in fact rhyme-dense (for example, it has a total of six rhyming words in the 49 syllables of the first stanza, whereas a comparable number of syllables in Pope's rhyming iambic pentameter would fall one syllable short of five rhymes). But we scarcely even perceive the rhyme in reading Auden's verse, whereas it is unmistakable in Pope's.

By declining to use a conventional, repetitive rhyme scheme, Auden willingly risks alienating those readers who feel his writing is "just not poetry" in order to capture that subtle sense of beauty and harmony that is the poem's theme. Auden is, indeed, attempting to describe the chalk cliffs, the surf-driven pebbles (or shingle), the perched gull, the urgent ships, and the drifting clouds, but he is even more interested in the process by which he and presumably all of us take such scenes of natural beauty to heart until "the full view/ Indeed may enter/ And move in memory as now these clouds do." Auden, no doubt, knows that a poet cannot hope to match the visual representation of the seaside in a photograph, a painter's landscape, or a film. But he knows as well that these visual media are not as effective as words in conveying the effects of rhythmic and natural movement on a human observor. Thus, his description of the setting is filled with activity: the "leaping light," "the pluck and knock of the tide," the "sucking surf," and even the memory of the whole scene that, like the drifting clouds, will "all the summer through the water saunter." And yet the actions he describes are not the purposeful and goal-oriented actions of hectic human life; they are sedate, rhythmic, and inherent in nature. Even the ships, which Auden knows "diverge on urgent voluntary errands," appear to him from the cliffs "like floating seeds."

What Auden wants, then, is not the methodical chime of repeated rhyme and not the businesslike stolidity of prose, but a more natural harmony that "through the channels of the ear/ May wander like a river" recreating "the swaying sound of the sea." Auden's idiosyncratic use of rhyme is but one of the musical devices that help him to do so. The similarity of vowel or consonant sounds, which we call imperfect rhyme when it occurs at the ends of lines, may also occur within lines where it is known more specifically as alliteration, assonance, or consonance.

Alliteration is the repetition in two or more nearby words of initial consonant sounds ("Where the chalk wall *f*alls to the *f*oam," line nine). *Assonance* is the repetition in two or more nearby words of similar vowel sounds ("ch*a*lk w*a*ll f*a*lls"). And *consonance* is the repetition in two or more nearby words of similar consonant sounds preceeded by different accented vowels ("cha*lk,*" "plu*ck,*" "kno*ck*"). Each of these devices is melodious—although less so than rhyme itself. For this reason, each is particularly appropriate in developing Auden's description of a natural and harmonious setting. Virtually every line reverberates with the subtle music of one or more of these three devices, and in some lines several musical effects are interwoven. Take, for example, the second stanza. The *aw* sound in "small" is repeated in "pause," and then in the next line this assonance is compounded by consonance and internal rhyme in the series "chalk wall falls." The *f* of "falls" alliterates with "foam," and the *all* sound is picked up again in "tall." In the third line, the *p*'s of "oppose" are reiterated in "pluck." (This hybrid of consonance and alliteration is one of many musical effects in verse with no formal name.) The fourth line has consonance ("pluck/knock"); the fifth has alliteration and assonance, which carry over into the sixth ("*s*hingle *s*crambles after the *s*uck-/ing *s*urf" and "s*u*ck-/ing s*u*rf and the g*u*ll"); and the seventh line combines alliteration ("*s*heer *s*ide") with the repetition of the *m* sounds in "*mom*ent." This high concentration of musical effects is repeated in both of the other stanzas.

As if all this were not enough, Auden also uses the emotional overtones of the various vowels and consonants to further heighten the beauty of his description. In general, those vowels that are produced through pursed and rounded lips tend to be soothing and *eupho-*

nious—although sometimes somber. We say "Oooh," "Ahh," and "Oh" in spontaneous expressions of pleasure and surprise. Conversely, those vowels that are produced with widely stretched lips tend to convey excitement, astonishment, or fright. Scared women "SHRIEEEK" and unhappy children "whine" and "wail." Such grating and unpleasant sounds are said to be *cacophonous.* Consonants, too, tend to divide into euphonious and cacophonous groups. Among the former we should list the liquid sounds of *r* and *l,* the nasal sounds of *m* and *n,* and such gentle sounds as *f, v, th,* and *sh.* Auden uses these soft consonants in "Look, Stranger" when he is describing the static appearance of the ships,

> Far off like floating seeds the ships,
> Diverge on urgent voluntary errands;

He also uses them to reinforce the idea that the very harmony of the scene makes it memorable:

> And the full view
> Indeed may enter
> And move in memory as now these clouds do.

Other consonants, called explosives—*p, b, d, k, t,* and hard *g*—create harsh, cacophonous effects. Auden uses these in his second stanza to describe the crash of the surf against the shore:

> . . . its tall ledges
> Oppose the pluck
> And knock of the tide,
> And the shingle scrambles after the suck-
> ing surf and the gull lodges
> A moment on its sheer side.

In fact, in "Look, Stranger" the meaning of the words may be less important than their rhythm and sound. To be sure, Auden describes the setting clearly, but it is a scene that, in one form or another, has been experienced by all men. We are impressed not so much by what Auden has to say, but by the way he says it.

In our analysis of Auden's poem perhaps we have emphasized too heavily the emotional overtones implicit in verbal sounds. If we examine any significant number of successful poems, we will find examples of harsh sounds used to create beauty or smooth sounds used with force and vigor. Few poets have ever been more conscious of the effects of sound than Pope in his lines on sound and sense in poetry (p. 179). It is indeed easy to applaud the liquid consonants (*f, r, n, m, th*) and melodious vowels ("s*o*ft," "bl*o*ws," "sm*oo*th") in his couplet on the sound of smooth verse:

> Soft is the strain when Zepher gently blows,
> And the smooth stream in smoother numbers flows.

In the next couplet, the sibilants (*s, sh*) and guttural vowels ("h*oar*se, r*ough* v*er*se") help to complement the stormy theme:

> But when loud surges lash the sounding shore
> The hoarse, rough verse should like the torrent roar.

And in the third couplet, a series of awkward consonantal combinations ("Aja*x* *str*ives some ro*ck's* *v*a*st* *w*eight") helps to slow the pace of the labored lines:

> When Ajax strives some rock's vast weight to throw,
> The line too labors, and the verse moves slow.

Yet Pope's lines also show us the dangers of generalization about the emotional effects of vowel and consonant sounds. The "hoarse, rough verse" in the second couplet is packed with liquid and nasal consonants, "whe*n* *l*oud su*r*ges *lash* the sou*nd*ing *sh*o*r*e," and the same is true in the third couplet where "*th*e *lin*e too *l*abo*r*s, a*nd* *th*e *v*e*rse* *mov*es s*l*ow." In these lines the liquid sounds have little moderating effect on the prevailing harshness of the verse. Obviously, the meaning of words can be more important than their sound in determining emotional connotations. Softness of vowels and consonants cannot make "foulness" fair or "murder" musical. With the exception of a few truly *onomatopoetic* words—for example, words like *moo, hiss,* and *clang,* whose sounds suggest their meanings—it is doubtful that the sounds of individual words often echo their senses. When "loud surges lash the sounding shore" in Pope's verse, the words *sound* harsh and forceful because of their denotations. And although the *l* and *s*-alliteration may in fact be pleasing to the ear, it does less to create a liquid beauty than to increase our sense of harshness by emphasizing the important words.

In the final analysis, the manipulations of sound that we have examined in this section are characteristic of all good writing. Authors base their word choice in large part on what "sounds" best. Theoretically, then, every piece of prose or poetry could be examined for the effect of sound on sense, but the problem is that our techniques of analysis are coarse and many of the decisions that authors make are complex, delicate, and even subconscious. We are like chemists struggling to determine a molecular weight using a physician's scale. In such circumstances one must concentrate on the macroscopic, cumulative effect of many microscopic interactions, for it is out of such interactions that the sounds of poetry are created.

6

Structure and Form in Poetry

Nearly all writing combines the narrative, dramatic, descriptive, and expository modes of expression. We rarely find any of these in a pure form in literature because an author's goal of creating interest and variety ordinarily requires that the modes be mixed. For the purpose of illustration, however, we can compose examples of how the same situation might be treated in each of the four modes:

Narrative: The boys crossed the street and entered the store.
Dramatic: "Look! There's a candy store."
"Let's cross over and buy some."
Descriptive: On one side of the street stood the two boys, jingling the coins in their pockets; on the other side were the large-paned windows of the store front, advertising in antique letters: DAN'S OLD-FASHIONED CANDIES.
Expository: The boys wanted to cross the street to buy some candy.

A narrative approach concentrates on action. In its pure form, it uses only nouns and transitive verbs, but such writing usually lacks appeal to the senses and to the intellect. As a result, narration does not necessarily predominate in narrative poetry; rather, the impulse to tell a story remains uppermost in the narrative poet's mind as he or she interweaves narration, description, dialogue, and explanation.

The principal forms of narrative poetry are the *epic,* which tells the book-length adventures of the founders of a nation or a culture (for example, *The Iliad, Paradise Lost*); the *romance,* which often resembles the epic in length and adventurousness but puts greater emphasis on love and supernatural events (*The Odyssey,* Tennyson's *Idylls of the King*); the *poetic tale* or short story in verse (Chaucer's *Miller's Tale,* Coleridge's *Rime of the Ancient Mariner*); and the ballad, a short narrative song (see pp. 203). The structure of narrative poetry closely resembles that of fiction, proceeding from an exposition of the setting, circumstances, and characters, through a period of complication (rising action), to a crisis and subsequent resolution.

The dramatic approach focuses on dialogue. Action and setting are conveyed through the spoken comments of the characters rather than through direct authorial description. Because poetry makes use of the aural qualities of language, most plays written before the twentieth century were composed in verse. Verse is, however, an artificial form of speech, and therefore twentieth-century realistic drama has mainly been written in prose, although the continuing popularity of musicals serves to remind us that poetic effects do appeal to theatrical audiences.

The *dramatic monologue,* which is the chief format for dramatic poetry is a fairly long speech by a fictional narrator that is usually addressed to a second, silent character. During the monologue the narrator reveals both his character and his motives at some crucial moment in his life. Because a monologue is basically reflective, the structure of a dramatic monologue rarely follows that of the conventional short story. It is likely to be digressive, argumentative, and analytic rather than strictly narrative.

A poem that is primarily descriptive or expository is called a *lyric.* Lyric poems range widely in subject, theme, and scope of treatment, but they are alike in their preoccupation with ideas, emotions, and the poet's state of mind. Although a narrative element is sometimes present, the lyric poet never concentrates on the story.

Many of the poems quoted in this text are lyrics, and by briefly examining a few of them, we can only begin to suggest the dozens of possible structures for lyric verse. A description may, for example, move from nearby objects to far-off ones, as in the second and third stanzas of Auden's "Look, Stranger" (p. 190). Or description may be followed by inquiry and analysis, as in Frost's "Design" (p. 114).

Frequently a specific incident leads up to a more general conclusion, as when Shakespeare (see p. 128) describes the emotions of an infant crawling after its mother as a symbol of his own passion for his mistress. The presentation may be chronological, like Herrick's in "Upon Julia's Clothes" (p. 156); may increase in emotional intensity, like Kipling's "Recessional" (p. 112); or may be analogical, like Donne's "A Valediction: Forbidding Mourning" (p. 99). In addition, descriptions can conceivably be organized according to the various senses or emotions evoked, and an argument can use comparison and contrast, order of importance, or parallelism to give structure to the whole. No exhaustive list of organizational structures is either possible or desirable.

In each of its formats—narrative, dramatic, and lyric—poetry varies more in length and content than either fiction or drama. Hence, the only useful generalizations about poetic structure are the broad ones that every element in a well-structure poem should have an identifiable function, and that the poem itself should build to a unified effect or series of effects.

STANDARD VERSE FORMS

In prose fiction, form is almost entirely subservient to meaning, but in poetry the verse form provides guidelines to the development of ideas. Verse is, as we argued earlier, a game played between the poet and his form. As in other games, the rules are essentially arbitrary. Why must a baseball cross the plate to be called a strike? What practical purpose is served by hitting a tennis ball over a mesh net and into a rectangular court? Why cannot a pawn move backward or a bishop sideways? Why must a sonnet have just 14 lines? The answer in each case is that the rules of the game help to provide a structure within which we can act and a standard against which we can measure our skills and the skills of others. A poet is challenged by his verse form to write as well as he can within certain restrictions. These restrictions do make the writing more difficult, but they also add to the achievement; and by forcing the poet to experiment with different means of expressing thoughts, they often help to better define what the poet really wants to say and how it can best be said.

Blank Verse

As we have seen, verse can be either rhymed or unrhymed. Unrhymed iambic pentameter is called blank verse. English blank verse was first written in 1557 by Henry Howard, the Earl of Surrey, in his translation of Virgil's *Aeneid.* It was then adopted for use in drama by Sackville and Norton in *Gorboduc* (1565); however, not until Marlowe and Shakespeare took up the line in the 1580s did its strength, sonority, and variety become evident, as illustrated in Shakespeare's famous characterization of Julius Caesar:

Why, man he doth bestride the narrow world
Like a colossus, and we petty men
Walk under his huge legs and peep about
To find ourselves dishonorable graves.
—from *Julius Caesar,*
William Shakespeare (c. 1600)

In 1664 Milton extended the uses of blank verse to the epic in his *Paradise Lost.* Although little blank verse was written in the eighteenth century, it has been used extensively since.

Stanzaic Verse

Although blank verse is normally organized, like prose, into paragraphs of variable length, rhymed verse is usually cast into units called stanzas. Often, the meter, rhyme scheme, and number of lines are identical in each stanza of a given poem (as in Auden's "Look, Stranger"). Occasionally, particularly in odes, the structure may vary from stanza to stanza, but no poem really deserves to be called stanzaic unless it regularly uses rhyme or a refrain. Individual stanzas must contain at least two lines and rarely exceed nine.

A *couplet,* formed of a single pair of rhymed lines, is the smallest possible stanzaic unit. When many of the couplets in a poem express a complete thought in two rhetorically balanced lines (as in Pope's lines on sound and sense, p. 179), the poet is said to use the *closed couplet.* The mere use of closed couplets does not, however, constitute a stanzaic structure. Pope's couplets are not visually separate from one another, nor are they always syntactically separate. Individual sentences frequently carry over into a third or fourth line. These run-on verses limit the utility of the couplet as an element of logical structure, and as a result Pope uses paragraphs instead of stanzas as his organizational units.

A few poems, however, are cast into stanzaic couplets, among them Stephen Vincent Benét's "The Mountain Whippoorwill: Or, How Hill-Billy Jim Won the Great Fiddler's Prize":

> Up in the mountains, it's lonesome all the time
> (Sof' win' slewin' thru' the sweet-potato vine.)
>
> Up in the mountains, it's lonesome for a child,
> (Whippoorwills a-callin' when the sap runs wild.)
>
> Up in the mountains, mountains in the fog,
> Everythin's as lazy as an old houn' dog.
>
> Born in the mountains, never raised a pet,
> Don't want nuthin' an' never got it yet.
>
> Born in the mountains, lonesome-born,
> Raised runnin' ragged thru' the cockleburrs and corn.
>
> Never knew my pappy, mebbe never should.
> Think he was a fiddle made of mountain laurel-wood.
>
> Never had a mammy to teach me pretty-please.
> Think she was a whippoorwill, a-skitin' thru' the trees.
>
> Never had a brother nor a whole pair of pants,
> But when I start to fiddle, why, yuh got to start to dance!
>
> *Listen to my fiddle—Kingdom Come—Kingdom Come!*
> *Hear the frogs a-chunkin' "Jug o' rum, Jug o' rum!"*
> *Hear that mountain whippoorwill be lonesome in the air,*
> *An' I'll tell yuh how I travelled to the Essex County Fair.*
>
> —from "The Mountain Whippoorwill,"
> Stephen Vincent Benét (1925)

In addition to the use of stanzaic couplets, Benét's poem is unusual in at least two ways. Each line of its accentual tetrameter is bisected by a caesura into units of two feet apiece (*dipodic meter*). Therefore, each couplet could easily be recast as four lines of accentual dimeter. Second, Benét does not commit himself to using stanzaic couplets throughout the remaining hundred lines of the poem. The quoted segment concludes with a quatrain, and Benét later abandons all stanzaic structure. Thus, for substantial segments of the poem, Benét has not overcome the limitations of stanzaic couplets; instead he has freely altered the structure of his poem in adapting to those limitations.

If couplets have rarely been used as independent stanzas, they have nevertheless been popular as complete poems. Most two-line poems are *epigrams*. An epigram is a concentrated witticism that can be written in either verse or prose—although the couplet is the dominant choice. Whatever its form, an epigram must be short, sharp, and swift—as startling as a wasp and as quick to sting. Both Belloc's "Lines for a Christmas Card" and Dryden's "Epitaph on His Wife" (p. 188) are epigrammatic. For a third example of an epigram, consider Coleridge's definition of the form:

> What is an epigram? A dwarfish whole;
> Its body brevity, and wit its soul.

Many epigrams are buried within longer poems. All of Pope's poems are packed with this form of wit (for example, the first two lines on sound and sense, p. 179); and the final couplets in many of the stanzas in Byron's *Don Juan* are epigrammatic (see pp. 118 and 120), as are the concluding couplets of many of Shakespeare's sonnets.

A three-line stanza is called a *tercet* or *triplet,* if all three lines rhyme together. Herrick's "Upon Julia's Clothes" (p. 156) is an example of a poem using this stanza. *Terza rima,* a form of three-line stanza popularized by the thirteenth-century Italian poet Dante, establishes an interlocking rhyme scheme in the following pattern: ABA BCB CDC, etc. The closing stanza is either a quatrain or a couplet. The most famous English poems in this stanza are Shelley's "Ode to the West Wind," Robert Browning's "The Statue and the Bust," and William Morris's "The Defence of Guenevere."

A unit of four lines, a *quatrain,* is the most common stanzaic form in English poetry. Although many different rhyme schemes have been used in quatrains, the most often used is *crossed rhyme,* in which the first line rhymes with the third and the second with the fourth, ABAB. Usually the first and third lines are tetrameter, the second and fourth trimeter. This is the pattern of Donne's "Valediction: Forbidding Mourning" (p. 99), Wordsworth's "She Dwelt Among the Untrodden Ways" and Poe's "Annabel Lee."

An iambic pentameter quatrain in which the first two lines rhyme with the last (AAXA) is known as a *rubais* because it was popularized in the *Rubáiyát of Omar Khayyám* (1859) by Edward FitzGerald. The stanza is particularly useful in epigrams because it is similar to a closed couplet, although it develops its point in four lines instead of just two. The first two lines in the quatrain are metrically identical to a closed couplet, but the next two lines, instead of developing a separate idea, extend and complement the first two. Thus, the entire quatrain is like a single couplet in which each line has twenty syllables and the first line has an internal rhyme:

Couplet 1 — Come, fill the Cup, and in the fire of Spring
Your Winter-garment of Repentance fling:
Couplet 2 ––––– The Bird of Time has but a little way
To flutter—and the Bird is on the Wing.
—from *The Rubáiyát of Omar Khayyám,*
Edward FitzGerald (1859)

In short, the *rubais* combines the unity and wit of a couplet with the freedom and scope of a quatrain.

Other quatrains use rhyme schemes based on a single rhyme (AAAA), a pair of couplets (AABB), or an "envelope" (ABBA), but the most important quatrain of all is the stanza used in traditional folk ballads—a stanza composed of alternating lines of iambic tetrameter and iambic trimeter rhyming (XAXA).

A *ballad* is a short narrative poem telling of a single, dramatic incident. The traditional ballad is part of our oral heritage, and one basic story may evolve into dozens of variant forms as it is recited or sung at different times to different audiences. "Bonny Barbara Allan" is certainly one of the most widely known and frequently altered of all ballads. It has gone through so many different versions over the years that one critic has observed wryly, "Barbara Allan's ninety-two progeny are something of a record achievement, certainly for a lady who, according to the ballad, scorned her lover. One is thankful that she did not encourage him!"[1]

BARBARA ALLAN

In Scarlet Town, where I was born,
There was a fair maid dwelling,
Made every youth cry well-a-way!
Her name was Barbara Allan.

All in the merry month of May,
When green buds they were swelling,

[1] Arthur Kyle Davis, Jr., *Traditional Ballads of Virginia.* (Cambridge, Mass.: Harvard University Press, 1929), p. 302.

Young Jemmy Grove on his death-bed lay,
  For love of Barbara Allan.

O slowly, slowly rose she up,
  To the place where he was lying,
And when she drew the curtain by,
  "Young man, I think you're dying."

"O 'tis I'm sick, and very, very sick,
  And 'tis a' for Barbara Allan;"
"O the better for me ye's never be,
  Tho your heart's blood were spilling."

"O dinna ye mind, young man," said she,
  "When ye was in the tavern drinking,
That ye made the healths go round and round
  And slighted Barbara Allan?"

He turned his face unto the wall,
  And death was with him dealing:
"Adieu, adieu, my dear friends all,
  And be kind to Barbara Allan!"

And slowly, slowly rose she up,
  And slowly, slowly left him,
And sighing said she could not stay,
  Since death of life had reft him.

She had not gone a mile but two,
  When she heard the dead-bell knelling,
And every toll that the dead-bell gave
  Cried, "Woe to Barbara Allan!"

"O mother, mother, make my bed!
  O make it soft and narrow!
Since my love died for me today,
  I'll die for him tomorrow."

—anonymous

Because traditional ballads (also referred to as folk or popular ballads) were composed for an oral presentation before an audience, they tell simple, direct stories using dialogue, repetition, and refrains in an effort to capture the interest and attention of an audience that may, after all, be hearing the story for the first time. Ballads tend to be objective, abrupt, and concise. The first few lines catch our interest with a question or a tense situation. Thereafter, the characters spring to life, acting and speaking with relatively little external commentary by the author. Some ballads use the refrain for the purpose of advancing or commenting on the narrative. The themes of ballads are those of continuing popular interest: unhappy love, feats of war or bravado, shipwrecks, murder, and domestic quarrels.

After the end of the Middle Ages and after the development of the printing press, concern for originality in composition naturally increased, and the circulation and communal creation of folk ballads declined. The ballad stanza has, however, remained popular, particularly in the former slave states of the South where Negro spirituals and blues evolved with the same format and vitality as in the traditional ballad. Furthermore, professional poets and songwriters ranging from Rudyard Kipling (*Barrack-Room Ballads*) to Bob Dylan ("The Ballad of the Thin Man," etc.) have composed delightful literary ballads that prove both the adaptability and the continuing popularity of the form.

Stanzas of five lines, or *quintets,* are infrequently found in English poetry and none of the many possible rhyme schemes has emerged as particularly prevalent. It says something about the unpopularity of this stanza that the best-known of the poems that employ it are such slight lyrics as Robert Herrick's "The Night-Piece, to Julia" (rhyming AABBA) and Edmund Waller's "Go, Lovely Rose" (rhyming ABABB). The two poems together total only forty lines.

The most common six-line stanza is the *Shakespearean sestet,* the pattern Shakespeare always used for the last six lines (or sestet) in his sonnets. It is composed of a crossed rhyme quatrain followed by a couplet (ABABCC), all in iambic pentameter. Shakespeare first used this sestet in his innovative and popular erotic tale, *Venus and Adonis* (1593), in which his handling of the stanza is light, humorous, and witty; he normally describes the action in the quatrain and cleverly summarizes it or introduces a new and incongruous image in the succeeding, epigrammatic couplet. In the following lines Venus has just seen Adonis and courted him with breathless, burning phrases:

With this she seizeth on his sweating palm,
The precedent of pith and livelihood,
And, trembling in her passion, calls it balm,
Earth's sovereign salve to do a goddess good.
    Being so enrag'd, desire doth lend her force
    Courageously to pluck him from his horse.

Over one arm the lusty courser's rein,
Under the other was the tender boy,

Who blush'd and pouted in a dull disdain,
With leaden appetite, unapt to toy;
She red and hot as coals of glowing fire,
He red for shame, but frosty in desire.
—from *Venus and Adonis,*
William Shakespeare (1593)

Here, the concluding couplets emphasize the comic reversal of roles in the poem: Venus manfully plucks Adonis from his horse in the first stanza, and in the second she is flushed with dissolute passion while Adonis blushes in virginal shame.

The *septet,* or seven-line stanza, is normally cast into the pattern known as *rhyme royal* because it was used in the only long poem written by an English-speaking king, *The King's Quhair* by James I of Scotland (ca. 1425). The rhyme scheme differs from that of the Shakespearean sestet by the addition of another B-rhyme at the end of the quatrain (ABABBCC); the line remains iambic pentameter.

Rhyme royal was first used in English poetry by Chaucer, who felt that the stanza was appropriate for the themes of "The Prioress's Tale," *Troilus and Criseyde,* and other serious poems. When Shakespeare came to write the "graver labour" that he had promised in the dedication to *Venus and Adonis,* he chose to use rhyme royal, and the result was the tragic and melodramatic *Rape of Lucrece* (1594). There is, however, nothing necessarily serious about poems written in this stanza. If anything, its closely packed rhymes and paired couplets may be most appropriate in witty verse, as in W. H. Auden's rambling and comic "Letter to Lord Byron."

The most important eight-line stanza is *ottava rima,* which is like a stretched Shakespearean sestet: eight lines of iambic pentameter rhyming (ABABABCC). Lord Byron stamped this stanza with the witty, satiric, and exuberant characteristics of his own personality by using it in his epic comedy, *Don Juan,* from which we have already quoted (see pp. 118 and 120).

Of all stanzaic patterns, the most intricate is the nine-line *Spenserian stanza.* First used by Edmund Spenser in *The Faerie Queene* (1590), this stanza is made up of eight lines of iambic pentameter rhyming ABABBCBC and a final C-rhyme of iambic hexameter (called an Alexandrine). The stanza has often been praised for its majesty and effectiveness in poems with serious themes. To a large extent, this praise is only a recognition that Spenser made majestic and effective use of the stanza in *The Faerie Queene.* Because the stanza inevitably recalls Spenser's poem, later poets have generally used it to create a Spenserian sense of romance, morality, and heroism. So, too, *ottava rima* connotes Byron's witty hedonism, and the Shakespearean sestet connotes the light eroticism of *Venus and Adonis.* The impact of each form on the tone and mood of poetry is often less a product of the stanza itself, than of one unforgettable use of the stanza. Unlike most other stanzas, however, the Spenserian is capable of great variety. Depending on how the poet breaks up his or her thoughts, the stanza can either produce the sound of two couplets (ABA *BB* CB *CC*), of a modified *terza rima* (*ABA* BB *CBC* C), or of many variations of couplets, tercets, quatrains, and quintets. Spenser frequently molds his stanza into two clear quatrains and a final stark Alexandrine, as in the following description of a knight who has lost his honor and his chastity in a luxurious "Bower of Bliss":

> His warlike armes, the idle instruments
> Of sleeping praise, were hong upon a tree,
> And his brave shield, full of old moniments,
> Was fowly ra'st, that none the signes might see;
> Ne for them, ne for honour cared hee,
> Ne ought, that did to his advancement tend,
> But in lewd loves, and wastefull luxuree,
> His dayes, his goods, his bodie he did spend:
> O horrible enchantment, that him so did blend.
>
> —from *The Faerie Queene,* Book II, Canto XII,
> Edmund Spenser (1590)

By avoiding a monotonous pattern, poets using Spenserian stanzas can vary the effect of their rhymes in much the same way that musicians create variations of a melody. This variety of sound patterns may explain why the Spenserian is the only complex stanza that has been repeatedly used in long poems. In addition to *The Faerie Queene,* it is the stanza of Robert Burns's *Cotter's Saturday Night,* Shelley's *Adonais,* Keats's *Eve of St. Agnes,* and Byron's *Childe Harold.*

The Spenserian is the longest of the well-known stanzas, and it includes in itself many of the lyrical possibilities of shorter stanzas. As such it reconfirms a number of general observations about the nature and function of stanzaic verse itself. First, stanzaic verse gives the poet an opportunity to impose something akin to the order and structure of prose (for stanzas have many of the virtues of paragraphs) without unduly restricting or sacrificing internally the peculiar expressiveness of poetry. Second, the type of stanza the poet chooses is important. Certain stanzaic patterns inevitably carry with them traditional associations which neither poet nor reader can ignore. The heroic couplet, for example, is unavoidably associated with Pope's satiric wit, in much the same way that ottava rima calls to mind Byron's risqué and exuberant humor. Finally, the less dense the rhymes in a particular stanza, the more frequently it is used in developing serious plots and themes; conversely, the more dense the rhyme, the less serious the subject matter and the greater the probability of a witty, satiric, or comic treatment.

Not all stanzaic poems are constructed out of regular and repeating structural units. *Odes* are particularly likely to be idiosyncratic, with each stanza differing from others in the same poem both in rhyme scheme and in length of line. This freedom is limited only by a common understanding that an ode must be a long lyric poem that is serious and dignified in subject, tone, and style. It strives to create a mood of meditative sublimity. Some of the more notable free-form odes in English include Wordsworth's "Intimations of Immortality," Coleridge's "Dejection," Shelley's "Ode to the West Wind," and Allen Tate's "Ode to the Confederate Dead."

Historically, odes were not always as free in form as they usually are today. In ancient Greece they were strictly organized choral songs that sometimes were written to signal the division between scenes in a play and at other times to celebrate an event or individual. These *Pindaric odes* (named after the Greek poet Pindar) develop through sequences of three different stanzas: *strophe, antistrophe,* and *epode.* The metrical pattern of each strophe remains the same throughout the ode, as does the pattern of each antistrophe and epode. Originally, the strophe was sung and danced by one half of the chorus, after which antistrophe was performed by the other half of the chorus using the same steps of the strophe in reverse. The epode was then performed by the combined chorus. Regular Pindaric odes are quite uncommon in English, the best known being Thomas Gray's "The Bard" and "The Progress of Poetry."

Horatian odes, patterned after those of the Roman poet Horace, retain one stanzaic structure throughout—that is, they are regular stanzaic poems dealing with lofty, lyrical subjects. Some of the better-known Horatian odes are Andrew Marvell's "An Horatian

Ode upon Cromwell's Return from Ireland" and Keats's "To Autumn" and "Ode on a Grecian Urn."

Fixed Poetic Forms

The stanzaic patterns we have described are only one way in which poets attempt to create a recognizable tune analogous to a songwriter's melody. The other way is to use one of the fixed poetic forms—the haiku, sonnet, ballade, villanelle, rondeau, sestina, limerick, and so on. Of these, the haiku, the limerick, and the sonnet have achieved a significant place in English poetry; however, all are alike in two respects: all are brief, and all create their moods through the combined effects of a fixed verse pattern and the traditional connotations associated with that pattern. The haiku, for example, is generally associated with brief suggestive images, the limerick with light humor, and the sonnet with love.

A *haiku* is a form of poetry that originated in Japan during the thirteenth century. It consists of three lines of five, seven, and five syllables, respectively. Because of the brevity of the form there is little room for anything more than the presentation of a single concentrated image or emotion. Thus, haiku poems, like this example by Moritake, tend to be allusive and suggestive:

What I thought to be
Flowers soaring to their boughs
Were bright butterflies.
—Moritake (1452–1540)

The influence of the Japanese haiku on the twentieth-century Imagist movement has been profound and is reflected in such familiar anthology pieces as Ezra Pound's "In a Station of the Metro" and William Carlos Williams's "Red Wheelbarrow."

A *limerick* is a form of light verse that is often scratched on the tiles of public rest rooms. Its five lines rhyme AABBA. The A-rhymed lines are in anapestic trimeter; the others are in dimeter. Surprisingly, many authors of good repute have tried their hand at this little form—among them Edward Lear (who wrote over two hundred limericks), Robert Louis Stevenson, Rudyard Kipling, and Oliver Wendell Holmes. The following pun attributed to Holmes on the name

"Henry Ward Beecher" helps to create one of the best of the printable limericks:

The Reverend Henry Ward Beecher
Called a hen a most elegant creature.
  The hen, pleased with that,
  Laid an egg in his hat.
And thus did the hen reward Beecher.
—anonymous

In comparison with the haiku and the limerick, the *sonnet* is a more distinguished and inspiring form. Indeed, poets often become so enamoured of the "little song" (the literal meaning of *sonnet*) that some have written nothing else and a few—including William Wordsworth and Dante Gabriel Rossetti—have composed rapturous sonnets on sonnetry.

Technically, a sonnet is a lyric poem of fourteen iambic pentameter lines, usually following one of two established models: the Italian form or the English form. The *Italian sonnet* (or *Petrarchan sonnet* named after the Italian Renaissance poet Petrarch) consists of an eight-line octave, rhyming ABBAABBA, followed by a six-line sestet, rhyming variously CDECDE, CDCDCD, etc. Normally, the octave presents a situation or issue, and the sestet explores or resolves it. Both "On First Looking into Chapman's Homer" (p. 103) and "Design" (p. 114) are Petrarchan sonnets. Keats's octave relates what he had heard about Homer before reading his poetry, while the sestet examines Keats's emotions after discovering the beauties of Homer through Chapman's translation. Frost uses his octave to describe the three objects he encounters on his morning walk, whereas his sestet raises questions about their origin and meaning.

The *English sonnet* (or *Shakespearean sonnet*) consists of three quatrains and a concluding couplet, rhyming ABAB CDCD EFEF GG. A variant of the English sonnet, the *Spenserian sonnet,* links its quatrains by employing the rhyme scheme ABAB BCBC CDCD EE. Although the English sonnet may describe an issue and its resolution using the same octave-sestet structure as in the Italian form, the three quatrains of the Shakespearean sonnet often present three successive images, actions, or arguments, which are then summed up in a final, epigrammatic couplet. A typical Shakespearean sonnet (number CXLIII) is quoted on page 128. Note that in this case the sonnet does take the form of an octave, presenting a hypothesis ("as a careful housewife"), and a sestet, presenting a conclusion ("So runn'st thou"). But the sonnet also breaks into three quatrains and a couplet. The first quatrain describes a housewife in pursuit of a stray cock or hen; the second tells how her neglected child chases after her; and the third explains that Shakespeare is in a situation like that of the child, whereas his mistress (who is presumably running after another man) is like the housewife. Finally, the concluding couplet summarizes and resolves the situation with a pun on William Shakespeare's first name:

> So I will pray that thou mayst have thy "Will,"
> If thou turn back and my loud crying still.

The sonnet became popular in England during the sixteenth century largely because of translations and imitations of Petrarch's passionate cycle of sonnets addressed to his mistress Laura. Similar sonnet sequences were written by Sir Philip Sidney (*Astrophel and Stella,* 1580), Samuel Daniel (*Delia,* 1592), Michael Drayton (*Idea,* 1593), Edmund Spenser (*Amoretti* and *Epithalamion,* 1595), and William Shapespeare (*Sonnets,* 1609). This deluge of amorous sonnets helped to establish the belief that the sonnet itself must always deal with love—a presumption that is still widespread. As early as 1631, Milton challenged this popular notion by writing sonnets of personal reflection, moral criticism, and political comment. The sonnets by Shakespeare, Keats, and Frost, quoted earlier in this text, demonstrate that Milton was correct and that the sonnet can be used in themes ranging from Shakespeare's illicit sexual proposal, to Keats's rapturous literary appreciation, to Frost's somber metaphysical brooding. It is this adaptability that makes the sonnet so much more important in literary history than other fixed forms, such as the haiku and the limerick.

VISUAL FORMS

All verse makes some appeal to the eye. We see where the lines begin and end, and from that information we can often tell something about the poetic emphasis and meaning. For some poets, however, this limited visual element is not enough. William Blake, for example, printed his poems himself so that he would be sure that both the calligraphy and the marginal illustrations would contribute to the overall effect. Thus, when we read the poems from his *Songs of Innocence* (1789) and *Songs of Experience* (1794), we must at the very least remember that the words only convey part of his intention. Few other poets have shared Blake's broad interests in both literature and graphic art, but many have experimented with three methods of expanding poetic meaning through visual form.

Typographical Analogies

Throughout history writers have underscored the content of their work by manipulating the way that words appear on the page. Capital letters convey urgency and loudness: STOP! HELP! COME HERE! Lower-case letters, particularly in names, suggest humility or timidity (but paradoxically also attract attention): *e.e. cummings, archie and mehitabel,* and so on. Additional letters or spaces in a line can suggest stuttering (*c-c-cold*), reverberation (*shockkk*), delay (*s l o w l y*), and distance (*l o n g*). Conversely, deleted letters or spaces indicate speed (*quickasawink*) and compactness (*huddld*). Misspellings, like *X-mass* and *Amerikkka,* make a visual statement by reminding us respectively of the cross borne by Christ and of the role played by the Ku Klux Klan during certain periods of American history. Furthermore, certain typesetting techniques allow the appearance of words to mirror their meanings: o^{ve}r, u$_{nde}$r, cramped, or t$_{a_{i_{l_{i_{ng.}}}}}$ E. e. cummings popularized the use of typographical analogies in modern poetry (see "Buffalo Bill's," p. 105); although these devices sometimes become contrived and gimmicky, other contemporary poets such as Robert Duncan, Allen Ginsberg, and Howard Nemerov have occasionally introduced tricks of typography into their poems.

Picture Poems

By careful word choice and clever typesetting, poets can sometimes create a visual image of the object or idea they are describing. Although picture poems have never been numerous, they are by no means new. One finds them in ancient Greek literature, as well as in the recent movement toward *concretism* (the concern with a poem's visual appearance rather than with its words). In most cases, visual poems tend to be frivolous, as in Lewis Carroll's *Alice in Wonderland* where the tale the Mouse tells Alice takes the form of a long, serpentine "tail" that wanders down half a page. The ingenious seventeenth-century poet George Herbert proved, however, that visual effects are not always frivolous. He formed his religious meditation on the altar of the human heart into the shape of an altar in the following poem:

THE ALTAR

A broken ALTAR, Lord, thy servant rears,
Made of a heart, and cemented with tears:
Whose parts are as thy hand did frame;
No workman's tool hath touched the same.
A HEART alone
Is such a stone,
As nothing but
Thy power doth cut.
Wherefore each part
Of my hard heart
Meets in this frame,
To praise thy Name:
That, if I chance to hold my peace,
These stones to praise thee may not cease.
O let thy blessed SACRIFICE be mine,
And sanctify this ALTAR to be thine.
—George Herbert (1633)

Acrostics

An acrostic is a poem in which certain letters (ordinarily the first in each line) spell out a word when read from top to bottom or bottom to top. The best-known acrostics in English literature are those by John Davies in praise of Queen Elizabeth I. Every poem in his volume of *Hymns of Astraea* (1599) spells out the words *Elizabetha Regina*—Elizabeth, the queen.

TO THE SPRING

E arth now is green and heaven is blue,
L ively spring which makes all new,
I olly spring, doth enter;
S weet young sun-beams do subdue
A ngry, aged winter.

B lasts are mild and seas are calm,
E very meadow flows with balm,
T he earth wears all her riches;
H armonious birds sing such a psalm
A s ear and heart bewitches.

R eserve, sweet spring, this nymph of ours
E ternal garlands of thy flowers;
G reen garlands never wasting;
I n her shall last our fair spring
N ow and forever flourishing
A s long as heaven is lasting.

—John Davies (1599)

All of these visual effects may occasionally play a useful role in good poetry, but they are more often signs of weakness—superficial and relatively easy techniques used by poets who are content to be ingenious. In the final analysis, the words of poetry and the energy, intellect, and feeling communicated by those words are of far more importance to truly great writing than even the most meticulous adherence to the external requirements of verse form.

7

Analyzing and Evaluating Poetry

In the preceding pages we have introduced and discussed the formal elements of poetry. An essential problem remains, a problem faced by any reader coming upon a new poem for the very first time: namely, how best to isolate and identify the chief elements of the poem for the purposes of analysis, understanding, and evaluation. There is, to be sure, no one "right" or "best" way to proceed, for individual poems vary greatly not only in their external formal characteristics, but in the way they handle and manipulate their internal elements as well. But the would-be critic must begin somewhere, and we will suggest here a series of questions that can be asked of any poem.

Before listing the questions, we should, however, add a few words of caution. First, poems differ greatly in their emphases. Not all of the questions that follow will be equally applicable to the analysis of every poem; therefore, the reader needs to follow to some extent his or her intuition in order to understand what makes a particular poem vital and appealing. Second, although analysis of an author's success in manipulating the elements of poetry can add to an appreciation and understanding of any poem, the reader should not assume that poems that *require* extensive explication to be understood are necessarily better than those that do not. Explication is one means—and generally the most important means—of coming to understand why an author has written what he or she has. Some poems require much explication and some little. But great poetry should be a pleasure to read, not a punishment. We can expect this pleasure to grow as analysis and mature reflection increase our understanding, but the enjoyment of poetry is, and should remain, visceral as well as intellectual.

Questions to Ask and Answer

First, read the poem carefully (aloud at least once), making sure that you understand the *denotative meaning* of each word. (Be sure to use both your dictionary and the editor's notes, if any.)

1. Does the poet manipulate the meanings of words using any of the following devices: *connotation, allusion, repetition, ambiguity, punning, paradox, irony?* How does the use of these devices add to the resonance and significance of the denotative meaning?
2. Examine the poem's *imagery.* Are any images repeated or otherwise emphasized? Does the imagery in the poem develop according to a logical pattern? Can you determine why the poet uses the images that he or she does?
3. What forms of poetic comparison (*metaphor, simile,* etc.) are used and what do they add to the poem's imagery and meaning?
4. Does the poem make use of *symbol* or *allegory?*
5. Who is the speaker? What kind of person does he or she seem to be? To whom is he speaking and what are his point of view and his relation to the subject? What is the general mood or *tone* of the poem? Is it consistent throughout, or is there a shift?
6. What is the situation or occasion of the poem? What is the setting in time and space?
7. *Paraphrase* and *summarize* the poem. What is the poem's *theme,* argument, or central idea and how is it developed? (Be alert to repeated images, the stanzaic pattern, rhetorical devices, etc.)
8. What is the *meter* and *rhyme scheme* of the poem? What other significant repetitions of sounds (*alliteration, assonance, consonance*) occur in the poem? How do they contribute to the effect of the poem? What is the form of the poem (*sonnet, ode, lyric, dramatic monologue,* etc.)? Are the meter, rhyme scheme, and form appropriate?

9. *Criticize* and *evaluate.* How well do you think the poet has achieved a total integration of his materials? What is *your* reaction to the poem? Do you like the poem? If so, why? If not, why not?

III
Drama

8

What Is Drama?

The word *drama* comes from the Greek verb *dran,* meaning "to perform." When we speak of a drama, we mean a story in dialogue performed by actors, on a stage, before an audience—in other words, a *play.* We also use the term *drama* in a more general sense to refer to the literary genre that encompasses all written plays and to the profession of writing, producing, and performing plays.

Because drama presupposes performance, it is not a purely literary genre. It combines the use of language with representational arts involving scenery, costuming, and the actors' physical appearance. It also makes use of vocal emphasis and tone of voice, along with such nonverbal forms of expression as physical gesture, facial expression, and sometimes music and dance. Thus, a drama only becomes a complete work of art when it is seen on the stage, and the written text of a play is only its skeletal frame—lacking flesh, blood, and a life of its own. This skeletal script is, however, the only permanent part of a play. The rest is ephemeral: it changes to some degree with each night's performance and, to a considerable extent, with each new production. Presentations of Greek tragedy, for example, have ranged from stately, historically accurate productions to loose, avant-garde adaptations. In one production of Euripides' *The Bacchae* we watch "larger than life" actors struggle to speak clearly while costumed in oversized masks, padded clothing, and sandals with thick platform soles. And in another production of the same play (renamed *Dionysus in 69*), we find naked women splashing their way through oceans of stage blood, engaging in simulated sex, and writhing through a savage "birth ritual."

Such extremes serve to remind us that the script is the only part of the play over which the author has complete control; the rest is the collaborative creation of many different artists, some of whom may misunderstand and therefore misrepresent what the author intended. Because we can never know exactly how Sophocles, Shakespeare, Molière, and other early dramatists staged their plays, we can never reproduce exactly the work of art they intended. But in reading the words of the play, we *can* share in the imaginative experience that—even more than success on the stage—is responsible for the survival and enduring popularity of great drama. We know, for example, that the plays of Euripides were not popular with the audience when first presented in ancient Greece. Yet Euripides' plays have survived through the ages, and those of his more popular contemporaries are all but forgotten. Apparently, Euripides' intense, introverted style and penetrating character analyses appealed to the readers who commissioned and preserved manuscripts of his plays. In contrast, the record for the longest continuous run for a single play is held by Agatha Christie's *The Mousetrap,* which, whatever its merit as drama, as of 1979 had been on stage for 27 years and almost 11,000 performances. Christie's play will not, of course, continue its run forever. Someday the show will close, and thereafter its survival will depend on readers. Only if the demand by the play-reading public is sufficient to keep a play in print, and only if the play in its written form appeals to a succession of producers and directors, can we expect that it will truly become a stage classic.

This is precisely what has happened in the case of Euripides, Shakespeare, and other great classic and modern dramatists, whose readers have always outnumbered their viewers. Even today, when the average citizen has an unparalleled opportunity to see outstanding theater on stage, copies of printed scripts continue to be sold in ever-increasing numbers. Although most lovers of the theater are adamant about *seeing* great drama performed, they are equally adamant about owning, reading, and studying the plays they love.

The reason for this phenomenon is clear enough: when we study drama as literature—that is, when we study the text of the play, apart from its staging—we may not see the entire work intended by the author, but we do see the words exactly as the playwright wrote them, or as they have been translated, without any cutting, rearranging, or rewriting by the director and without the interpretive assistance (or hindrance) of the actors. The written script may be skeletal compared to a stage presentation, but that limitation can help us to concentrate on the play's structure and on those elements of drama that fall directly under the author's control.

DRAMA AND POETRY

As soon as we think of drama as a form of literature, it is evident that a play shares many similarities with a long narrative poem. In fact, from the days of ancient Greece through the first half of the nineteenth century, most plays were written in verse. The dramatic works of Aeschylus, Sophocles, Euripides, Aristophanes, Marlowe, Shakespeare, Jonson, Molière, Racine, Corneille, and many others are largely or entirely poetic. Even Ibsen, who probably did more than any other dramatist to make prose acceptable in tragedy, wrote two of his most famous plays, *Brand* and *Peer Gynt,* in verse.

The reasons for the historical predominance of verse in drama are not difficult to discover. Drama, like poetry, is meant to be heard. As a result, like poetry, it makes use of the aural qualities of rhythm and rhyme. Furthermore, because Greek drama originally grew out of choral songs, it was only natural that the musical elements in the songs should be preserved in the plays; and because Greek drama served as a model for most subsequent generations, verse remained an integral part of most playwriting until the preoccupation with realism near the end of the nineteenth century made the contrivance of dialogue in verse both unnecessary and undesirable. Finally, many of the stages used for drama were relatively barren, and the playwright was required to evoke through poetic language any characteristics of the setting that he wished the audience to envision. Thus, poetic diction, imagery, and techniques of versification became thoroughly integrated into the drama.

One can not conclude, however, that drama is inevitably a form of poetry. Indeed, in the last century new poetic dramas have rarely been successful on the stage. Popular taste has changed, and audiences now demand realism instead of poetic flourishes. Of course, many of these realistic plays—especially those of Tennessee Williams and Eugene O'Neill—are written in prose which is so imagistic and suggestive that it may be studied as a form of free verse, but even if we confine this discussion to plays more obviously written in verse, we will find some differences between poetry and drama. In the first place, a poem is meant for only one speaker; a play for two or more. Similarly, a poem can be written in virtually any verse form, while a play (in English) is limited by tradition to blank verse, heroic couplets, or prose. Finally, most poems are quite short, while most plays are comparatively long. When we speak of the poetry in Shakespeare's plays, we ordinarily refer to only a few well-known passages: the descriptions of Cleopatra's barge or her death in *Antony and Cleopatra,* Marc Antony's oration in *Julius Caesar,* Portia's speech on mercy in *The Merchant of Venice,* Hamlet's soliloquies, and so on. Such passages, and others like them, are memorized and anthologized almost as if they were separate poems, while the rest of each play, whether it is truly poetic or not, is read, performed, and analyzed in much the same way as if it were prose. Shakespeare, after all, was human and like other men was apt to put in an occasional dull day at his desk. Take, for example, the following brief scene from *Othello:*

SCENE 2. *A room in the castle. Enter* OTHELLO, IAGO, *and* GENTLEMEN.

OTHELLO: These letters give, Iago, to the pilot,
And by him do my duties to the Senate.
That done, I will be walking on the works.
Repair there to me.
IAGO: Well, my good lord, I'll do 't.
OTHELLO: This fortification, gentlemen, shall we see 't?
GENTLEMEN: We'll wait upon your lordship.
(*Exeunt.*)

—from *Othello,* act 3, scene 2,
William Shakespeare (1604)

Even if this scene of only six lines served some dramatic function, it would be uninspired writing. Othello's letters to the Senate have no further significance, nor does his inspection of the fortifications. The scene is an encounter of no substance that serves only to waste a little stage time, allowing Cassio to begin the interview with Desdemona that was promised in the preceding scene and that we join in progress in the subsequent one.

The same kind of mechanical drama is even more common in the works of lesser dramatists. The quantity of true poetry in a play is always slight when compared with the larger body of dialogue that is necessary to move the characters around and push the action forward. Indeed, the preponderance of prosaic and merely capable lines in a play helps to make the poetic moments stand out more clearly so that they seem (to quote Shakespeare) "as the spots of heaven,/ More fiery by the night's blackness."

DRAMA AND FICTION

If we take it as axiomatic that the best of a play approaches the status of poetry while the bulk of it remains prosaic, then it follows that most drama is closer to fiction than poetry. Plays are fictitious both in the factual sense that their plots are generally untrue and in the figurative sense that they intend to convey general truths. Like a novel, a play always tells a story. A play cannot be purely lyric, descriptive, or argumentative—although each of these modes of expression has a place in drama. Instead, it begins like a typical short story with an introduction to the characters, the situation, and the setting. It rapidly develops some conflict among the characters that typically reaches a crisis in the fourth act and finds its resolution in the fifth. And in presenting its action, a play manipulates many of the elements found in a short story. Aristotle, the first theoretician of drama, identified six basic elements in the genre: setting, character, plot, language, theme, and music. All but the last are also elements of fiction, and music is no longer requisite or even common in modern drama.

Despite these similarities, a play clearly differs from a short story and drama differs from fiction. Some of the main differences between the genres emerge in the handling of point of view, time, and structure. Unlike a short story, which can present the action from many different points of view, a play is obliged to present its story dramatically. The characters speak directly to one another, and the audience observes their actions without the assistance of a narrator to fill in background information, draw conclusions, and generally serve as a guide to the significance of unfolding events.[1] The playwright cannot pry into the minds of the characters as an omniscient narrator might, and the audience can have no knowledge of a character's thoughts, emotions, or past unless these emerge through dialogue, physical action, or the use of soliloquy.

Because of its dramatic point of view, a play takes place in the perpetual present tense. Where the short story or the novel always implicitly begins, "Once upon a time . . . ," a play both begins and proceeds with "now . . . now . . . now!" The audience always knows what the characters *are doing* while they are onstage, but the playwright has no unobtrusive means of showing what they *have done* either before the curtain rises or while they are offstage. The confidant, who is made privy to another's past, and the messenger, who reports offstage activities, are obvious and sometimes inadequate substitutes for fictional omniscience. Indeed, the author's desire to supply characters with a past helps us to understand why many plays focus on heroes whose exploits are already known to the audience through history or legend.

Another way of stating the difference between fiction and drama is to observe that a play is structured around a succession of *scenes*. A new scene is needed whenever there is a change of setting or time. (In many French and a few English dramas, a new scene also begins with the entrance or exit of any major character.) The scenes are often then grouped into *acts,* which indicate the major units in the development of the plot. The formal division of plays into acts and scenes represents a major difference between the structure of drama and that of fiction. In the latter, the plot *may* unfold as a chronological series of scenes, but there is nothing to keep an author from reminiscing within a scene. Thus, fiction may present a convoluted series of stories within stories—*The Arabian Nights* provides many examples—but drama is obliged to present only those plots that can be developed continuously and chronologically.[2]

In the following pages, as we examine the influence of the actors, the audience, and the stage, we will discover other ways in which

[1] *Our Town* (1938) by Thornton Wilder, *The Glass Menagerie* (1944) by Tennessee Williams, *After the Fall* (1964) by Arthur Miller and a number of other modern plays use a narrator to introduce and control the action, but even in these plays the narrator must eventually step aside and allow the events to unfold objectively and dramatically.

[2] There are, to be sure, exceptions, as usual. In *Our Town,* to cite Wilder's play again, the action returns to the past in the last act.

drama differs from poetry and fiction; it should now be clear, however, that the major elements of drama are also the major elements of poetry and fiction. Our present task is not to describe new literary elements, but rather to explain how the special conditions of dramatic presentation influence the playwright's handling of fictional and poetic devices.

THE ACTORS

Because drama is primarily designed for performance, we can expect that the greatest plays will encourage and successfully incorporate the creative potential of the actors. A dramatist writes with the knowledge that his or her lines will be presented on stage in a way that emphasizes tonal implications and fulfills the incidents suggested by the dialogue. But while a professional playwright seeks to encourage the actors to interpret their lines creatively, he may wish to be sure that the larger thematic impact of the play remains unchanged by different acting styles. By writing their plays for specific stage companies, some dramatists are able to retain a greater measure of control over the initial stage production. These dramatists can not only conceive the play and write the first draft with the strengths and limitations of key actors and actresses already in mind, but they can also supervise the rehearsals and revise the parts of the play that seem ill-suited to the actors. In many cases, therefore, the text of the play that emerges is the result of some form of collaboration between the playwright and the actors.

Because a playwright must assume that the roles in the script will be played by real people, with real idiosyncracies in personality and appearance, there is no need to describe any character's external appearance. The audience can see for itself what Ibsen's Hedda Gabler looks like, and a description of Hedda's appearance, such as one might find in a novel, becomes redundant and unnecessary in the dialogue of a play. Of course, the author's parenthetic stage directions sometimes do include a description of the characters. Hedda, for example, is introduced as

> a woman of nine-and-twenty. Her face and figure show refinement and distinction. Her complexion is pale and opaque. Her steel-gray eyes express a cold, unruffled repose. Her hair is of an agreeable medium

brown but not particularly abundant. She is dressed in a tasteful, somewhat loose-fitting morning gown.

—from *Hedda Gabler,* act 1, Henrik Ibsen (1890)

But such comments are directed at readers, not viewers. They underscore the fact that a playwright often writes simultaneously for two audiences: one in the theater and the other in the armchair.

In writing for the theater, the dramatist has in the actors a great advantage over the novelist, for the characters in a play *are* real. They live and breathe, stand up and sit down, sigh and smile, enter and exit—all with greater realism than even the most competent novelist can create. The actions and expressions of several characters can be conveyed on stage in a matter of seconds, whereas a novelist might have to devote several pages to a description of the same incidents. As a result, drama has an immediate impact that fiction and poetry can never equal. The illusion of reality in some plays or films is as close as art can ever come to bringing its fictional incidents to life.

But although the playwright is relieved from describing the physical appearance or actions of his characters at length, he *cannot* analyze their personalities and motives concisely. An omniscient inquiry into how and why a character speaks, moves, and thinks as he or she does is both desirable and entertaining in a novel by Dickens, but it is not easy to present through dialogue on a stage. Instead, a dramatist individualizes his characters by giving them distinctive habits or quirks of speech and by allowing them to express their personalities through action. Soon after Hedda Gabler first appears on stage, for example, we see her impatience with any references to her femininity or possible pregnancy:

TESMAN: . . . Auntie, take a good look at Hedda before you go! See how handsome she is!

MISS TESMAN: Oh, my dear boy, there's nothing new in that. Hedda was always lovely. [*She nods and goes toward the right.*]

TESMAN [*following*]: Yes, but have you noticed what splendid condition she is in? How she has filled out on the journey?

HEDDA [*crossing the room*]: Oh, do be quiet!

MISS TESMAN [*who has stopped and turned*]: Filled out?

TESMAN: Of course you don't notice it so much now that she has that dress on. But I, who can see—

HEDDA [*at the glass door, impatient*]: Oh, you can't see anything.

TESMAN: It must be the mountain air in the Tyrol—

HEDDA [*curtly interrupting*]: I am exactly as I was when I started.

TESMAN: So you insist, but I'm quite certain you are not. Don't you agree with me, Auntie?

MISS TESMAN [*who has been gazing at her with folded hands*]: Hedda is lovely—lovely—lovely. [*Goes up to her, takes her head between both hands, draws it downward and kisses her hair.*] God bless and preserve Hedda Tesman—for George's sake.

HEDDA [*gently freeing herself*]: Oh! Let me go.

MISS TESMAN [*in quiet emotion*]: I shall not let a day pass without coming to see you.

TESMAN: No, you won't, will you, Auntie? Eh?

MISS TESMAN: Good-by—good-by! [*She goes out by the hall door.* TESMAN *accompanies her. The door remains half open.* TESMAN *can be heard repeating his message to Aunt Rina and his thanks for the slippers. In the meantime* HEDDA *walks about the room raising her arms and clenching her hands as if in desperation. Then she flings back the curtains from the glass door and stands there looking out.*]

—from *Hedda Gabler,* act 1, Henrik Ibsen (1890)

Even here the superiority of fictional omniscience in describing motives and emotions is obvious. Ibsen's parenthetic stage directions succinctly and unambiguously inform the reader about the attitudes of the characters. Where these describe actions ("She nods and goes toward the right"), there is no problem presenting them on the stage. Where they describe a tone of voice ("HEDDA [at the glass door, impatient]"), they can be a challenge to acting skills but are still likely to be understood by the audience. When, however, they indicate a state of mind more than a tone of voice, the reader is apt to fare very much better than the viewer. How, for example, is Miss Tesman's "quiet emotion" to be conveyed in her final comment to Hedda?

Usually, Ibsen avoids vague instructions about an actor's tone of voice and strives instead to bring out his characters' attitudes through their words and actions. Hedda, for example, is frustrated by the timid and retiring role that nineteenth-century women were expected to play. She, like many other women of the day, feels imprisoned by the one-sided decorum imposed by her male-dominated society. To dramatize this, Ibsen never allows her to leave her own constricting household during the play's four acts. Through her conversations with Eilert Lovborg and Judge Brack, we discover that she wishes she could participate in the excitement and dissipations of masculine life, but is hindered by a dread of scandal. Thus, although she tries to satisfy her adventurous urges by manipulating the lives of others—particularly Tesman and Eilert—her repressed passions continually break out. These aspects of her personality are given dramatic form by her actions in the brief scene quoted here. She grows irritated at the allusions to pregnancy, clenches her fists, restlessly paces to and from the windows of the parlor, and a few moments later begins to toy with guns. Using these and other dramatic indications of Hedda's underlying turmoil, Ibsen is able to expose the hidden core of her personality without access to the novelist's omniscient narration.

While writing into the script words and actions that help to define the characters, a playwright must also allow some room for the actors' interpretation and self-expression. In other words, a successful play will stimulate and inspire the actors to use their talents creatively in presenting the play before an audience. In practice, the meaning of the play and the vital intellectual substance that animates each character should be suggested in the script but not rigidly imposed on it. Thus, Ibsen wisely leaves it unclear whether Hedda truly wishes she were a man or is simply rebelling against the traditionally subdued role of her sex. Part of the pleasure of the theater for habitual playgoers derives from this artistic ambiguity. In successive productions of established classics, those who follow the theater closely are able to see how different actresses and actors interpret their roles and are able to compare those interpretations with perceptions based on a study of the text.

But while a dramatist is required to leave some slack in the characterizations to accommodate the actors' differences in the physical appearance as well as their need for creative self-expression, he or she must not allow these freedoms to get out of hand. A play, like most other literary works, ordinarily presents an ethical point or some thematic statement about the world and our place in it that the playwright feels to be both relevant and signifcant. Because drama is a collaborative art—drawing on the talents of the actors, director, musicians, stagehands, scenic artists, and others—a playwright must learn to sketch theme and plot in simple, vigorous, and bold strokes, to be certain that the "message" will come through to the audience. Good drama implies the successsive unfolding of the implications of one overarching idea: Hedda's desire to control a human destiny, Tartuffe's hypocrisy, Othello's jealousy, Oedipus's false pride. In each case the central idea is traced by the course of seemingly inevitable events. It is not in the power of the actors to change the concept of the play, just as it is not in the power of an engineer to change the downhill flow of a river. The natural path may be momentarily blocked, but its ultimate course cannot be stopped or stayed.

A careful and single-minded plot development is but one means by which playwrights sometimes seek to control the influence of the cast on the impact of a play. As already noted, many dramatists have composed their plays with the specific abilities of specific actors in mind in an effort to minimize the risk of misplayed parts. The parts in Shakespeare's plays, for example, are often carefully tailored to suit his fellow members of the Lord Chamberlain's Men (later the King's Men), a professional acting company with which Shakespeare was associated throughout his career. Thus, we find that while Will Kempe was with the company, Shakespeare wrote into his plays a part for a boisterous and farcical clown; but when Kempe was replaced by Robert Armin, the role of the clown became more subtle and witty. Similarly, Shakespeare could confidently create the demanding roles of Hamlet, Lear, and Othello because he knew that in Richard Burbage the company had an actor capable of playing such diverse parts. One of the many contemporary tributes to Burbage's skill describes him as follows:

> His stature small, but every thought and mood
> Might thoroughly from the face be understood
> And his whole action he could change with ease
> From ancient Lear to youthful Pericles.

Shakespeare himself is said to have specialized in playing old men—the old servant Adam in *As You Like It,* the ghost in *Hamlet,* and so on.

In addition to writing specific roles for specific actors, Shakespeare and other Renaissance playwrights had to write all the female parts in such a way that they could be played by preadolescent boys. (Up until about 1660, acting was considered a profession too depraved for women. Men played all the women's parts, even in ancient Greece and Rome.) Naturally, the nude scenes that now abound in films and on the stage would have been out of the question in Shakespeare's day—for reasons other than moral decorum. Indeed, demonstrations of physical passion are comparatively rare in Shakespearean drama because too much kissing and clutching between characters whom the audience knows full well to be a man and a boy might break down the dramatic illusion and become either ludicrous or offensive. In all of *Othello,* a play about sexual conduct and misconduct, there are only four kisses. Three are mere courtesy kisses given to Desdemona in public by Cassio and Othello after she has survived a fierce storm at sea. The only kiss in private is the one Othello gives the sleeping Desdemona just before he suffocates her. Similarly, the height of the balcony in *Romeo and Juliet* keeps the lovers apart during their most passionate moments, and in *Antony and Cleopatra* there is but one embrace before the death scene.

The influence of the actors on the script of a play is not unique to Shakesperean drama. All playwrights must work within the limitations imposed by the medium. Dramatists are, for example, obviously limited in the number of characters they can use. Even though Aristophanes in *Lysistrata* wanted to show the effects of a sex strike by the entire female population of Greece, he actually used only one Athenian, one Spartan, and one Anagyran in speaking roles—with perhaps a score of nonspeaking women to stand for all the rest. Apart from the fact that only a limited number of actors can fit on a stage, the number of speaking roles in a play must be few enough so that the director can round up (and pay) enough accomplished actors and so that the audience can remember who they all are. By convention, as well as by economic and practical necessity, Greek dramatists limited themselves to three speakers and a chorus. This does not mean that there were only three parts in a play, but rather that only three speaking characters could be on stage at any one time. Because the same actors might play several roles (changing masks and costumes offstage), the number of speaking roles could range anywhere from two to twenty, but the dramatist had at all times to balance the requirements of his story with the practical concerns of allowing the actors sufficient time to change costume and matching the physical and vocal demands of the roles to those of the actors available to play them. It would not do, for example, to send an actor playing a husky, deep-voiced king offstage and then to bring him back as a petite princess. The same character would be physically unable to play both parts. These restrictions are less stringent in plays written after the golden age of Greek drama (c. 480–380 B.C.), but accomplished playwrights have always manipulated their plots to allow some doubling up of parts and have always been aware that the stage does not allow them to portray the assembled masses of contending armies. Hence, in the prologue to *Henry the Fifth,* Shakespeare asks the audience to

Suppose within the girdle of these walls
Are now confin'd two mighty monarchies,

. . .

Into a thousand parts divide one man;
And make imaginary puissance;
Think, when we talk of horses, that you see them
Printing their proud hoofs i' th' receiving earth.
For 'tis your thoughts that now must deck our kings.
—from *Henry the Fifth,* "Prologue,"
William Shakespeare (1599)

One final way in which the actors influence the drama deserves mention: plays are sometimes conceived, and often revised, as a result of the advice of the actors and the director. Indeed, contemporary plays normally open off-Broadway to allow time for revision before risking an expensive production—and facing the critics—in the heart of New York City. A similar process has operated throughout the history of the theater, and Shakespeare's plays, in this sense at least, are probably much the better for having remained unpublished until long experience on the stage had taught the members of his company which lines played well and which were in need of revision.

THE AUDIENCE

A few plays are intended only to be read and therefore are known as *closet dramas* (*Samson Agonistes* by Milton, *Cain* by Bryon, and *Prometheus Unbound* by Shelley are notable examples); but most plays make an effort to please an audience massed in a theater. Playwrights who compose for the stage have learned by experience the truth of Samuel Johnson's dictum that

The drama's laws the drama's patrons give,
And we who live to please, must please to live.

The goal of a playwright is to fill the theater and to keep on filling it for as long as possible. A play must have popular appeal, and the quest for it naturally influences the choice and treatment of dramatic subjects.

Alexander Dumas (the elder) once claimed that all he needed for success on the stage was "four boards, two actors, and a passion."

Dumas knew, as all of us now do, that the ingredients for a popular play (and certainly popular TV) always include sex and violence. As the tragedian in Tom Stoppard's *Rosencrantz and Guildenstern Are Dead* (1967) put it, well-liked plays are of "the blood, love, and rhetoric school":

> . . . I can do you blood and love without the rhetoric, and I can do you blood and rhetoric without the love, and I can do you all three concurrent or consecutive, but I can't do you love and rhetoric without the blood. Blood is compulsory—they're all blood [in tragedy], you see.
>
> —from *Rosencrantz and Guildenstern Are Dead,* act 1,
> Tom Stoppard (1967)

The plots of most plays do in fact focus on one of the violent passions (anger, jealousy, revenge, lust, treachery) or on some form of love (love of woman, love of home, love of country, love of justice). Aristophanes' *Lysistrata,* for example, cleverly combines love of woman, love of country, and simple lust; *Othello* builds on jealousy; and much of the plot of *Hedda Gabler* revolves on Hedda's envy of Thea. Other plays examine the effect of less violent, but still powerful, passions: pride in *Oedipus Rex,* hypocrisy in *Tartuffe,* and fear of the unknown in *Rosencrantz and Guildenstern Are Dead.*

Plays do differ, however, as John Dryden once observed, because of the historical differences in the play-going audience:

> They who have best succeeded on the stage
> Have still conformed their genius to the age.

Greek dramas were presented before huge audiences drawn from all levels of society, from poor to rich and from illiterate to sophisticated. Attendance was viewed as a religious duty. As a result, the tragedies dealt with simple and well-known stories that all members of the audience could understand; but they did have to deal with the play's subject in a way that underscored the necessity of reverence for the gods and their decrees. Elizabethan dramas were also aimed at an audience drawn from all levels of society, but by then the connection of the theater with religion had been severed. Thus, Shakespeare's plays contained enough blood and love to keep the illiterate mob in the pit entertained and enough lofty rhetoric to please the lords and ladies in the box seats, but they did not seek to inculcate any particular religious or philosophic views.

By the late nineteenth century, the price of a theater ticket exceeded the means of the laboring classes, and therefore plays like *Hedda Gabler* portray the problems and conditions of life in the upper or middle classes. There is occasionally a bit of gentlemanly poverty in the plays of this period, but the degrading and impoverished conditions of factory labor are almost entirely ignored. More recently, the technological revolution of the twentieth century has meant that people can often find their entertainment at home on television or at the local movie theater. Most of the people who attend plays today do so because they want to combine culture with entertainment. As a result, much contemporary drama tends to be intellectual and allusive, as in the witty manipulations of *Hamlet* in Tom Stoppard's *Rosencrantz and Guildenstern Are Dead* (1967).

Even in modern drama, however, the plot usually makes an appeal to mass psychology. The playwright must cling first to those elemental passions and emotions common to all men and only secondarily, if at all, stimulate the qualities of intellect, in which men differ. The audience in a theater is, after all, a crowd and therefore "less intellectual and more emotional than the individuals that compose it. It is less reasonable, less judicious, less disinterested, more credulous, more primitive, more partisan."[3] In a theater, the sophisticated responses of the few are outnumbered by the instinctive responses of the many. As a result, the dramatist writes for a live audience that is spontaneous and unreflective both in its approval and disapproval.

Because most members of the audience can be expected to see the play once and only once, a successful play must be clearly plotted, easy to understand, and both familiar and acceptable in its theme. Playwrights satisfy the tastes of the times, but they rarely guide them. A novel may survive, even if its initial acclaim is slight, so long as those who first read and understand it are able to influence subsequent intellectual and literary thinking. But a play that fails in its first performance is unlikely to be published at all. Even if a few enthusiasts keep it from sinking immediately into oblivion, one costly failure on Broadway is usually sufficient to scare away future producers. The financial risks in producing plays are more clear-cut than those in publishing novels. If a new play proves to be unpopular, the initial costs involved in scenery, costuming, and rehearsal are not recouped, and the debts mount every day that actors play before a

[3] Clayton Hamilton, as quoted by Brander Matthews, *A Study of the Drama* (New York: Houghton Mifflin, 1910), p. 88.

half-filled house. In contrast, if a new novel at first seems unpopular, the cost of storing a few thousand copies will scarcely distress the publisher as long as the demand is constant and seems likely to grow. Thus, a play, unlike a novel, must please upon first acquaintance; and if it is to have durable literary value, it must continue to please during successive viewings or readings. The challenge in writing drama is, thus, to be at once popular *and* intellectually stimulating. Comparatively few playwrights have succeeded at being both.

There are a number of good reasons for the frequent failures in the theater. Even if a playwright chooses a popular subject and develops the plot with simplicity and grace, he cannot be confident of pleasing an audience unless the structure of the play is carefully crafted to meet the physical needs of spectators: the duration of scenes and the mixture of dialogue and action, for example, must be adapted to the audience's attention span. A play, like other forms of literature, is principally composed of words, but too much talk and too little action may produce a result about as exciting as a town council meeting. Conversely, actions that remain uninterpreted by dialogue quickly become chaotic. A sword fight on stage may show the physical agility of the actors and the conflict between characters; but if it is continued too long, it threatens to turn the drama into a gladiatorial exhibition, in which most of the interest is drained by the recognition that the swords are wooden, the blood is artificial, and each thrust or parry has been carefully choreographed in advance.

In some ways, of course, the playwright has a tremendous amount of control. Once the theater is darkened and the play begins, the audience is captive: the seats all face the stage, the only well lit part of the theater. When the curtain rises, any lingering conversations are "shushed." The closely packed patrons watch and listen attentively because they have paid to do so, because there is little else they *can* do in a dark theater, and because the seating arrangement makes it difficult to leave before the intermission.

These theatrical conditions directly influence the structure of the play. As much as dramatists may lust after the novelist's right to a leisurely introduction, they must resign themselves to the bald fact that, because no audience can sit still for more than about an hour at a time, the play must be at its intriguing best by the intermission. Similarly, a play that begins at 8:00 P.M must certainly end by 11:00 P.M., lest all the teenagers with curfews, all the parents with babysitters, and all the young couples with "other things on their minds" leave en masse before the final curtain.

THE THEATER

In writing a play, a dramatist is always aware of the physical conditions of the theater. These conditions often govern the actions and settings that can be presented, as well as the way in which the scenes are developed. The size of the theater, the promixity of the audience to the stage, and the characteristics of the stage itself influence the scenery, the costuming, and the actors' methods.

As we will see, the conditions for staging Greek drama were unlike those for Elizabethan drama, Elizabethan unlike neoclassical, and neoclassical unlike modern. Nonetheless, each stage provides an arena within which the words and actions of the performers are observed by an audience of substantial size. It follows that some actions are too minute and others too grand to be staged effectively. When, for example, Tom Stoppard's characters bet on the toss of a coin in the first scene of *Rosencrantz and Guildenstern Are Dead,* the audience cannot actually see whether the coin comes down heads or tails. Common sense tells us that the coin should come down tails about as often as heads, and no doubt it does each time the scene is acted. But Stoppard is able to take advantage of our inability to see so small a happening. By having Rosencrantz study each coin, announce it "heads," and put it in his purse as Guildenstern looks on in growing consternation, Stoppard builds in us the sense that the times are indeed "out of joint."

Similar considerations in staging influenced Shakespeare's *Othello.* Desdemona's handkerchief is a vital element in the plot, but this piece of cloth, which is too small to bind Othello's forehead, is also too small to be seen clearly by the most distant members of the audience. Thus, Shakespeare takes care to identify it in the dialogue whenever he introduces it on stage. For example, when Bianca flings the handkerchief back to Cassio in act 4, scene 1, Othello, who is watching from a distance, says, "By heaven, that should be my handkerchief!" And then, to clear up any posible confusion, Iago, who has had a closer vantage point, drives home the identification:

IAGO: And did you see the handkerchief?
OTHELLO: Was that mine?
IAGO: Yours, by this hand. And to see how he prizes the foolish woman your wife! She gave it him, and he hath given it his whore.

Large events can be even more difficult to present on stage. In the second act of *Othello,* Shakespeare wishes to describe the arrival at Cyprus of Cassio, Desdemona, and Othello after they have been separated by a storm at sea. Naturally it is difficult to depict either the turbulent sea or the arrival of the shattered flotilla. Instead Shakespeare introduces three minor characters whose primary function is to help us imagine the setting and events offstage:

SCENE 1. *A seaport in Cyprus. An open place near the wharf.*
Enter MONTANO *and* TWO GENTLEMEN.

MONTANO: What from the cape can you discern at sea?
FIRST GENTLEMAN: Nothing at all. It is a high-wrought flood.
I cannot 'twixt the heaven and the main
Descry a sail.
MONTANO: Methinks the wind hath spoke aloud at land,
A fuller blast ne'er shook our battlements.
If it hath ruffianed so upon the sea,
What ribs of oak, when mountains melt on them,
Can hold the mortise? What shall we hear of this?
SECOND GENTLEMAN: A segregation of the Turkish fleet.
For do but stand upon the foaming shore,
The chidden billow seems to pelt the clouds;
The wind-shaked surge, with high and monstrous mane,
Seems to cast water on the burning Bear,
And quench the guards of the ever-fixed Pole.
I never did like molestation view
On the enchafed flood.
MONTANO: If that the Turkish fleet
Be not ensheltered and embayed, they are drowned.
It is impossible to bear it out.
(*Enter a* THIRD GENTLEMAN.)
THIRD GENTLEMAN: News, lads! Our wars are done.
The desperate tempest hath so banged the Turks
That their designment halts. A noble ship of Venice
Hath seen a grievous wreck and sufference
On most part of their fleet.
MONTANO: How! Is this true?
THIRD GENTLEMAN: The ship is here put in,
A Veronesa. Michael Cassio,
Lieutenant to the warlike Moor Othello,

Is come on shore, the Moor himself at sea,
And is in full commission here for Cyprus.
—from *Othello,* act 2, scene 1,
William Shakespeare (1604)

Presumably the first gentleman is standing at one edge of the stage looking into the distance as though out to sea. He shouts back to the others that he sees nothing but enormous waves. The second gentleman, who has recently stood on the shore, gives a fuller and more poetic account of the storm. Then the third gentleman, having just come from the wharf, brings news of the destruction of the Turkish fleet and the arrival of Cassio's ship. Thus, events that Shakespeare would had difficulty portraying on stage are made vivid and convincing through the dramatic accounts of three different reporters.

Just as the actions in a drama are limited by the size of the stage and its distance from the audience, so, too, the settings are influenced by the practical problems associated with a visual presentation. Some scenes are next to impossible to stage. Act 2 of Lord Byron's *Cain* (1822), for example, opens in "the Abyss of Space" and a stage direction in act 3 (which is set outside of Eden) reads: "The fire upon the altar of Abel kindles into a column of the brightest flame, and ascends to heaven; while a whirlwind throws down the altar of Cain, and scatters the fruits abroad upon the earth."

As a *closet drama,* Byron's play was never intended to be staged, but similar difficulties sometimes present themselves in conventional plays. Shortly after Byron's death, in fact, his poem "Mazeppa" was dramatized. We can only pity the poor director who was asked in one scene to show the hero "strapped to the back of a wild horse, while birds peck at his eyes, lightning destroys a tree on stage, and wolves pursue the horse."

During the late nineteenth century, in response to a demand for greater realism, playwrights began to specify the arrangement of furniture in a room, the number of pictures on the walls, and sometimes even the thickness of the butter on a piece of stage toast. Here is the first stage direction in Ibsen's *Hedda Gabler:*

SCENE: *A spacious, handsome and tastefully furnished drawing room, decorated in dark colors. In the back a wide doorway with curtains drawn back, leading into a smaller room decorated in the same style as the drawing room. In the right-hand wall of the front room a folding door leading out to the hall. In the opposite wall, on the left, a glass door, also with curtains drawn back. Through the panes can be seen part of a veranda outside and trees covered with autumn foliage. An oval table, with a cover on it and surrounded by chairs, stands well forward. In front, by the wall on the right, a wide stove of dark porcelain, a high-backed armchair, a cushioned footrest and two footstools. A settee with a small round table in front of it fills the upper right-hand corner. In front, on the left, a little way from the wall, a sofa. Further back than the glass door a piano. On either side of the doorway at the back a whatnot with terra-cotta and majolica ornaments. Against the back wall of the inner room a sofa, with a table, and one or two chairs. Over the sofa hangs the portrait of a handsome elderly man in a general's uniform. Over the table, a hanging lamp with an opal glass shade. A number of bouquets are arranged about the drawing room in vases and glasses. Others lie upon the tables. The floors in both rooms are covered with thick carpets. Morning light. The sun shines in through the glass door.*

—from *Hedda Gabler,* act 1, Henrik Ibsen (1890)

Clearly, a setting as complex as this cannot be changed for every new scene. As it so happens, all of the action in *Hedda Gabler* takes place in the same two rooms. Similarly, the entire action of *Oedipus Rex* takes place in front of the royal palace at Thebes, that of *Lysistrata* before the Acropolis, and that of *Tartuffe* in Organ's house. Although *Rosencrantz and Guildenstern Are Dead* uses two sets, these differ only by the addition of an umbrella, a lawn chair, and three barrels. In a fair number of plays, however, the scene changes with every act, and in a few, like *Othello,* it changes for virtually every scene. Yet, even in *Othello,* a stage with a half-dozen different acting areas and a few movable props can be made to convey the whole range of settings.

Unlike the novelist or the film maker, the playwright cannot allow the plot to flow freely across unlimited fields of action. If the scenery is to be at all realistic, very few settings can be used unless the playwright is prepared to have the work produced only in the few modern theaters with "revolving stages," on which several realistic sets can be erected and alternately used. Even if the scenery is only suggestive, the playwright is much more limited by his genre than other narrative artists. In general, the action of a play takes place in only one or two locales. These may be quite narrowly and specifically defined in realistic drama (Hedda's drawing room, for example) or broadly conceived in more imaginative works (Venice and Cyprus in *Othello*), but a play that uses too many settings risks confusing the audience and consequently failing in the theater. Shakespeare's *Antony and Cleopatra,* for example, is a poetic masterpiece, but it has rarely been successful on the stage because its forty-two scenes skip bewilderingly around the Roman Empire, and the action spans years rather than days. Ordinarily, it is only through the devices of a film maker or a novelist that such action can be presented clearly and convincingly.

Thus far, we have been discussing the general effects of any theater on the scenes and actions of drama, but different theaters in different historical periods have had quite different impacts on the drama. A play like *Othello* is written for the intimate Elizabethan stage. The subtle and insinuating facial expressions necessary for a convincing portrayal of Iago's manipulation of Othello would have been lost in the vast amphitheaters of ancient Greece. Similarly, the stark plots and grand rhetoric of Greek tragedy might seem histrionic and ridiculous in the confines of a small modern theater. In order to understand a play, in short, we must know something about the stage for which it was written. In the past, most masterpieces of the drama have been produced in one of four basic theaters: the classical Greek theater, the Elizabethan theater, the neoclassical French theater, and the realistic "box set." Modern drama, however, has moved toward a more flexible theater that can easily be adapted to suit the specific needs of each new play.

The Classical Greek Theater (c. 480–380 B.C.)

Greek Drama grew out of the primitive rituals performed in conjunction with the three annual festivals dedicated to Dionysus (or Bacchus), the god of fertility, regeneration, and wine.[4] Although, in time, such rituals evolved into the drama of Aeschylus, Euripides, Sophocles, and Aristophanes and the uninhibited revels of Dionysus were exchanged for more dignified role playing within a formal theatrical setting, the classic drama of the ancient Greeks retained, however loosely, its original ties with religion. It continued to be performed only three times a year and then in massive doses of four or five plays a day—circumstances that had an important impact on the audience, the content, and the structure of Greek drama.

In the first place, the audience in a Greek theater was enormous.

[4] Indeed, the very names for the three forms of Greek drama—tragedy, comedy, and satyr play—derive from the worship of Dionysus. The word *tragedy* means "goat song," probably referring to the goat-skinned satyrs; the derivation of the term *satyr play* is obvious; and the word comedy comes from *comos,* Greek for "revelry."

Everyone who wanted to see a play had only a few opportunities each year to do so, and the idea of attending was all the more attractive because of the sporting element inherent in the prizes awarded for the best tragedies and comedies. The theater of Dionysus at Athens (see Figures 8-1 and 8-2), which was used in the first productions of all the great fifth-century Greek plays, probably seated about 17,000. The theater at Epidaurus, built a century later, seated 20,000; and the theater at Ephesus held more than 50,000. Because no existing building was large enough to accommodate so vast a crowd, the plays were performed outdoors in the natural basin formed where two hills met.

During the life of Sophocles (495–406 B.C.) the audience sat on wooden benches that ascended the hillside, more than half encircling an *orchestra* or "dancing place" some 78 feet in diameter. A wooden building called the *skene* (from which we derive the term *scene*)

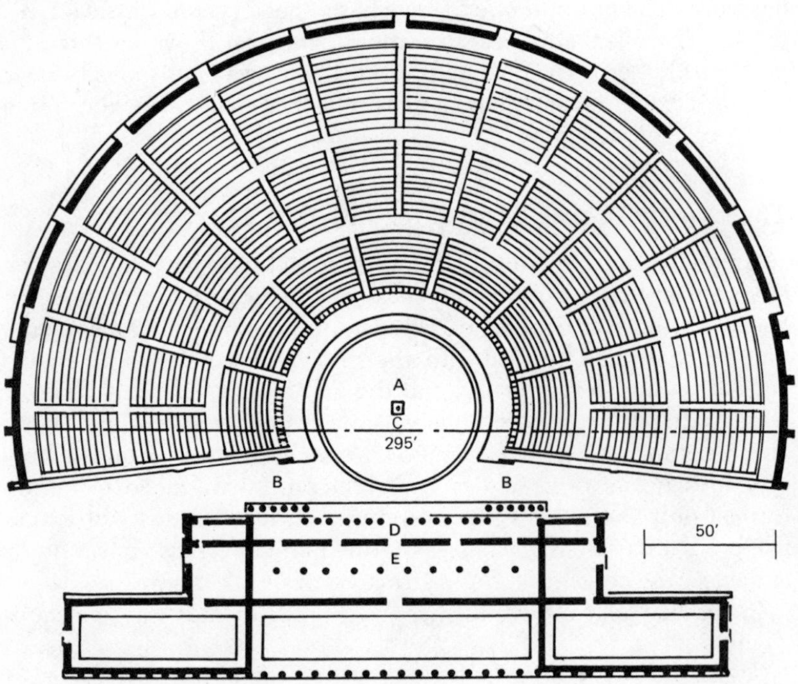

Figure 8.1. Plan of the Theater of Dionysus at Athens. *A. orchestra; B. chorus entrance; C. altar to Dionysus; D. proskenion; E. skene.*

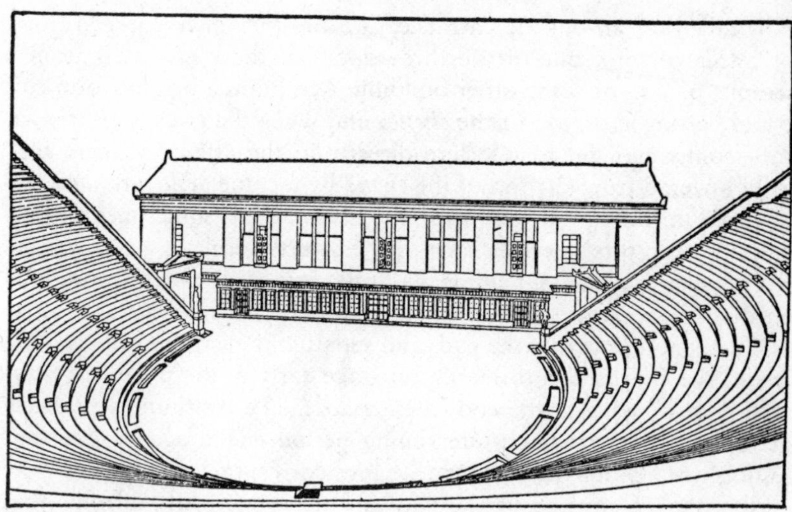

Figure 8.2. A reconstruction of a Classical Greek Theater. Note the large "dancing place" or *orchestra,* the encircling tiers of benches, and the scene building or *skene* at the rear. In this case the *skene* includes a raised platform stage. (From Ernst Robert Fiechter's *Die Baugeschichtliche Entwicklung des Antiken Theaters.*)

closed off the second half of the amphitheater and served simultaneously as an acoustical wall (reflecting the voices of the actors back into the audience), a scenic background (representing any building central to the action), and a convenient place for the three principal actors to change masks and costumes. The narrow space between the *skene* and the *orchestra* was known as the *proskenion* and served as the main acting area.[5]

The chorus normally remained in the *orchestra,* while the major characters moved from the *proskenion* to the *orchestra* and back again, according to the script. The chorus and any processions entered and exited along the edge of the stands to the far right or left of the *skene.* Although the major characters used these aisles when the

[5] There is much confusion over what the Greeks actually meant by the term *proskenion.* Some scholars think that it referred to the wall of the *skene;* others that it referred to a row of columns that supported the roof of a porch extending out from the *skene;* and still others agree with our interpretation. Literally, the word means "before" (*pro-*) "the skene" (*skenion*). The *proscenium,* in modern stagecraft, is the forward part of the stage between the curtain and the orchestra. The arch from which the curtain hangs is the *proscenium arch.*

plot called for an outside entrance, at times they also emerged from, or retreated into, one of the three doors of the *skene* as if from a temple, palace, or some other building. Action on a balcony or a cliff could be staged on top of the *skene,* and when the gods appeared, as they sometimes did to interfere directly in the affairs of men, they were lowered from the top of the *skene* by a crane. The term *deus ex machina* (meaning "the god from the machine") is sometimes used to describe (and often deride) such divine interventions.

This massive open-air arena naturally imposed special conditions on the plays performed in it. First of all, there was no curtain to rise at the beginning, fall at the end, and separate the various scenes. As a result, the chorus had to march on stage early in the play (the *parados*) and off stage at the end (the *exodos*). The continuous presence of the chorus during the intervening period encouraged a constant setting throughout the play and a close correspondence between the period of time covered by the play and the amount of real time that elapsed during the actual on-stage presence of the chorus. As a result, Greek drama tended to concentrate on a single complex situation.[6] The typical Greek tragedy begins only a matter of hours before its catastrophe is to occur. The characters stand on the brink of disaster, and the playwright swiftly tells us how they got there, using a formal prologue and sometimes also a series of interviews with messengers, nurses, and other minor characters. In the prologue to *Oedipus Rex,* for example, we learn that a plague afflicts Thebes because the murderer of the former king, Laios, has not been punished. Oedipus immediately vows to find the killer and drive him from the land. The remainder of the play works out the consequences of this impetuous vow by revealing that Oedipus himself is the killer, that Laios was his father, and therefore that Laios's wife, Iocaste, is actually Oedipus's mother as well as his wife and the mother of his children.

The four secenes, or *episodes,* during which Oedipus discovers the tragedy of his past are separated from one another not by the fall of a curtain, but by a series of choral interludes called odes. Each *ode* (or *stasimon*) was accompanied by music, to which the chorus danced back and forth across the stage in a sober and symbolic fashion. During these odes the chorus was able to provide essential background information, reflect on past actions, or anticipate future ones.

[6] The unity of place, time, and action demanded in neoclassical drama was an outgrowth of these tendencies. Greek playwrights did not, however, formally require adherence to these three unities.

Often, too, the responses of the chorus represent those of an ideal audience or provide a lyric respite from the intense emotions of the episodes. In addition these interludes may symbolize the passage of time necessary to send for a character or accomplish some other offstage action.

Because the theater was unenclosed and the plays were performed during the daytime, the action of Greek drama normally also took place during the daytime, out-of-doors. However, some events in Greek drama did require an interior setting—Iocaste's suicide is an example—and, accordingly, Greeks were forced to improvise. One frequently used technique was to have a messenger, or some other character, come outside and describe in detail what had taken place within. This is exactly how Sophocles handled the death of Iocaste:

> The full horror of what happened you cannot know,
> For you did not see it; but I, who did, will tell you
> As clearly as I can how she met her death.
>
> . . .
>
> Exactly how she died I do not know:
> For Oedipus burst in moaning and would not let us
> Keep vigil to the end: it was by him
> As he stormed about the room that our eyes were caught.
> From one to another of us he went, begging a sword,
> Hunting the wife who was not his wife, the mother
> Whose womb had carried his own children and himself.
> I do not know: it was none of us aided him,
> But surely one of the gods was in control!
> For with a dreadful cry
> He hurled his weight, as though wrenched out of himself,
> At the twin doors: the bolts gave, and he rushed in.
> And there we saw her hanging, her body swaying
> From the cruel cord she had noosed about her neck.
> A great sob broke from him, heartbreaking to hear,
> As he loosed the rope and lowered her to the ground.
>
> —from *Oedipus Rex,* Sophocles (430 B.C.)

A second possibility was simply to throw open the doors of the *skene* and allow the audience to peer inside. Although this technique later worked in the smaller Elizabethan theater, the size of the Greek theater and the unavoidable obscurity of the interior of the *skene* rendered this approach unsatisfactory. To overcome this obstacle, the Greeks constructed a platform on wheels (the *eccyclema*) that could be rolled out of the *skene* as required, and this device became the accepted convention for portraying an interior scene or tableau.

The size of the Greek theater had still other effects on the nature of Greek drama. The actors wore large masks, padded clothing, and platform sandals in order to increase their stature and expressiveness for the viewers at the rear of the ampitheater. Although those costumes must have significantly restricted mobility and made physical actions awkward, the masks were designed to function like primitive megaphones and improved the carrying power of the actors' voices. As such, it is little wonder that Greek drama came to be made up of words rather than actions. This verbal emphasis complements the Greek dramatist's preoccupation with motive and character rather than plot, for the state of mind and feelings of an individual can only be fully explained and analyzed using words. The pre-eminence of Greek tragedy came about in part because it was a drama of the mind and not the body.

Then, as now, the audience exerted its influence on both the structure and the content of the plays presented. Because Greek audiences remained in the theater all day, lapses of attention, and periods of jostling, munching, joking, and dozing were inevitable. It was nevertheless essential that all the members of the audience understand the key turning points of the action if the play were to succeed at all; as a result, playwrights preferred to present bold, simple stories that were either familiar to the audience (for example, the story of Oedipus) or, in the case of comedy, predicated on a simple, straightforward hypothesis (in *Lysistrata* that sexual denial can put an end to war). Not surprisingly, given the religious traditions associated with drama and the stylization imposed by the use of masks, many tragic plots were drawn from mythology. The comedies, on the other hand, sought a similar ease of understanding by burlesquing contemporary personalities and events.

The Elizabethan Theater (c. 1550–1620)

The decline of the Roman Empire brought an end to the Greek theater, and for nearly a thousand years Europe produced little drama of significant literary merit. It is true that the Catholic church, in about the tenth century, began to encourage the production of plays filled with moral or religious instruction, but these anonymous creations are more important as historical curiosities than as dramatic achievements. As a result, when the rediscovery of Greek and Roman literature first spread through Europe to England, few people had any idea what a theater ought to look like. Plays were put on wherever a stage could be erected or a crowd could gather. Amateur groups performing at a university and professionals performing at an inn found that the courtyard provided a ready-made theater. A fairly large stage could be easily set up at one end, and the audience could watch the play from the surrounding yard or balconies. The balcony immediately above the stage, in turn, could be conveniently used by the actors for playing scenes that called for a hill, a cliff, an upstairs window, or any other high place.

No doubt innkeepers found that an afternoon play stimulated business. Those standing in the courtyard watching the play could take their minds off their aching feet by calling for more beer, and the surrounding bedchambers encouraged other forms of trade—so much so that the municipal officials of London (who were staunch puritans) soon began to regulate the production of plays, denouncing the "eavell practizes of incontinencye in great Inns havinge chambers and secrete places adjoyninge to their open stagies and gallyries, inveglynge and alleur [enticement] of maides." As a result of these regulations, several of the theatrical companies decided to build their own playhouses just outside of the city limits. It is hardly surprising that when they did so, beginning in about 1576, they patterned their theaters on the very courtyards to which they had become accustomed.

The existing evidence about the size, shape, and structure of the Elizabethan stage and theater is scanty, but it does allow us to state some facts positively and to make other educated guesses. From a contract for the construction of the Fortune Theater (see Figures 8-3 and 8-4) we know that the building was square and relatively small, measuring 80 feet on each side. (The Globe Theater, where Shakespeare's plays were performed, was about the same size, but octagonal.) The pit, or inner yard, of the Fortune measured 55 feet per side, and the stage, which was 43 feet wide, projected halfway (exactly 27½ feet) into the yard. Three galleries were partitioned into "twopenny rooms" and "convenient divisions for gentlemen's rooms"—presumably the equivalent of box seats. When filled to capacity, the theater probably held a crowd of about a thousand, with the common folk pressed elbow to elbow around three sides of the stage.

Because the stage intruded so far into the middle of the audience, most spectators sat or stood within thirty feet of the actors, and even the distant corners of the third balcony were but sixty feet away. As

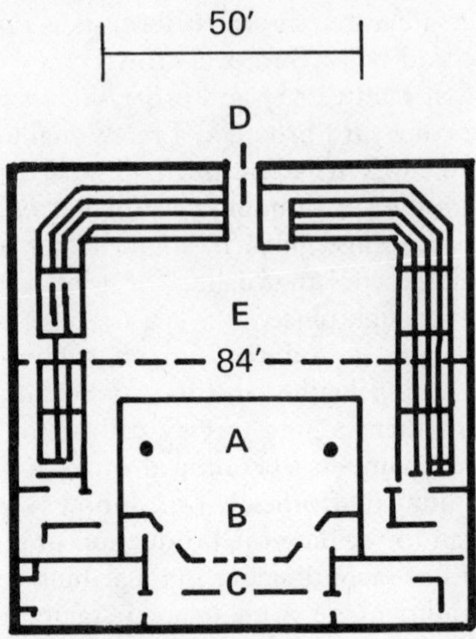

Figure 8.3. Plan of the Fortune Theater, London. A. *front stage;* B. *back stage;* C. *inner stage;* D. *entrance;* E. *courtyard.*

a result, the Elizabethan theater fostered a sense of intimacy utterly foreign to its predecessor. *Asides* and *soliloquies,* which would seem contrived if the actor had to visibly strain to make his stage whisper carry to a distant audience, here seemed natural and unaffected; as a consequence, Elizabethan plays came to be filled with lines intended for the audience alone. In the third act of *Othello,* when Iago comes *downstage*[7] toward the audience, with Desdemona's handkerchief in his hand, he is so near the audience that his low reflections are delivered almost conspiratorially into their ears:

> I will in Cassio's lodging lose this napkin,
> And let him find it. Trifles light as air
> Are to the jealous confirmations strong
> As proofs of Holy Writ. This may do something.
> The Moor already changes with my poison.
> Dangerous conceits are in their natures poisons,
> Which at the first are scarce found to distaste,

[7]The terms *downstage* and *upstage* derive from the period when the stage was raked, or tilted, toward the audience. When actors moved toward the audience they literally moved down the stage, and in moving away they climbed slightly up.

But with a little act upon the blood
Burn like the mines of sulphur.
—from *Othello,* act 3, scene 3, William Shakespeare (1604)

When Othello subsequently enters *upstage,* he is some forty to fifty feet away from Iago; consequently, Iago can comment on Othello's visible agitation without fear of being overheard. He sees that, in fact, jealousy does "burn like the mines of sulphur" within Othello's breast, and he addresses the spectators directly: "I did say so. / Look where he comes!"

In addition to intimacy, the Elizabethan stage also had versatility. It contained at least six different acting areas (see Figure 8-4). The main one was, of course, the 27½- by 43-foot platform. In this large neutral area, characters could meet and interact without raising any question in the minds of the Elizabethan audience about the exact setting; In the original text of *Othello,* for example, there are only three directions for setting, and all of them are quite indefinite: two call for the use of an inner chamber and one for an upstairs window. If, for some reason, a specific setting *was* important, the characters themselves would describe it, as in the seaport scene quoted earlier (p. 238).

An inner stage behind the main platform was used to represent the interior of a council chamber, a bedroom, a tent, a tomb, a throne room, and so on. Act 1, scene 3, of *Othello* requires that this inner stage be screened by curtains that can be drawn to reveal "the Duke and Senators set at a table." Similarly, act 5, scene 2, opens on "Desdemona in bed." Because every other scene in the play calls for each character to enter, speak his lines, and then exit, only these two scenes need to be staged in the curtained inner chamber.

According to the records available to us, a balcony, bounded by two window stages, apparently extended above the inner stage. In act 1, scene 1, of *Othello,* Roderigo and Iago converse in the street before calling up to Brabantio who "appears above, at a window." Similarly, Juliet appears at a window in her first balcony scene. Such stage directions, together with the "convenient windows" called for in the contract for the Fortune Theater, imply that these areas were either shuttered or curtained so that the characters could suddenly "appear." But the balcony must also on occasion have provided a fairly large area in which several characters could meet, as indicated by such stage directions as "Enter Cleopatra and her maids aloft."

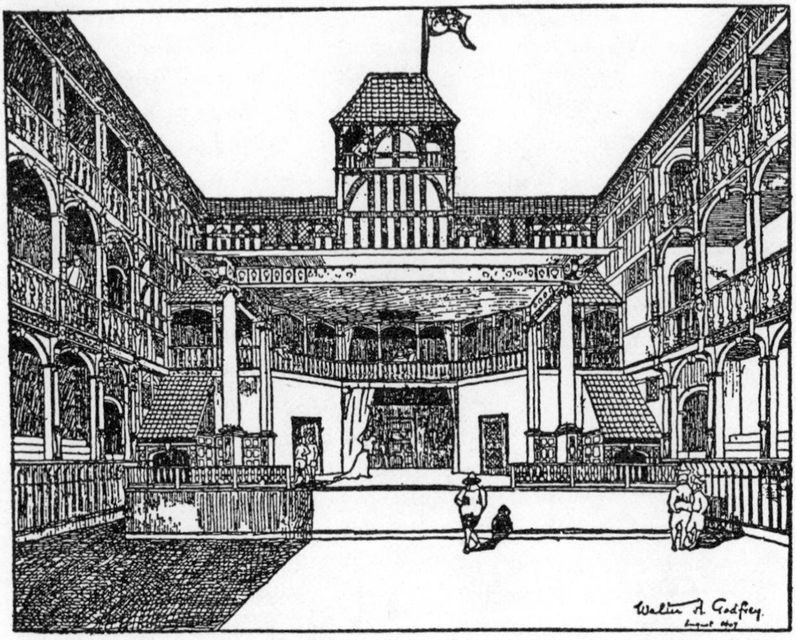

Figure 8.4. A reconstruction of the Fortune Theater by Walter H. Godfrey. Note the platform stage projecting into the "pit," the curtained inner stage, the two side entrances, the balcony, the "crow's nest," and the three rows of galleries for spectators. (From *Shakespeare's Theatre* by Ashley H. Thorndike.)

Although there may also have been an even higher balcony for the musicians (or for action taking place in a tower or in the crow's nest of a ship), few scenes—none in *Othello*—were staged very far above the crowd assembled in the yard. In fact, the vast majority of the scenes in Elizabethan drama were presented on the main stage, so that the audience was able to see and hear clearly.

Because the audience stood around three sides of the main stage, it was impossible to use a curtain to separate scenes. And because the public theaters were unenclosed and plays were performed during the daytime, it was impossible to throw the stage into darkness during a change of scene. Hence, a scene would start with the entrance of one or more characters, and the locale would remain the same until all of the characters left the stage—or were carted off, if dead ("Exeunt severally; Hamlet dragging in [i.e., offstage] Polonius"). Action in a new locale would then commence with a new set of entrances. Usually the characters would enter from one side door and exit through the other—although in conflicts the entrances were made simultaneously from opposing doors ("Enter Pompey at one door, with drum and trumpet: at another, Caesar, Lepidus, Antony, Maecenas, Agrippa, with soldiers marching").

The different settings in an Elizabethan play were rarely indicated by any change in props or scenery. *Othello* contains fifteen different scenes, and if the suggested stage directions of modern editions are followed, a production would require at least eleven different settings. Obviously, such changes were impossible on an open stage. Indeed, if the list of properties owned by the Fortune Theater is indicative of the period, scenery was used mainly to adorn the inner stage and even there only sparingly:

> i rock, i cage, i Hell mouth.
> i tomb of Guido, i comb of Dido, i bedstead.
> i wooden hatchet, i leather hatchet
> Iris head, & rainbow; i little altar.
> i copper target, & xvii foils.
> iii timbrels; i dragon in Faustus.
> i Pope's miter.
> iii imperial crowns; i plain crown.

For the most part, Elizabethans relied on words rather than props to give a sense of locale.

All of this means that the Elizabethan theater, with its multiple acting areas and its imaginary settings, was well suited to plays with rapidly shifting scenes and continuous action. It gave rise to a form of drama entirely unlike that of ancient Greece. Instead of the play starting a few fictional hours before the crisis (as in *Oedipus*), the Renaissance play starts at the beginning of a story and skips from time to time and place to place until the crisis is reached. Act 1 of *Othello,* for example, begins in Venice on the night of Othello and Desdemona's marriage. Then act 2 skips more than a week ahead to a period when all of the principals arrive in Cyprus, and there the action requires two more nights and a day. Because Elizabethan plays range freely in time and setting, all of the most dramatic moments in a story are presented on stage. Thus, if *Oedipus Rex* had been written by Shakespeare, the audience might have seen and heard events that Sophocles included only as reminiscences—particularly, the original prophecies of the oracle to Oedipus, Oedipus' flight from

Corinth, and his murder of Laios at the place where three roads meet. Scenes of violence, which occur offstage in Greek tragedy (like the death of Iocaste) were physically enacted before the Elizabethan audience. *Othello* includes several sword fights, three murders, and a suicide—all on stage. And this carnage is only moderate by Renaissance standards. (Note that despite its general paucity of props, the Fortune Theater inventoried *seventeen* foils!) The audience standing in the yard demanded action, and the versatile Elizabethan stage made this demand easy to fulfill.

The Neoclassical French Theater (c. 1660–1800)

The early acting companies of France, like those of England, toured the countryside, playing wherever they could. As luck would have it, tennis had been popular in France during the fifteenth century, and many noblemen had erected indoor tennis courts, some of which were transformed during the next two centuries into primitive theaters. A temporary stage would be erected on one half of the court; ordinary folk would stand or sit on wooden benches in the other half, and the nobles would be seated in the galleries overlooking the playing area. It was in such converted quarters that Corneille and Molière, two of the greatest of the neoclassical playwrights, saw their first plays produced.

Thus, early French theaters evolved in a direction that differed radically from their Elizabethan counterparts. The single most significant change was the increased separation of the actors from the audience. Whereas the Elizabethan audience had been nearly encircled by the actors, the seventeenth-century French audience sat along one side of the stage and looked in on the action, as if peering through an invisible wall (see Figures 8-5 and 8-6). This arrangement eventually led to the use of a front curtain to conceal the stage between acts and made possible elaborate changes of scenery.

Because all members of the audience watched the play from a similar vantage point, the setting could be vividly depicted on huge flat canvases, using the devices of perspective developed by the painters of the Italian Renaissance (see figure 8-6). These flats could easily be replaced between acts, providing the opportunity for changes in setting. The curtain concealed the scene before the start of the play, but thereafter any changes in scenery were made mechanically in full view of the audience, as a form of special effect. Molière himself was

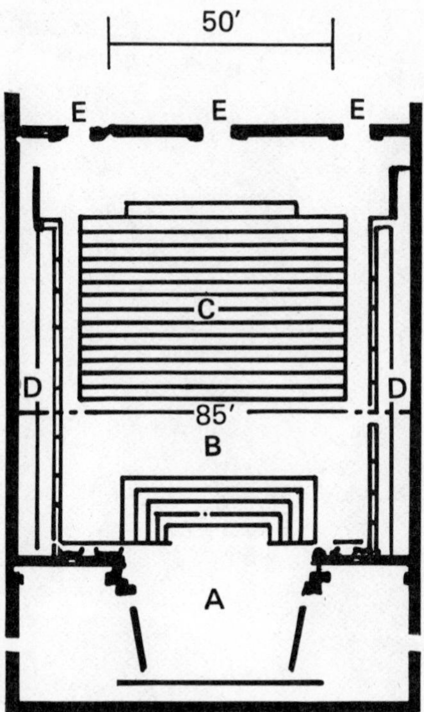

Figure 8.5. Plan of the Richelieu-Moliere Theater, Paris. *A. stage; B. parterre; C. seats; D. galleries; E. entrances.*

not beyond using fountains, aerial chariots, the descent of a god in a cloud, or a maiden emerging from a sea shell to bring the crowd to its feet and to delight the king.

It is almost axiomatic in theater that whenever innovations in staging begin to turn drama into spectacle, the quality of the writing in plays declines. However, at least three factors kept seventeenth-century French drama from degenerating into exhibitionistic extravaganzas. First, neoclassical scholars and critics imposed their standards on the age by requiring that every play fulfill the three unities: *unity of time* mandated that the play's action should be confined to a single day; *unity of action* forbade subplots and irrelevant episodes; and *unity of place* required that all of the action take place in a single setting or vicinity. The exclusion of digressions and the limitation on settings greatly constricted the use that French playwrights could

Figure 8.6. A Neoclassical Theater in Strasburg (1655). Note the flat wings representing rows of buildings, the painted backdrop showing the continuation of the street, and the actors at the forefront of the stage beneath the chandeliers. (From *Wierner Szenische Kunst* by Joseph Gregor.)

make of their curtained stage. Molière's *Tartuffe,* for example, takes place in fewer than twelve hours, in a single setting that has a simple dinner table as its most elaborate prop. Those plays by Molière that do include spectacular stage effects usually confine them to a prologue or epilogue, so that formal adherence to the unities is preserved.

The simplicity of Molière's settings was encouraged by two physical characteristics of the neoclassical theater: weak lighting and the presence of spectators on the stage itself. French drama was performed indoors, often under artificial light and the tallow candles then in use burned dimly. As a result, most of the acting took place immediately under the chandeliers and as far downstage (as close to the audience) as possible. Thus, the elaborately painted flats served less as the setting for the play than as a general backdrop to the action, which often took place on the narrow strip or *apron* in front of the *proscenium arch*. The dark interior also presented problems for the fops and dandies who came to the theater as much to be seen as to see the play itself. The box seats were likely to remain in the shadows, and because many of those vain creatures were wealthy patrons, the theater owners accommodated them with seats (sometimes as many as two hundred) on the stage. Naturally, such seating cut down the available acting area and limited the ability of stagehands to move bulky properties around.

As a result of the seating, the lighting, and the neoclassical rules of composition, most of the plays in this period were set in a single place of general resort—a courtyard, a street, a drawing room. The plots developed scenes of emotional intensity, but because decorum and probability were required by unity of action, they rarely erupted into the violent activity that so often left the Elizabethan stage littered with bodies. The drama of the period is witty, intellectual, and refined. Characteristically, it depicts highly idealized and artificial conversations among men and women representing broad human types—classical heroes or gods in tragedy, contemporary scoundrels or buffoons in comedy. It is an intentionally stylized drama based on the premise that fixed rules of structure are necessary in refined literature.

The Development of the Box Set (c. 1830–1920)

In 1642 Oliver Cromwell and his Puritan followers closed down all the playhouses in England, and by the time they were reopened in 1660, the Elizabethan theater was dead. Not surprisingly, given the predilection of Charles II and his court for all things French, the English drama that succeeded the Restoration was heavily influenced by the neoclassical conventions of the French theater—a condition that persisted throughout most of the eighteenth century. In the nineteenth century, however, the situation changed. A series of important technical innovations encouraged dramatists to abandon neoclassicism in favor of a drama characterized by realistic (mimetic) plots performed within equally realistic settings.

The first of these changes was the introduction, between 1820 and

1840, of gas lighting. Not only were gas lights brighter than the candles and oil lamps that had hitherto served, but now all the lights in the house could be controlled from a single instrument panel. For the first time, a director could focus the audience's attention on the lighted stage by leaving the rest of the auditorium in total darkness; this increased control over stage lights allowed playwrights to switch their scenes from day to night without recourse to cumbersome passages of dialogue calling attention to the fact. The improved lighting also allowed the actors to move more or less freely about the setting, instead of forcing them to remain out in front of the proscenium arch. Such maneuverability naturally called greater attention to the setting, which could now become a functional, rather than simply an ornamental, feature of the play. As a consequence, directors began to eliminate the backdrops and the artificial perspective of movable flats.

Soon after 1830, the *box set* was introduced in England. In its ultimate development, the box set is identical to a real room with one wall removed. Even though the audience can peer through this "invisible" fourth wall to eavesdrop on the action taking place within, the actors pretend that the invisible wall exists. Thus, asides directed to the audience can no longer occur and soliloquies must be strictly limited to those emotional moments during which a character might logically be overheard talking to himself. Nineteenth-century producers understandably relished these innovations and some went so far even as to boast in their advertisements of having sets with real ceilings, real doors, and working locks. The description of the set for *Hedda Gabler* (p. 239) is a typical example of the meticulous care with which late nineteenth-century playwrights envisioned the locale of their plays.

At about the same time that candlelight was being replaced by gas, directors also discovered ways to focus spotlights on single characters. This was first achieved by burning small chunks of lime and reflecting the light off of curved mirrors onto the leading man or leading lady (who was then, quite literally, "in the limelight"). Most directors, understandably, became enamored with the technique, and throughout the nineteenth century talented actors and actresses often held to the limelight to the detriment of the play as a whole. A particularly fine speech by Edmund Kean or Sarah Kemble Siddons, for example, might bring the audience to its feet in midscene. And if the applause were long and loud enough, Mr. Kean or Mrs. Siddons would simply recite the speech again as an encore. The inevitable effect of such an emphasis was to encourage dramatists to concentrate on writing good parts for the leading roles without giving equal attention to plot, structure, and theme.

A further development in nineteenth-century stagecraft was the increasing use made of the curtain spanning the proscenium arch. Until about 1875, the curtain was used only to screen the stage before the start of the play; once raised, it did not fall again until the end of the last act. The intention, of course, was to startle and delight the spectators when the curtain first rose on the fanciful world of the theater and then to entertain them by magically transforming that world before their eyes. So long as the scenery was mainly composed of paintings on flats that could be slid off stage mechanically and replaced by others, such changes of scene could occur swiftly and smoothly. But the advent of the realistic box set inevitably brought with it an increasing number of unwieldy props. The stage became cluttered with footstools, sofas, armchairs, end tables, vases, and portraits that stagehands were required to cart off or rearrange during any change of scene. The whole process soon became more frantic than magical and more distracting than entertaining. Furthermore, to effect such changes before the eyes of the audience only served to break down the illusion of reality. In order to sustain the illusion, directors and playwrights began to use the curtain between acts and even between scenes.

This had an immediate and important influence on the text of plays written in the final quarter of the nineteenth century. Before then a scene or an act necessarily began with a set of entrances and concluded with some pretext calling for the characters to exit—usually a variant of "Come! Let's be off to dine [or drink, or dance, or what have you]." The increased use of the curtain freed the dramatist from such constrictions. The emphasis changed from finding a way of getting the characters offstage, to finding a way of building dramatic tension and emphasizing basic themes at the end of acts or scenes. The resulting *curtain line* is perhaps the most distinctive feature of modern drama. Ibsen was among the first to employ the curtain line, and in *Hedda Gabler* he honed it to perfection. Each act ends on a note of high drama, but for the purpose of illustration, we will look at the conclusion to the third act:

LÖVBORG: Good-by, Mrs Tesman. And give George Tesman my love. [*He is on the point of going.*]

HEDDA: No, wait! I must give you a memento to take with you. [*She goes to the writing table and opens the drawer and the pistol case, then returns to* LÖVBORG *with one of the pistols.*]

LÖVBORG [*looks at her*]: This? Is this the memento?

HEDDA [*nodding slowly*]: Do you recognize it? It was aimed at you once.

LÖVBORG: You should have used it then.

HEDDA: Take it—and do you use it now.

LÖVBORG [*puts the pistol in his breast pocket*]: Thanks!

HEDDA: And beautifully, Eilert Lövborg. Promise me that!

LÖVBORG: Good-by, Hedda Gabler. [*He goes out by the hall door.*]

[HEDDA *listens for a moment at the door. Then she goes up to the writing table, takes out the packet of manuscript, peeps under the cover, draws a few of the sheets half out and looks at them. Next she goes over and seats herself in the armchair beside the stove, with the packet in her lap. Presently she opens the stove door and then the packet.*]

HEDDA [*throws one of the quires into the fire and whispers to herself*]: Now I am burning your child, Thea! Burning it, curlylocks! [*Throwing one or two more quires into the stove.*] Your child and Eilert Lövborg's. [*Throws the rest in.*] I am burning—I am burning your child.

—from *Hedda Gabler,* act 3, Henrik Ibsen (1890)

With growing horror, we realize not only that Hedda is encouraging Eilert to kill himself, but also that she could have prevented his death by returning the manuscript. She burns the only copy of Eilert's book because she is insanely jealous that Thea, "that pretty little fool" as Hedda thinks of her, should after all have had "her fingers in a man's destiny." The curtain drops just as Hedda reaches her deepest and most chilling insight into her own actions: "I am burning—I am burning your child."

The Modern Theater

Twentieth-century stagecraft has been characterized by flexibility. An improved understanding of the past has allowed us to stage the plays of Sophocles, Shakespeare, Molière, and others with greater fidelity to the original intentions of the author. Furthermore, modern critical principles encourage playwrights, and directors to put aside their *a priori* notions about staging and recognize that each play requires and deserves a separate approach. Continuing technical developments in the twentieth century have facilitated this flexibility both through further refinements in lighting and through machinery that can easily manipulate the sets and sometimes even the seating arrangement in the theater.

Although most modern theaters retain the proscenium arch and a clear division between the audience and the actors, many small theaters (especially temporary ones) have experimented with other structures. The most innovative of these have tried to recreate the intimacy and versatility of the Elizabethan stage either in small semicircular amphitheaters or in arena theaters. *Arena staging* or *theater-in-the-round* has emerged as the most distinctive twentieth-century contribution to stagecraft. The audience totally surrounds the stage and is therefore as close to the action of the play as is physically possible. Entrances and exits are made through the aisles normally used by the spectators and in some cases these become secondary acting areas, as well. Inevitably, however, the actors cannot simultaneously face all members of the audience. So long as the play focuses on the conflict between at least two characters, this presents no problem. When the two square off, all members of the audience will have at least a frontal view of one character or a profile of both. When the dramatic interest is focused totally on one character, however, as it is in the final moments of *Othello,* one fourth of the audience is apt to feel frustrated at being unable to see and hear properly his climactic speech. For this reason, arena staging is less successful than other approaches for plays with one dominant role.

Most of the major playhouses in America were built long before arena staging became widely accepted, but they, too, have adapted to the twentieth-century demand for flexibility. Modern set designs have been transformed by a consensus that their primary purpose is to provide three-dimensional areas for acting. The movable flats that were used well into the twentieth century to create perspective in outdoor settings have now been all but eliminated. Playwrights and directors seem to agree that everything depicted on stage should be functional and esthetically pleasing but not necessarily realistic. The sets should draw no attention to themselves or away from the acting. The general trend has been toward a simple, almost architectural stage, with platforms at various levels linked by stairways and ramps. The modern set strives to be suggestive and intellectually stimulating instead of purely pictorial, and this aim is facilitated by modern electrical lighting, which can actually create moods by "drawing" on the stage with shadows and prismatic colors to transform a single set into a constantly changing environment.

The trends in the modern theater have imposed no new conditions on playwrights; instead, they have been freed from many of the old limitations of the stage. This flexibility is best illustrated by the range of settings used in the classics of modern drama. Eugene O'Neill's *Desire Under the Elms* (1931), for example, takes place in, and immediately outside of, the Cabot farmhouse. O'Neill's own sketches show the exterior of the farmhouse, with various sections of the wall removed as the action shifts from one room to another. In effect, it is a stage with multiple box sets. Arthur Miller's *Death of a Salesman* (1949) also calls for the interior of a house, but in this case all of the walls are invisible and the house itself becomes a large, skeletal structure of various platforms for acting or observing actions. Finally, Tom Stoppard's *Rosencrantz and Guildenstern Are Dead* (1967) is set on a barren stage, "a place without any visible character"; it requires only a platform with two different levels and a few simple properties.

The causes of the modern trend toward flexibility, suggestivity, and simplicity of setting are complex, but certainly television and the movies have had something to do with it. Before films became popular, there had been an ever-increasing trend toward spectacle in the theater. Although crowds once flocked to playhouses to see a theatrical railroad engine steaming along toward the bound heroine or baying bloodhounds pursuing the bleeding hero, they soon found that the movies—through close-ups, cuts, and editing—could present those thrills more realistically while indulging in the additional expensive luxuries of having the train explode or the hero slog through miles of snake-infested swamp. Within a few years, therefore, playhouses ceased to stage spectacular extravaganzas, and drama once again became the verbal and intellectual experience previously enjoyed by the Elizabethans and the Greeks.

9

The Elements of Drama

For the most part, the elements of drama are identical to those of fiction and poetry. Plays have plots, themes, characters, and settings and make use of the many devices of poetic diction. Thus, many of the steps in the analysis of a play should parallel those used for a poem or a short story. At the same time, however, drama is a different literary genre and it imposes its own constraints on the playwright's use of certain elements of literature. These unique aspects of dramatic writing are our present concern.

Every play unfolds a story through the dialogue and actions of its characters. An understanding of these four elements—story, dialogue, action, and character—is therefore crucial to the appreciation of drama.

DIALOGUE

Tom Stoppard's *Rosencrantz and Guildenstern Are Dead* has no story apart from that already told in *Hamlet;* its principle characters are notably mainly because no one can distinguish between them; and the most significant action in the play is prolonged waiting. Part of the fun of Stoppard's work is that he has nearly stripped drama to its one indispensible element, dialogue.

A theatrical production without dialogue can be a mime or a ballet, but it is never a play. As Stoppard himself might have put it: a play can give you talk and characters without much action. And a play can give you talk and action without strong characters. But a play cannot give you characters and action without talk. It is all talk in drama.

Dramatic dialogue, however, is very different from the kind of dialogue that makes up so much of our ordinary lives. Actual conversation is full of hesitations, pauses, fragments, misunderstandings, and repetitions. The communication itself is often as much a product of inflections, gestures, and facial expressions as it is of the spoken word. It depends so much on innuendo and allusions to previous conversations that an outsider is often unable to determine the exact meaning of a discussion heard out of context. This in fact was Richard Nixon's contention when he protested in July and August 1973 against the release of the transcripts of his conversations about Watergate. The following selection from the Nixon tapes may have been one of the most important moments in the history of the United States presidency; its release shocked the nation and eventually led to Nixon's resignation in August 1974. As we will see, however, it is far from being good drama:

THE SETTING: *March 21, 1973, 10:12 A.M. The Oval Office*
THE PARTICIPANTS: *Richard Nixon and John Dean*
THE SITUATION: *Dean has just reviewed the history of the Watergate cover-up, calling it a "cancer" close to the presidency. Having described the continual demands for hush money by the Watergate burglars, he continues:*

DEAN: . . . It will cost money. It is dangerous. People around here are not pros at this sort of thing. This is the sort of thing Mafia people can do: washing money, getting clean money, and things like that. We just don't know about those things, because we are not criminals and not used to dealing in that business.
NIXON: That's right.
DEAN: It is a tough thing to know how to do.
NIXON: Maybe it takes a gang to do that.
DEAN: That's right. There is a real problem as to whether we could even do it. Plus there is a real problem in raising money. Mitchell has been working on raising some money. He is one of the ones with the most to lose. But there is no denying the fact that the White House, in Ehrlich-

man, Haldeman, and Dean, are involved in some of the early money decisions.

NIXON: How much money do you need?

DEAN: I would say these people are going to cost a million dollars over the next two years.

NIXON: We could get that. On the money, if you need the money you could get that. You could get a million dollars. You could get it in cash. I know where it could be gotten. It is not easy, but it could be done. But the question is who the hell would handle it? Any ideas on that?

DEAN: That's right. Well, I think that is something that Mitchell ought to be charged with.

NIXON: I would think so too.

DEAN: And get some pros to help him.

—from *Submission of Recorded Presidential Conversations,* April 30, 1974

It is clear enough that the president and his chief counsel are discussing obstruction of justice, acquiescence in blackmail, and involvement with professional criminals. The very topics of conversation are momentous and appalling. Yet the passage is stylistically weak and grammatically inept. The conversation redundantly returns to the difficulty of raising the money and the need for "pros" to handle the payoffs; and when Dean digresses into a discussion of the White House involvement, the president brings him back to the point by asking, "How much money do you need?" The sentences are choppy and inelegant, and the participants do not come to a clear decision until many exchanges later. Even then the discussion does not end. It meanders along for at least another hour, with the participants drifting away from the central issue and then darting back to it like minnows chasing a spinner.

In contrast, important conversations in drama slash past trivial details and strike the lure with vigor and directness. A play necessarily packs a story of significance into two or three hours of stage time. As a result, each sentence is hard and muscular—made up of concrete nouns and active verbs. The dialogue continuously and clearly builds toward its point, eliminating irrelevancies and unnecessary repetitions. When trimmed to its dramatic core, a real conversation, like the one between Richard Nixon and John Dean, might well be cut by half.

Dramatic dialogue ordinarily carries with it still another burden: it must include sufficient background information to fix the time, place, and circumstances of the action firmly in the mind of the audience. Nixon and Dean, after all, knew each other well and also knew the circumstances surrounding the issues described in their conversation; the playwright, however, must introduce the characters and provide background information before the audience can really understand what is going on. Although some playwrights prefer to have a narrator set the scene in a formal prologue—as, for example, in Williams's *The Glass Menagerie* or Wilder's *Our Town*—most try to bring out the background information gradually during the play's first act. Ibsen was a master of the gradual introduction, as illustrated in the first few moments of *Hedda Gabler:*

MISS JULIANA TESMAN, *with her bonnet on and carrying a parasol, comes in from the hall, followed by* BERTA, *who carries a bouquet wrapped in paper.* MISS TESMAN *is a comely and pleasant-looking lady of about sixty-five. She is nicely but simply dressed in a gray walking costume.* BERTA *is a middle-aged woman of plain and rather countrified appearance.*

MISS TESMAN [*stops close to the door, listens and says softly*]: Upon my word, I don't believe they are stirring yet!

BERTA [*also softly*]: I told you so, miss. Remember how late the steamboat got in last night. And then, when they got home!—good lord, what a lot the young mistress had to unpack before she could get to bed.

MISS TESMAN: Well, well—let them have their sleep out. But let us see that they get a good breath of the fresh morning air when they do appear. [*She goes to the glass door and throws it open.*]

BERTA [*beside table, at a loss what to do with the bouquet in her hand*]: I declare, there isn't a bit of room left. I think I'll put it down here, miss. [*She places it on the piano.*]

MISS TESMAN: So you've got a new mistress now, my dear Berta. Heaven knows it was a wrench to me to part with you.

BERTA [*on the point of weeping*]: And do you think it wasn't hard for me too, miss? After all the blessed years I've been with you and Miss Rina.

MISS TESMAN: We must make the best of it, Berta. There was nothing else to be done. George can't do without you, you see—he absolutely can't. He has had you to look after him ever since he was a little boy.

BERTA: Ah, but, Miss Julia, I can't help thinking of Miss Rina lying helpless at home there, poor thing. And with only that new girl too! She'll never learn to take proper care of an invalid.

MISS TESMAN: Oh, I shall manage to train her. And of course, you know, I shall take most of it upon myself. You needn't be uneasy about my poor sister, my dear Berta.

BERTA: Well, but there's another thing, miss. I'm so mortally afraid I shan't be able to suit the young mistress.

MISS TESMAN: Oh well—just at first there may be one or two things—

BERTA: Most like she'll be terrible grand in her ways.

MISS TESMAN: Well, you can't wonder at that—General Gabler's daughter!

Think of the sort of life she was accustomed to in her father's time. Don't you remember how we used to see her riding down the road along with the general? In that long black habit—and with feathers in her hat?

BERTA: Yes indeed—I remember well enough! But, good lord, I should never have dreamt in those days that she and Master George would make a match of it.

MISS TESMAN: Nor I. But by-the-bye, Berta—while I think of it: in future you mustn't say Master George. You must say Doctor Tesman.

BERTA: Yes, the young mistress spoke of that too—last night—the moment they set foot in the house. Is it true then, miss?

MISS TESMAN: Yes, indeed it is. Only think, Berta—some foreign university has made him a doctor—while he has been abroad, you understand. I hadn't heard a word about it until he told me himself upon the pier.

BERTA: Well, well, he's clever enough for anything, he is. But I didn't think he'd have gone in for doctoring people too.

MISS TESMAN: No, no, it's not that sort of doctor he is. [*Nods significantly.*] But let me tell you, we may have to call him something still grander before long.

BERTA: You don't say so! What can that be, miss?

MISS TESMAN [*smiling*]: H'm—wouldn't you like to know!

—from *Hedda Gabler,* Henrik Ibsen (1890)

Everything in this conversation is natural and unstrained, yet it tells us all that we immediately need to know about the main characters and their relationships with one another. We learn that George Tesman and his new wife have just returned from their honeymoon, that no one had ever dreamt the two would wed, that prior to his marriage George had lived with his two aunts and the maid Berta, and that George has recently been awarded a doctorate by "some foreign university." These few facts give us our bearings and prepare us for the entrance of George and Hedda. They also hint at Hedda's romantic past and George's professorial ambitions, thus preparing us for the entrance of Eilert Lövborg, who is about to compete for George's academic position as he had once competed for Hedda's affections.

But we learn even more. Ibsen is so economical a craftsman that these few lines of dialogue also contribute to the characterization of George, Hedda, and Aunt Julia. We learn, for example, that George is helpless and relies on others to provide him with the comforts of life. When Aunt Julia must choose whether Berta should stay with Aunt Rina or go with George, she decides that her invalid sister is more self-sufficient than her nephew. We also learn that George is not the elegant sort of man one would expect to marry a general's daughter, although his aunts and Berta are genuinely fond of him. Thus, when we first see Tesman on stage we have been prepared, subtly, for his kindly, methodical, sentimental, and slightly incompetent approach to life. Hedda, on the other hand, is a far more formidable character. She is mentioned by Berta and Julia with anxiety. Because Hedda is so "grand in her ways," Berta fears that she "shan't be able to suit the young mistress" and Aunt Julia agrees that "at first there may be one or two things." Aunt Julia's reminiscences about how Hedda used to ride in a long black habit with feathers in her hat prepare us for a woman of aristocratic and romantic disposition. And Hedda's insistence that her husband be called Doctor Tesman hints at her desire for a dignified and proper place in society. These few introductory remarks, then, indicate that Hedda is likely to be emotionally unsuited to a drab life with Tesman and suggest that her romantic predilections may eventually come into conflict with her equally strong desire for propriety. Finally, the lines indirectly characterize Aunt Julia. She is a fussy, meddling, and kindly woman who habitually thinks of others first. She listens carefully to find out if the newlyweds are stirring, throws open the glass door to give them plenty of air, and gives up her own maid to be sure they will be well served. Berta's mistaken assumption that George has become a medical doctor apparently triggers one of the preoccupations of Aunt Julia's prying mind. The allusion to a medical doctor in the context of George's marriage arouses her hope that the household may soon need an obstetrical physician and that George will become a father as well as a doctor of philosophy. She nods significantly and says mysteriously, "we may have to call him something still grander [than doctor] before long."

A third function of the dialogue in this introductory scene is to foreshadow themes of later importance. The oblique reference to Hedda's possible pregnancy is but one such example. In a more overt and pragmatic way, the opening dialogue and accompanying actions often help to initiate events that are further developed as the play progresses. The bouquet that is in Berta's hand as the play opens carries a card promising a visit from Thea Elvsted, a visit that will develop into a competition between Hedda and Thea for control over Eilert Lövborg. Similarly, Aunt Julia's well-intentioned opening of the glass doors will later irritate Hedda, who prefers a "softer light" and complains, "Oh—there the servant has gone and opened the veranda door and let in a whole flood of sunshine." From that point on, Hedda maliciously seeks opportunities to goad Aunt Julia and to prevent any attempt to create a tight family circle that will include George's aunts. As the play unfolds, the expressed anxieties of Aunt Julia and Berta that "there may be one or two" points of conflict between them and Hedda are amply confirmed.

In summary, the dialogue in Ibsen's plays, as in most other plays, serves many simultaneous functions. It is used to provide necessary factual information, to reminisce, to characterize, to speculate, and to foreshadow. Such dialogue may take the form of discussion (as in the quoted scene), argument, or inquiry. It may accompany and clarify actions or simply reveal attitudes and opinions. In short, good dialogue is a very flexible narrative tool.

Dialogue is not, however, an easy tool to use. A playwright, unlike a novelist, cannot simply halt proceedings to introduce formal character sketches or to set a scene; nor can a playwright exert the same direct control over the "story." A fictional "yarn" is spun out of a voice that the author, as narrator, can fully control. But the dramatist has no voice of his or her own. When the curtain rises, the fabric of the plot must emerge naturally from interwoven and independent threads of conversation.

When we argue that the plot of a play must emerge naturally from its dialogue, we do not mean that the dialogue itself must inevitably be "natural" or "realistic." As the Watergate tapes demonstrate, the real words of real people often seem awkward and unnatural in transcript. But art is not life. We hold art to a higher standard of probability, eloquence, and organization; therefore, nearly all dramatic dialogue is more rhetorical—more poetic, if you will—than real dialogue. Even so, however, there is an enormous range between the dialogue of *Hedda Gabler,* for example, and that of *Oedipus Rex.* Part of the difference results from the fact that the former is written in prose, the latter in verse; and verse is always much richer than prose in sound, rhythm, and imagery.

There is, however, also the matter of level of style. Both in the original Greek and in faithful translations, the language of *Oedipus* is lofty and formal; the language of *Hedda Gabler,* by contrast, is colloquial and informal. Listen to the opening lines of *Oedipus:*

OEDIPUS: My children, generations of the living
In the line of Kadmos, nursed at his ancient hearth:
Why have you strewn yourselves before these altars

In supplication, with your boughs and garlands?
The breath of incense rises from the city
With a sound of prayer and lamentation.
Children,
I would not have you speak through messengers,
And therefore I have come myself to hear you—
I, Oedipus, who bear the famous name.
—from *Oedipus Rex,* Sophocles (430 B.C.)

The three sentences are grammatically complete and relatively long—the first and third especially so because of the elaborate epithets that Oedipus uses to describe first his people and then himself. Furthermore, the first two sentences contain implied comparisons: the people are strewn before the altars like their boughs and garlands, and their lamentations rise like the smoke from incense. Plays like *Oedipus,* which are careful both in grammar and in their use of poetic devices, are said to be written in the "high" style.

The language of *Hedda Gabler* is, of course, far different. Notice, for example, the casual and conversational tone. Phrases are inserted to capture the flavor of everyday speech ("upon my word," "good lord," "well, well," "I declare"). Grammatical relationships, too, are informal: the dialogue is sprinkled with dashes to indicate incomplete thoughts or sudden changes in direction. And Ibsen makes no attempt to use poetical devices. Playwrights occasionally carry this colloquial, or "low," style even further and use ungrammatical and dialectical speech as a tool of characterization. The back-country accents and diction of the Cabots, for example, help Eugene O'Neill explore crude and elemental passions in *Desire Under the Elms.* Similarly, Stanley Kowalski's inarticulate speech in Tennessee Williams's *A Streetcar Named Desire* underscores his assertive, uneducated, and violent character.

Dramatic theory during the classical and neoclassical periods held that tragedy should be written in the high style and that the colloquial, or low, style was appropriate only to comedy. In practice, however, as the plays of Shakespeare amply demonstrate, such a distinction need not be rigidly observed, and in more modern times it has been all but abandoned. Most drama is mixed in style, rising to eloquence or falling to informality according to the inherent demands of the practical dramatic situation.

STORY

People come to the theater because they wish to be entertained. Although they may be willing to admire fine writing or to tolerate moral instruction, they demand an engrossing story. An audience is, after all, a crowd, and the principal desire of a crowd is to find out "what happens next." Drama, however, would emphasize story even if it were not demanded by the audience, for the dramatic point of view necessitates a fundamentally chronological development of action. Reminiscences can be, and often are, used to precipitate the action, but once the play has begun, the events on the stage inevitably unfold according to the simple time sequence of a story.

Dramatic actions as they unfold upon the stage do not, of course, simply "happen"; they are premeditated and artistically arranged by the playwright to yield a dramatic plot. The ability to understand the story (the "what happens") may satisfy our basic desire as theatergoers to be entertained, but as literary critics we also need to understand not only "what happens" but "why"—a question that invariably forces us to consider the dynamics of plot.

Like a typical short story, the plot of nearly every play contains five structural elements: *exposition, complication, crisis, falling action,* and *resolution.* The principal difference between fictional and dramatic plots is that the latter are more regular in their use of these five elements, as is illustrated in the following paragraphs.

Exposition

The exposition provides essential background information, introduces the cast, begins the characterization, and initiates the action. Some exposition is always provided in the first scene, and all of the essential background material is usually provided by the end of the first act. Sometimes a formal prologue or introduction by a narrator helps to set the scene, but more often there is no sharp division between the exposition and the complication that follows. In fact, most plays begin *in medias res* (in the middle of things), just after some event has taken place that will eventually lead to the crisis.

EXAMPLES OF THE SITUATION AT THE COMMENCEMENT OF DRAMATIC ACTION

Oedipus Rex: A plague afflicts Thebes because the murderer of King Laios has never been punished.

Othello: Othello and Desdemona have secretly married; and Cassio, rather than Iago, has been made Othello's lieutenant.

Tartuffe: To be nearer to his religious adviser, Orgon has installed Tartuffe in his home.

Hedda Gabler: After their honeymoon, Hedda and George have returned to town, as has Eilert Lövborg, who is seeking to publish a new book. Rumor has it that George's faculty appointment must await the outcome of a competition with Eilert.

The situation at the outset of a play usually gives us important clues to its direction and meaning. We do not, for example, see Oedipus at his moment of early triumph over the Sphinx; instead we first see him as he proudly promises that he will discover Laios's killer just as he once discovered the meaning of the Sphinx's riddle. The play explores the consequences of this rash promise. Similarly, *Othello* does not begin with a scene showing Othello's wedding ceremony, but rather with the conspiracy between Roderigo and Iago, in order to focus the audience's attention immediately on Iago's thirst for revenge.

Complication

This section of the plot introduces and develops the conflict. It commences when one or more of the main characters first become aware of an impending difficulty or when their relationships first begin to change.

Examples of Initial Complication

Oedipus Rex: Teiresias alleges that Oedipus has murdered Laios.

Othello: Iago recognizes that Cassio's courteous attentions to Desdemona can be used to make Othello jealous (act 2, scene 2).

Tartuffe: Orgon reveals his decision that Mariane must marry Tartuffe instead of Valère, whom she loves (act 2, scene 1).

Hedda Gabler: Thea informs Hedda that Eilert Lövborg is in town and that he is still preoccupied by the memory of an unknown woman (act 1).

It is not always possible to identify the precise point at which the complication of the plot begins. The plot of *Othello,* for example, obviously turns on Iago's ability to make Othello suspect Desdemona of infidelity. But how does this suspicion originate? Does it begin as a scheme in Iago's brain when, having seen Cassio take Desdemona by the hand (act 2, scene 2), he whispers slyly, "With as little a web as this will I ensnare as great a fly as Cassio"? Or does it begin somewhat later (act 3, scene 3), when (as Cassio parts from Desdemona) Iago says to Othello, "Ha! I like not that"? Or did Othello's jealousy start as early as act 1, scene 3, when Brabantio exclaimed, "Look to her, Moor, if thou has eyes to see. She has deceived her father, and may thee"? In a sense it begins at each place. It was foreshadowed in act 1, scene 3; first plotted by Iago in act 2, scene 2; and first felt by Othello in act 3, scene 3. From relatively small beginnings, Othello's jealousy grows until it dominates his entire personality. Much of the impact of the play results from the fact that the tragedy that ultimately destroys Othello has its roots in such indefinite beginnings.

In other plays, however, the conflict and its thematic significance are immediately clear. Oedipus's pride and impetuosity are implicit in his very first speech, but they only take on the aspect of tragic flaws when he refuses to check the accuracy of the prophesies reported by Teiresias and rashly concludes that the priest has joined with Creon in conspiring to usurp his throne. Similarly, Orgon's excessive faith in Tartuffe is clear throughout the first act, but only becomes dangerous and destructive when it leads him to break his promise that Valère shall marry Mariane. In both plays, the tensions that dramatically affect the protagonist's subsequent conduct are implicit in the opening scenes.

Crisis

The crisis, or turning point of the play, occurs at the moment of peak emotional intensity and usually involves a decision, a decisive action, or an open conflict between the protagonist and antagonist. It is often called the *obligatory scene* because the audience demands to *see* such moments acted out on stage.

Examples of the Crisis

Oedipus Rex: The shepherd's information about Oedipus's birth finally convinces the king that he has murdered his father and married his mother.

Othello: Through the machinations of Iago, Othello sees Desdemona's handkerchief in the hand of Cassio and concludes that she must die for her infidelity (act 4, scene 1).

Tartuffe: While hidden under a table, Orgon hears Tartuffe trying to seduce his wife and finally recognizes Tartuffe's hypocrisy for what it is (act 4, scene 5).

Hedda Gabler: Instead of returning Eilert's manuscript, Hedda encourages him to believe it is lost and gives him a pistol with which to commit suicide. After he has left, she burns the manuscript (act 3).

Just as it is sometimes difficult to determine where the conflict originates, it is sometimes also difficult to determine when the crisis takes place. Once Othello has seen Cassio with Desdemona's handkerchief, he is convinced of her guilt and the tragic conclusion of the play is foreordained. The scene, then, marks an important turning point in the characterization of Othello. But the dramatic tension continues to mount until the confrontation between Othello and Desdemona in her bedchamber (act 5, scene 2). We do not *know* that Othello will actually kill Desdemona until he does so. And only when he does so in spite of Desdemona's moving pleas and his own obvious reluctance, do we recognize the extent to which his jealousy has blinded him. Clearly, this scene, too, is a crisis in the plot and another turning point in the characterization of Othello. A hundred lines further into the scene we find yet another crisis and another turning point when Emilia tells Othello that Desdemona could not have given the handkerchief to Cassio for she, Emilia, had found it and given it to Iago. This revelation is the turning point in Iago's fortunes; it finally shows Othello how mistaken he has been all along. In the few remaining moments of the play, Othello rises again to the dignity and nobility that had first characterized him.

It is a mistake, therefore, in plays like *Othello* always to seek the crisis within a single moment of emotional intensity. Great literature is never bound by formula. Instead, as critics we must learn to look carefully at each moment of high drama in an effort to determine what we can learn from it about the play, its characters, and their relationship to the playwright's overall intention.

Falling Action and Resolution

As the consequences of the crisis accumulate, events develop a momentum of their own. Especially in tragedy, the falling action of the play results from the protagonist's loss of control and a final catastrophe often appears inevitable. The resolution of a comedy, however, frequently includes some unexpected twist in the plot (for example, the intervention of the king or the revelation of the hero's true parents). This twist cuts sharply through all difficulties and allows the play to end on a happy note. In both tragedy and comedy, the resolution brings to an end the conflict that has been implicit (or explicit) since the play's opening scenes. When the curtain falls, the relationships among the characters have once more stabilized.

EXAMPLES OF THE FALLING ACTION AND RESOLUTION

Oedipus Rex: Oedipus blinds himself in sorrow and then is banished by the new king, Creon.

Othello: After smothering Desdemona, Othello learns of her innocence and slays himself.

Tartuffe: Using a deed that Orgon had foolishly signed, Tartuffe attempts to expel Orgon and his family from their own home. At the last moment, Tartuffe is arrested and imprisoned by order of the king.

Hedda Gabler: After Eilert's death, George and Thea set to work reproducing the lost manuscript. Hedda, whom George has commended to Judge Brack's attention, finds herself in Brack's power when he threatens to reveal information that would involve her in scandal. Rather than become Brack's mistress or tolerate scandal, Hedda shoots herself.

The resolution, or dénouement, merits special attention because it is the author's last chance to get the point across. Thus, it is not surprising that the resolution often contains a clear statement (or restatement) of the theme and a full revelation of character. In the last lines of *Hedda Gabler,* for example, Hedda realizes that Thea will indeed inspire Tesman just as she had Eilert Lövborg, while she, Hedda, can do "nothing in the world to help them." And Othello, in his last lines, begs that, when relating his story, Lodovico and Gratiano will speak

Of one that loved not wisely but too well,
Of one not easily jealous, but, being wrought,
Perplexed in the extreme, of one whose hand,
Like the base Indian, threw a pearl away
Richer than all his tribe—of one whose subdued eyes,
Albeit unused to the melting mood,
Drop tears as fast as the Arabian trees
Their medicinal gum.

—from *Othello,* act 5, scene 2, William Shakespeare (1604)

In the last lines of *Tartuffe,* the officer presents Molière's conception of the ideal man:

His royal soul, though generous and human,
Views all things with discernment and acumen;
His sovereign reason is not lightly swayed,

And all his judgments are discreetly weighed.
He honors righteous men of every kind,
And yet his zeal for virtue is not blind,
Nor does his love of piety numb his wits
And make him tolerant of hypocrites.
—from *Tartuffe,* act 5, scene 7, Molière (1664)

And finally, the Choragos pronounces a telling judgment upon Oedipus, as that play closes:

CHORAGOS. Men of Thebes: look upon Oedipus.
This is the king who solved the famous riddle
And towered up, most powerful of men.
No mortal eyes but looked on him with envy,
Yet in the end ruin swept over him.
Let every man in mankind's frailty
Consider his last day; and let none
Presume on his good fortune until he find
Life, at his death, a memory without pain.
—from *Oedipus Rex,* Sophocles (430 B.C.)

In each case the lines are so crucial and so clearly a summary of what the author finds most important that literary critics often use them as keys to unlock the riches of each play.

Although virtually all plays include an exposition, complication, crisis, falling action, and resolution, and all take approximately the same amount of time to perform, they differ drastically in the amount of fictional time covered by the action shown on stage. In plays like *Oedipus Rex, Tartuffe,* and *Hedda Gabler,* the action begins just a few hours before the crisis. This allows the drama to unfold before the spectators' eyes, much as if they were looking in on real events. But because nearly any plot of significance builds to a crisis that caps a series of events dating back months or years, these *unfolding plots* necessarily make use of reminiscences introduced via the testimony of elderly step-parents, conversations between servants, or other similar strategies. The manipulation of these reminiscences requires considerable ingenuity in order to avoid a sense of obvious contrivance. One alternative is to present the action episodically, skipping weeks, months, or years between scenes as the chief events leading up to the crisis are acted out on stage. *Othello* and most other Elizabethan plays employ such *episodic plots.*

Whether a plot is unfolding or episodic, it ought to be tightly structured and pruned of unnecessary characters, actions, speeches, and scenes. The term *well-made play,* or "*pièce bien faite,*" was coined by Eugène Scribe, a French playwright (1791–1861), to describe such plots—especially when they proceed logically from cause to effect in building toward a climactic scene in which the hero triumphs by revealing some adeptly foreshadowed secret. Although the formula prescribed by Scribe is now out-of-date, the craftsmanship he advocated will never be. It is, and always has been, an unmistakable sign of good drama. The first truly well-made plays were not written by Scribe or Ibsen, but by Aeschylus and Sophocles. And the latter's *Oedipus Rex* probably conforms more closely than any later drama to the description of the well-made play first given in Aristotle's *Poetics:*

> The plot, being an imitation of an action must imitate one action and that a whole, the structural union of the parts being such that, if any one of them is displaced or removed, the whole will be disjointed and disturbed.[1]

CHARACTER

For many of us, an interest in literature is an outgrowth of our interest in people and their personalities. Drama is particularly satisfying in this respect, for plays are inevitably and immediately concerned with the human beings who are impersonated by live actors and actresses on the stage. The terms used to describe characters in drama are, for the most part, the same as those used for fiction. In fact, some of these terms were originally borrowed from drama to describe fictional qualities. The *dramatis personae* of a play usually include a *protagonist* and an *antagonist* or an antagonistic force. (The protagonist in a tragedy, however, is often called the *tragic hero.*) Othello and Oedipus are clearly protagonists; Iago is Othello's antagonist; and the will of the gods is the antagonistic force opposing Oedipus. A great many plays also include a *confidant* (*confidante* if female) to whom a major character "confides" his or her most private thoughts and feelings. Emilia, for example, serves as Desdemona's confidante, just as Dorine is Mariane's confidante in *Tartuffe.* A *foil* is a minor figure whose contrasting personality in some way clarifies or enhances that of a major character, as Cléante's mod-

[1] *The Poetics of Aristotle,* 3rd ed., trans. by S. H. Butcher (New York: Macmillan Publishing Company, 1902), p. 35.

eration serves as a foil for Orgon's zealotry and as Laertes becomes a foil for Hamlet while both are seeking to revenge their fathers' deaths. A *caricature* is a character with one motive or trait that is carried to a ridiculous extreme. George Tesman, who has spent his honeymoon researching a book on "the domestic industries of Brabant during the Middle Ages" is a caricature of the scholarly temperament. And nearly everyone in *Tartuffe* is a caricature of some aspect of seventeenth-century French society.

This terminology underscores the obvious difference between major and minor characters. The parts of the protagonist and antagonist are major, whereas those of the confidant and foil are often (but not always) minor. Because it is only reasonable to assume that most of a playwright's attention will be focused on his major characters, one of our first steps in the analysis of a play should be to identify the characters who have leading roles. The most obvious clue is the number of lines spoken by each character: major characters have many, and minor characters few. But more importantly, major characters are usually individualized and given both complex motives and a past, while minor characters often have no past at all and sometimes represent no more than a common character type. One has said all that need be said about the characters of the messenger and the shepherd in *Oedipus Rex* as soon as their titles are mentioned. They have few individual traits and serve primarily to convey information to Oedipus and the audience. Similarly, Judge Brack in *Hedda Gabler* is a middle-aged rake whose single motive is to establish a comfortable triangular friendship in which Hedda becomes his mistress while George remains his friend. No such simple statements, however, can accurately describe the personalities of major characters like Oedipus, Othello, and Hedda. In order to understand these individuals, we must look carefully at the various means of characterization used to bring them to life.

Characterizing details in drama come to us from many different sources. We immediately learn something from the *name and physical appearance* of each character—although this information is often unreliable. The characters in *Othello,* for example, so often use the adjective *honest* when they refer to Iago that it seems (ironically) a part of his name, and they mistakenly take his coarse manner and military bearing as signs of simplicity and firmness. A second method of characterization is through an individual's *patterns of action* over the course of the play. Hedda Gabler's pacing, for example, is an indication of her sense of suffocating confinement in her role as a woman. Most characterization, however, is accomplished through dialogue in one of four ways. A character can reveal his or her personality and motives, as Iago often does, through *asides and soliloquies.* There may also be self-revelation in *the way a character speaks* because dialect, word choice, and grammar all provide clues to a person's background and intelligence. Othello's "perfect soul" is partially revealed through his eloquence, while Iago's idiomatic slang marks him as a "profane wretch" (according to Brabantio) in the very first scene of the play. *The way a character responds* to others is also important. Adversity seems at first only to make Othello more self-confident. When swords on both sides are drawn as Brabantio seeks to arrest Othello, the latter averts a crisis with composure: "Good signior, you shall more command with years / Than with your weapons." Yet the violent temper of this eminent soldier eventually surfaces, and he himself recognizes that he is one not easily made jealous or moved to anger, "but, being wrought,/ Perplexed in the extreme." Finally, *what others say about a character* can help us to understand him. As we have seen, the conversation between Aunt Julia and Berta is packed with observations, speculations, reminiscences, and judgments about Hedda and Tesman. These characterizing details come at us in fragmentary glimpses during the normal ebb and flow of the conversation. Occasionally, however, an author may provide a more concentrated sketch of a character's actions or personality—usually in the form of such *hidden narration* as the messenger's account of Oedipus' rage after learning his true parentage (see p. 245).

The process of understanding drama is very closely linked to our ability to understand the personalities and motives of the major characters. As we read and study a play, we inevitably raise a host of questions: Why does Iago dedicate himself to tormenting Othello? Why is Othello so susceptible to Iago's manipulations? What makes the lost handkerchief so important to Othello? Why does Desdemona lie about the handkerchief? What stops Othello and Desdemona from talking about their misunderstanding openly and fully? Is Othello thoroughly noble or is his character seriously flawed in some way? These questions, and others like them, are concerned with fundamental character traits and express our expectation that the actions of the characters should be plausible, consistent, and adequately motivated. In attempting to answer them, we continually compare what is said by or about a character with the way in which that character acts on stage, searching for the thread of unity that creates a convincing personality.

At the same time, however, characters who are too consistent generally seem unrealistic. Conventional wisdom tells us that real people are full of surprises and so, in literature, we tend to demand characters who are capable of surprising us in a convincing way. Their motives should be complex and even competing, as Othello's obvious love for Desdemona competes with his injured pride when he thinks that she has been unfaithful to him. Moreover, those characters who most interest us usually undergo a process of growth and change during the course of the play. Othello fascinates us as he sinks from his initial nobility to an all-consuming jealousy, before rising again in the tragic self-knowledge of his last speech. Similarly, Oedipus's blind complacency and self-satisfaction break down as the unfolding events force him to see the criminal actions of his past. At the end of the play, this banished and self-blinded man realizes that, although his eyes once were clear, he has had "neither sight nor knowledge."

We must be careful, however, not to push too far the demand for growth and change in character. Many fine plays, including *Tartuffe* and *Hedda Gabler,* present personalities or dilemmas without even hinting at the possibility of moral improvement or permanent solutions. Apparently Molière felt that a man like Tartuffe can be imprisoned but rarely improved, and that Orgon is as naturally impetuous in desiring Tartuffe's punishment as he had earlier been in praising him. Similarly, *Hedda Gabler* is a bleak study of a fundamentally pathological personality. The value of such drama is not that it creates characters just like our next-door neighbors, but rather that it shows how only slight distortions in personality can destabilize the whole structure of ordinary social relationships.

ACTION

John Wilmot, the Earl of Rochester, once criticized Charles II as a king who "never said a foolish thing / Nor ever did a wise one." Many a dramatist, after seeing his plays poorly acted, must have sympathized with the response of Charles II: "This is very true: for my words are my own, and my actions are my ministers'." The playwright must live with the parallel and sometimes melancholy realization that, while his words are his own, his actions are the actors'. Fortunately for the play-going public, actors are much more successful at putting the words of a play into action than bureaucrats are at implementing those of the head of government.

Although the actions in a play may sometimes be indicated or suggested in the script, they are just as often the inevitable by-products of the performance. When Berta and Aunt Julia are talking in the first scene of *Hedda Gabler* (see p. 264), we should not assume that they face each other motionlessly throughout their conversation. Ibsen himself directs them to perform a few actions—close the front door, open the door to the veranda, put down the bouquet, and so on—but twelve consecutive exchanges take place without a single stage direction. What do these women do with their hands during these exchanges? Do they remain motionless or move about the room? Do they face each other, the audience, or neither? Ibsen doesn't say, but surely some actions must take place—if only an averted glance here and a penetrating look there. Although the lines must be spoken, the director is free to present them as he wishes, and this presentation will affect both the characterization of the speakers and the degree of dramatic emphasis given to their words.

As readers of drama, we may attempt to be our own director, moving the characters about an imaginary stage and endowing them with gestures and expressions suitable to the dialogue. Most of us, however, are content to concentrate on the words in the play and leave the accompanying actions vague, except where they are demanded by the script. In either approach, however, we must be very sensitive to actions implied in the dialogue. This is especially true when we read plays written before the middle of the nineteenth century. Thereafter the techniques of the novel began to infiltrate drama and the playwright's stage directions became more frequent and more detailed. But early playwrights kept their stage directions to an absolute minimum. Here, for example, is part of a scene from Shakespeare's *Othello* as it was published in the famous *First Folio* (1623):

(*Enter* LODOVICO, DESDEMONA, *and* ATTENDANTS)

LODOVICO: Save you worthy General!
OTHELLO: With all my heart, sir.
LODOVICO: The Duke and Senators of Venice greet you.
OTHELLO: I kiss the instrument of their pleasures.

DESDEMONA: And what's the news, good Cousin Lodovico?
IAGO: I am very glad to see you, signior.
Welcome to Cyprus.
LODOVICO: I thank you. How does Lieutenant Cassio?
IAGO: Lives, sir.
DESDEMONA: Cousin, there's fall'n between him and my lord
An unkind breach, but you shall make all well.
OTHELLO: Are you sure of that?
DESDEMONA: My lord?
OTHELLO: "This fail you not to do, as you will—"
LODOVICO: He did not call, he's busy in the paper.
Is there division 'twixt my lord and Cassio?
DESDEMONA: A most unhappy one. I would do much
To atone them, for the love I bear to Cassio.
OTHELLO: Fire and brimstone!
DESDEMONA: My lord?
OTHELLO: Are you wise?
DESDEMONA: What, is he angry?
LODOVICO: Maybe the letter moved him,
For, as I think, they do command him home,
Deputing Cassio in his government.
DESDEMONA: By my troth, I am glad on 't.
OTHELLO: Indeed!
DESDEMONA: My lord?
OTHELLO: I am glad to see you mad.
DESDEMONA: Why, sweet Othello?
OTHELLO: Devil!
DESDEMONA: I have not deserved this.
LODOVICO: My lord, this would not be believed in Venice.
Though I should swear I saw 't. 'Tis very much.
Make her amends, she weeps.
OTHELLO: O devil, devil!
If that the earth could teem with a woman's tears,
Each drop she falls would prove a crocodile.
Out of my sight!
DESDEMONA: I will not stay to offend you.
LODOVICO: Truly, an obedient lady.
I do beseech your lordship, call her back.

—from *Othello,* act 4, scene 1, William Shakespeare (1604)

The only stage direction is that calling for the entrance of Lodovico, Desdemona, and attendants. But if we read the lines with care, we realize that Lodovico has brought a letter from Venice that he gives to Othello at line 199, and that Othello refers to this letter when he says, "I kiss the instrument of their pleasures." Presumably, Othello does kiss the letter, and he must open it before line 210, when he pretends to be deeply engrossed in his reading. We can also conclude that Othello slaps Desdemona when he calls her a devil in line 221, for Lodovico later exclaims to Iago, "What, strike his wife!" And we know that Desdemona must start to leave the stage after saying, "I will not stay to offend you" (line 228), because Lodovico asks Othello to call her back in line 230.

All of these actions are implicit in the dialogue, and most modern texts of the play formally incorporate them into editorial stage directions. Even so, however, the questions, counterquestions, exclamations, and asides in the rapid exchanges between lines 201 and 221 presume many additional actions and interactions. As readers we may not pause to speculate on the exact nature of this interplay, but we should realize that here, as in all drama, the script itself is only a partial guide to the dramatic action, as any glance at a director's prompt book would quickly prove. Both the formal stage directions and the creative contributions of the actors and director are designed either to emphasize the themes and character traits introduced in the dialogue or to stimulate further dialogue. The relationship between dialogue and dramatic action is like that between a diamond and its setting in a ring: in both cases the latter enhances and emphasizes the value and clarity of the former.

10

The Classifications of Drama

No one denies that *tragedy* and *comedy* are the major subgenres of drama, but the debate over their precise meaning has persisted through at least one hundred generations of philosophers and literary critics. Can this immense investment of intellectual energy have been worthwhile? The ability to classify plays does not help us in any important way to understand what a playwright has done, why he or she has done it, or what makes the play interesting. Yet these are the questions with which we must always deal in order to understand literature. Moreover, making a simple distinction between tragedy and comedy is about as easy as determining whether we more often sorrow or smile in reading or viewing a particular play. It is only when we demand precision in defining the kinds of plot, character, and action that create tragic or comic emotions that the issue becomes complex and irresolvable.

Most playwrights have been indifferent to these matters of classification, preferring simply to write their plays and let others worry about categorizing them. Plato tells us that Socrates once cornered Agathon, a respected tragic playwright, and Aristophanes, the greatest comic playwright, at the end of a party in Athens. In his enthusiasm for philosophy, Socrates began to bend their ears with his theory that the genius of comedy is the same as that of tragedy. Being drowsy and half drunk, both poets agreed, shared another cup of wine, and promptly dozed off, leaving Socrates to peddle his theory elsewhere.

If the responses of Agathon and Aristophanes were universal, we would not need to discuss tragedy and comedy any further. However, some playwrights do write plays according to some theory of the formal principles for each subgenre, and therefore we need to have at least rudimentary knowledge of the theories behind tragedy and comedy.

TRAGEDY

The first, and most influential, literary theorist was Aristotle (384–322 B.C.) whose famous definition of tragedy remains the cornerstone upon which all discussions of the subject must build. Tragedy, Aristotle contended,

> is an imitation of an action of high importance, complete and of some amplitude; in language enhanced by distinct and varying beauties; acted not narrated; by means of pity and fear effecting its purgation of these emotions.[1]

This definition puts much of its emphasis on the tragic action, or story, which Aristotle thought should be serious, complex, and tightly structured. Tragedy does not need to show events that have happened, but only those that would happen, given a certain set of circumstances. The events must be arranged in a causal progression, so that no action in the play can be eliminated or displaced without damaging the whole structure. Ideally the plot should include both irony and a disclosure, each evolving naturally out of the story. In *Oedipus Rex,* for example, the arrival of the messenger is ironic because the news of Polybos's death might be expected to release Oedipus from any fear of murdering his father, but instead it leads directly to the disclosure of his incest and parricide. Thus, the plot interweaves the irony with the fatal disclosure.

The requirement that the action of a tragedy be of "high importance" led Aristotle to demand that the protagonist be nobly born

[1] Aristotle on *The Art of Fiction,* trans. by L. J. Potts (Cambridge, England: Cambridge University Press, 1962), p. 24.

and more admirable than ordinary men. He cannot, however, be morally perfect because the best plots arise when his downfall is the inevitable consequence of some defect in character (or *tragic flaw*). The spectacle of a good man dragged to destruction by a single error arouses in the audience both pity and fear, leading to a *catharsis,* a psychological state through which those emotions are purged; the audience leaves the theater relieved, or even exalted, rather than depressed.

This Aristotelian definition accurately reflects the goal of most Greek, Roman, and neoclassical tragedy, but it is too narrow to include many serious and important plays written during other periods. Richard III, Macbeth, and Hedda Gabler, for example, are certainly *less* virtuous than ordinary men and women; it is debatable whether Romeo, Juliet, Hamlet, and Othello have tragic flaws; and very few of the characters in modern drama are nobly born. A definition of tragedy that excludes most of the work of Shakespeare and all of Ibsen—not to mention that of more recent playwrights—cannot be complete.

A more modern view is that there are at least three variations of the tragic situation or tragic emotion.[2] Some plays ask us to look on the sufferings of the tragic hero as a human sacrifice that is necessary to cleanse society. The fall of Oedipus, for example, is necessary to purge Thebes of hidden crime and to free the city from a plague imposed by the gods. Similarly, Richard III, Iago, and Macbeth can all be viewed as warped personalities who must perish before ordinary and stable social relationships can reassert themselves. As these examples suggest, the plots of sacrificial tragedies take one of two forms. The tragic hero suffers either through the will of the gods (like Oedipus) or through a rejection by society (like Macbeth). And in either form the protagonist may merit his suffering, as Oedipus and Macbeth do, or he may be an innocent victim of forces beyond his control, as are Romeo and Juliet.

A second tragic pattern arises from the paradox of the fortunate fall. As plots of this kind unfold, we realize that the hero's destruction is necessary if he is to rise to a higher level of personal awareness and development. Othello, for example, must be brought to recognize his responsibility for Desdemona's death if he is to change from a man who once spoke smugly of his "perfect soul" into a tragic fig-

[2] See E. M. W. Tillyard, *Shakespeare's Problem Plays* (Toronto: University of Toronto Press, 1949), pp. 14–17.

ure who accepts himself as one who "Like the base Indian, threw away a pearl / Richer than all his tribe." Oedipus must be blinded before he can truly see. And King Lear must be stripped of his regal pride and forced to "hovel . . . with swine and rogues forlorn in short and musty straw" before he can find his humanity. Tragedies of this second kind reaffirm our human capacity to learn from our experiences; they extend to us the reassurance that even in defeat we can rise above our limitations to an immortal grandeur.

A third tragic pattern involves the simple spectacle of sufferings that greatly exceed normal bounds. The tragic characters struggle helplessly to survive in an environment weighted against them. Like small insects entangled in a web, their futile flutterings express their surprise, regret, and bewilderment at the difference between their own fate and that of other men. Such plays usually include an inquiry by the characters and the playwright into the purpose (or futility) of the tragic individual's sufferings and the role of all human suffering in the scheme of the universe. If *Rosencrantz and Guildenstern Are Dead* is a tragedy at all, it is a tragedy of inexplicable suffering. From the first scene to the last, the characters question the reasons for their involvement in the action and the nature of the world into which they are unwillingly cast. Ultimately their plight becomes a symbol of our plight, and Stoppard persuades us that the death they experience is not simply a variant of the player's phoney "deaths for all ages and occasions," but rather, like real death, "the endless time of never coming back . . . a gap you can't see, and when the wind blows through it, it makes no sound. . . ."

Should we, however, define *Rosencrantz and Guildenstern Are Dead* as a tragedy? It is tragic in the sense that the main characters are victims of forces beyond their control; it is tragic in the sense that the protagonists are destroyed; and, moreover, it is tragic in the sense that the plot deals with issues of high importance, such as reality, fate, and death. But from start to finish, the dialogue is hilarious. If comedy has anything to do with humor, then surely this play qualifies as comic. The situation of Stoppard's characters, and by extension that of all human beings, is absurd—both macabre and wildly funny. It is senseless, silly, and sobering, all at the same time. In contemporary theater, we call this mixture of tragedy and comedy the *theater of the absurd;* its very existence reminds us that there need be no sharp distinction between the frowning mask of tragedy and the smiling mask of comedy.

COMEDY

Horace Walpole, the eighteenth-century man of letters, once observed that "the world is a comedy to those that think, a tragedy to those who feel." Walpole's comparison is as good a guide as any to the key differences between these two modes of drama. The tragic hero is closely examined and portrayed as an individual; the comic character is viewed intellectually from a distance and represents a broad human "type"—a young lover, a hypocrite, an elegant fop, and so on. The tragic mode asks us to sympathize with the hero and imagine ourselves in his position; the comic mode suggests that we step back from life and look with amusement on the humorous predicament of others. The subject matter of comedy is often as serious as that of tragedy, but the comic playwright consciously distorts events and personalities in order to remind the audience that the play deals with fantasy and not fact. The plots of comedy are usually convoluted exercises in authorial imagination; the plots of tragedy are sobering revelations of our emotional and psychological core.

A lighthearted but intellectual approach to comedy has prevailed from the very beginning. The extant plays of Aristophanes (called *Old Comedy*) are carefully structured explorations of a bizarre intellectual hypothesis. What would happen, he asks in *Lysistrata,* if all Greek women refused to participate in sexual relations until the Peloponnesian War was brought to an end? Suppose (in *The Birds*) that one could found an empire in the air and starve the gods by intercepting the smoke from earthly sacrifices. Imagine (in *The Clouds*) that a farmer attends the school of Socrates in hopes of learning how to avoid paying his debts. In each case the idea and background of the situation are presented in the prologue. The merits and deficiencies of the hypothesis are then formally explored in an *agon,* or debate. The application of the debate is then illustrated in a series of episodes that conclude with a final song and a scene of merriment. In addition, each play contains a number of elements that apparently were required by convention: the entrance of a wildly costumed chorus, an elaborately structured song (*parabasis*) in which the playwright lectures the audience and satirizes the society, and a host of meticulous rules ranging from a required form of *agon* to the necessity of reciting the *pignos* or "choking song" in only one breath.

Within this highly structured form, Aristophanes continually sought to satirize the society at large and its most prominent individuals. He repeatedly attacked the Peloponnesian War and decadent innovations in religion, education, and poetry. He created ridiculous caricatures of Socrates, Euripides, Aeschylus, the politicians of Athens, and even the Greek gods. And throughout it all he continually explored and distorted the implications of his initial intellectual hypothesis.

Although *Rosencrantz and Guildenstern Are Dead* shows traces of the Aristophanic tradition by rewriting *Hamlet* from the point of view of two of its minor characters, the hypothetical postulate with which Old Comedy begins tends to favor a rather limiting form of social satire. The plays of Aristophanes are so filled with topical and personal allusions that many parts of them are now unintelligible. In order to survive as a literary form, comedy had to begin using plots and characters that could be universally understood and enjoyed.

By the time Aristophanes wrote his last comedy, *Plutus,* in 388 B.C., he had already evolved beyond the conventions of Old Comedy. The *New Comedy* that ensued has proven to be remarkably durable. Even today most comedies continue to follow the same plot structure:

> What normally happens is that a young man wants a young woman, that his desire is resisted by some opposition, usually paternal, and that near the end of the play some twist in the plot enables the hero to have his will. . . . The movement of comedy is usually a movement from one kind of society to another. At the beginning of the play the obstructing characters are in charge of the play's society, and the audience recognizes that they are usurpers. At the end of the play the device in the plot that brings the hero and heroine together causes a new society to crystallize around the hero. . . .
>
> The appearance of this new society is frequently signalized by some kind of party or festive ritual, which either appears at the end of the play or is assumed to take place immediately afterward.[3]

Northrop Frye, the critic cited here, has also identified most of the other conventional elements of comedy. He argues that the form appeals most directly to the young men and women in the audience, who identify with the hero and heroine precisely because these protagonists are unindividualized representatives of youth in whom each member of the audience can find his or her own traits. The antago-

[3] Northrop Frye, *Anatomy of Criticism: Four Essays* (Princeton: Princeton University Press, 1957), p. 163.

nist who blocks the hero's wishes is either a father or a father-figure and is often made ridiculous by the exaggeration of a single character trait. Molière's Tartuffe and Orgon are typical blocking figures, just as Mariane and Valère are the nondescript protagonists. The plot itself usually overflows with complications that place all of the characters in ticklish situations, and these complications are often resolved by an unexpected twist in the plot, such as the miraculous intervention of the king at the end of *Tartuffe*. At the beginning of *Tartuffe*, hypocrisy dominates the play's society, but by the end a more sensible and honest social structure has emerged that will be celebrated through the marriage of Valère and Mariane.

When the main sources of humor in a play are the ludicrous complications of love, the play is called a *romantic comedy*. When the emphasis is on the ridiculous foibles or characteristics of the blocking figures, it is called a *comedy of humours*. (This term derives from the medieval physiological theory of the "four humours," four identifiable elements believed to determine and control individual temperament and personality; an imbalance was thought to result in a lopsided, eccentric personality who became a natural object for comic treatment.) When the play makes fun of the affectations, manners, and conventions of human behavior, it is called a *comedy of manners*. And when it achieves its effects through buffoonery, horseplay, and crude jokes, it is called a *farce*.

Minute subcategories such as those defined in the preceding paragraph can be compounded almost indefinitely by considering that broad middle ground between tragedy and comedy. The players who performed before the court in *Hamlet* were supposed to be capable of acting "tragedy, comedy, history, pastoral, pastoral-comical, historical-pastoral, tragical-historical, tragical-comical-historical-pastoral, scene individable, or poem unlimited." Shakespeare's mockery of such generic hair splitting is implicit in the exaggerations of the list and in his satire of Polonius, who utters it. Contemporary drama criticism may have moved away from pastoral, historical, and the various hyphenated couplings, but it has developed a myriad of other terms to describe minor classifications of the tone and structure of drama. The most significant of these (*domestic tragedy, melodrama, naturalism, realism, revenge tragedy, thesis play*, etc.) are defined in the glossary appended to this text.

11

Analyzing and Evaluating Drama

Although all plays differ from one another, at times radically, certain fundamental questions can be asked of virtually every play as an aid in identifying and understanding its major features. As noted in our discussion of drama, plays inevitably share many elements with both fiction and poetry; as a result, a number of the questions that follow assume a general familiarity with the two earlier sections of this book.

QUESTIONS TO ASK AND ANSWER

Plot

1. Describe the plot in terms of its *exposition, complication, crisis, falling action,* and *conclusion.* Is the plot unified? Do the individual acts and scenes seem logically related to each other? Are there any scenes that seem to be unnecessary?
2. What is the essential problem or conflict on which the plot turns? Where does the turning point seem to occur? How is the plot resolved? Does the resolution seem to be an appropriate and satisfactory one?

3. Compare the end of the play with its beginning. What are the major changes that have taken place?
4. Describe the function of each act and scene. Do certain scenes seem to be linked in some way in order to contrast with or reinforce one another? Do any of the scenes seem to present a microcosm, condensation, or metaphor of the play as a whole?
5. In what ways does the opening act or scene serve the purpose of exposition, and how is this exposition achieved? What important events have taken place before the play opens? In what ways does the exposition serve to introduce or *foreshadow* the major problems or conflicts of the plot?
6. Does the play contain one or more *subplots?* If so, what is their relationship to the main plot of the play? Are they, for example, intended to reinforce, contrast, or parody the main action?

Character

1. Who is the *protagonist* of the play, and who is the *antagonist?*
2. What is the function of the play's other major characters? What is their relationship to the protagonist and antagonist and to each other?
3. What is the function of the play's minor characters? Is their role mainly one of exposition or interpretation, or are they used as *foils* to oppose, contrast, or caricature certain of the major characters?
4. What methods does the playwright employ to establish and reveal the characters?
5. Are the actions of the characters properly motivated, consistent, and plausible?
6. Do any of the characters serve *symbolic* or *allegorical* functions?
7. To what extent does the playwright rely on the reader's or audience's prior knowledge of one or more of the characters? (Remember that many of the major figures of Greek tragedy were well known in advance to their audiences.)

Dialogue

1. Is the dialogue written in *high style, low style,* or some combination of the two?
2. How does the dialogue of the characters differ? How do such differences serve as an aid in characterization?

3. What stylistic devices contribute most to the play's dialogue? (Consider, for example, the use the playwright makes of patterns of poetic rhythm and sound, repetition, puns or word play, comparison, allusion, imagery, irony, symbolism, etc.)
4. Does the playwright make use of certain key words or phrases that gain a cumulative effect and added significance through repetition in a succession of contexts?

Setting

1. What is the play's setting in time and space?
2. To what extent does the setting functionally serve to aid in characterization, establish and sustain atmosphere, and/or influence plot?
3. What is the relationship of the setting to the play's action? Does it serve to reinforce the action, or is the relationship one of contrast?
4. Does the setting have symbolic overtones?

Theme

1. What is the play's theme or controlling idea?
2. How is the theme presented? Is it explicitly stated by one or more of the characters or is it merely implied by the action? What specific passages of dialogue or action contribute most clearly to the revelation or presentation of theme? To what extent do such moments occur at or near the ends of acts or scenes as a way of building dramatic tension?
3. What is the value or significance of the play's theme? Is it topical or universal in its application?

Other Aspects of Drama

1. *Title.* Consider the play's title. What clues does it provide, if any, in identifying the playwright's emphasis?
2. *Dramatic conventions.* To what extent does the playwright make use of such dramatic conventions as *asides, soliloquies,* a *chorus,* or the *three unities* of time, place, and action? What function or functions do these conventions serve? To what extent do these conventions reflect the kind of theater in which the play was originally staged?

3. *Actions and stage directions.* Identify the major physical actions of the play and explain their significance.
4. What help, if any, do the author's stage directions provide in helping the reader to understand the play?
5. *Classification.* Is the play a *tragedy,* a *comedy,* or some hybrid of two or more types? (Be prepared to explain your answer by making reference to the discussion in the text.)
6. *Audience appeal.* To what extent is the appeal of the play topical (that is, to what extent does it contain certain elements that reflect the manners, customs, attitudes, and beliefs of the society for which it was originally written)? To what extent is its appeal permanent and universal?

Evaluating the Whole

1. How well do you think the playwright has managed to achieve a total integration of his or her materials?
2. What is *your* reaction to the play? Do you like the play? If so, why? If not, why not?

Glossary

Abstract: The opposite of *concrete;* used to describe a word or group of words representing attitudes, generalities, ideas, or qualities that cannot be apprehended directly through the senses. The language of philosophy and science tends to be abstract.

Absurd, Theater of the: A type of modern drama (often associated with Edward Albee, Samuel Beckett, Jean Genet, Eugène Ionesco, Arthur Kopit, and Harold Pinter) that attempts to convey the playwright's vision of an absurd, frustrating, illogical, and essentially meaningless human condition by ignoring or distorting the usual conventions of plot, characterization, structure, setting, and dialogue.

Accent (pp. 167–169): Used in English poetry to describe the stress or emphasis accorded to certain syllables. When a pronounced syllable receives no stress or emphasis it is, by contrast, referred to as unaccented. In English poetry, *meter* depends on the pattern of accented and unaccented syllables.

Acrostic (pp. 213–214): A poem in which certain letters (ordinarily the first in each line) spell out a word or words.

Act (p. 226): A major division of a play; sometimes subdivided into a number of separate *scenes.*

Alexandrine (p. 206): A line of poetry consisting of six iambic feet (iambic hexameter).

Allegory (pp. 76–79; 150–155): A type of narrative that attempts to reinforce its thesis by making its characters (and sometimes its events and setting, as well) represent specific abstract ideas or qualities; see also *fable, parable,* and *symbol.*

Alliteration (pp. 193–196): The repetition in two or more nearby words of identical consonant sounds. See also *Assonance* and *Consonance*.

Alliterative verse (pp. 181–182): A metrical system in which each line contains a fixed number of accented syllables and a variable number of unaccented ones.

Allusion (pp. 118–120): A reference, generally brief, to a person, place, thing, or event with which the reader is presumably familiar.

Ambiguity (pp. 124–127): A word, phrase, event, or situation that may be understood or interpreted in two or more ways, each valid in the immediate context.

Ambivalence: The existence of two mutually opposed or contradictory feelings about a given issue, idea, person, or object.

Anachronism: A person or thing that is chronologically out of place.

Anapest (anapestic) (p. 178): A foot of two unaccented syllables followed by an accented one.

Anecdote: A brief, unadorned narrative about a particular person or incident. Short stories differ from anecdotes by virtue of their greater length and the deliberate artistic arrangement of their elements.

Animism (pp. 147–148): A poetic figure of speech in which an idea or inanimate object is described as though it were living, without attributing human traits to it; see also *personification.*

Annotation: The explanatory note (or notes) that an author or editor supplies for a given text.

Antagonist (pp. 15; 24–25; 275): The rival or opponent against whom the major character (the *protagonist* or *hero*) is contending.

Anticlimax: A sudden transition from the important (or serious) to the trivial (or ludicrous). We speak of something being anticlimatic when it occurs after the *crisis* (or *climax*) of the plot has been reached.

Antihero: A *protagonist* whose distinctive qualities are directly opposite to, or incompatible with, those associated with the traditional hero. Such an opposition by no means implies that the character is evil or villainous but often tends to reflect the author's belief that modern life no longer tolerates or produces individuals capable of genuine heroism, in its classic sense.

Anti-novel (anti-story): A type of experimental novel (or short story), usually associated with the French school of Alain Robbe-Grillet, that attempts to convey to the reader the experience of objective reality without authorial direction by dispensing with the traditional aspects of realistic ("mimetic") fiction, e.g., plot, character, theme, dialogue.

Apostrophe (pp. 146–147): A figure of speech in which a person (usually present) or a personified quality or object is addressed as if present.

Archaism: An obsolete word or phrase.

Archetype (pp. 71–72; 151): Used in literary analysis to describe certain basic and recurrent patterns of plot, character, or theme; see also *symbol.*

Arena stage/ arena theater (p. 259): A theater with seating surrounding, or nearly surrounding, the stage.

Argument: A summary statement of the content or thesis of a literary work.

Aside (pp. 248–249): A dramatic convention in which the lines addressed by a character to the audience are presumed to go unheard by the other characters.

Assonance (pp. 193–194): The repetition in two or more nearby words of similar vowel sounds; see also *consonance* and *alliteration.*

Atmosphere (pp. 40–41): The mood or feeling pervading a literary work.

Ballad (pp. 203–205): A narrative poem consisting of a series of four-line stanzas, originally sung or recited as part of the oral tradition of an unsophisticated rural folk society.

Blank verse (p. 200): Lines of unrhymed iambic pentameter.

Bombast: Language that is inflated, extravagant, verbose, and insincere.

Burlesque: A form of humor that ridicules persons, attitudes, actions, or things by means of distortion and exaggeration. Burlesque of a particular literary work or style is referred to as *parody. Caricature,* on the other hand, creates humor by distorting or exaggerating an individual's prominent physical features; see also *satire.*

Cacophony: See *euphony.*

Caesura (pp. 173–175): A pause or break occuring near the middle of a line of poetry.

Canto: Sections or divisions of a long poem.

Caricature: See *burlesque.*

Carpe diem: A Latin phrase meaning "seize the day," generally applied to lyric poems that urge the celebration of the fleeting present, e.g., Robert Herrick's "To the Virgins, to Make Much of Time."

Catastrophe: A form of *conclusion* (or *dénouement*), usually tragic in its outcome.

Catharsis (p. 284): See *classical tragedy.*

Chance and Coincidence (p. 22): Chance refers to events or "happenings" within a plot that occur without sufficient preparation; coincidence to the accidental occurence of two (or more) events that have a certain correspondence.

Character (pp. 23–36; 275–278): An individual within a literary work.

Characterization: The process by which an author creates, develops, and presents a character.

Chaucerian stanza: See *rhyme royal.*

Chorus (pp. 243–245): In Greek drama the chorus was a group of singers and dancers who sometimes served as actors to comment on or interpret the significance of the action.

Classical tragedy (pp. 283–284): Refers to Greek and Roman tragedies or plays written imitating their subjects or conventions.

Climax: See *crisis.*

Closed couplet (pp. 200–201): See *couplet.*

Closet drama (p. 239): A drama written to be read rather than staged and acted.

Coincidence: See *chance and coincidence.*

Comedy (pp. 286–288): Broadly, any literary work designed primarily to amuse. The term is usually reserved for plays whose tone is lighthearted and humorous, that are amusing, and that have a happy ending.

Comic relief: A comic scene introduced into an otherwise serious or tragic fictional or dramatic work, usually to relieve, if only momentarily, the tension of the plot; often heightens, by contrast, the emotional intensity of the work.

Complication (pp. 17–18; 270–271): That part of the plot in which the conflict is developed and intensified; sometimes referred to as the *rising action.*

Conceit (pp. 98–101): Usually refers to a startling, ingenious, perhaps even far-fetched, metaphor establishing an analogy or comparison between two apparently incongruous things.

Conclusion: See *resolution.*

Concrete: Opposite of *abstract.* Language referring directly to what we see, hear, touch, taste, or smell is concrete. Most literature uses concrete language and expresses even abstract concepts concretely through images and metaphors.

Confidant/confidante (pp. 54; 275): The individual, often a minor character, to whom a major character reveals, or "confesses," his or her most private thoughts and feelings. Authors and playwrights use the confidant as a device to communicate necessary information to the reader and audience.

Conflict (pp. 15–16): The struggle or encounter within the plot of two opposing forces that serves to create reader or audience interest and suspense.

Connotation (pp. 115–118; 155–157): The meaning suggested or implied by a given word or phrase, as opposed to its literal meaning; see *denotation.*

Consonance (pp. 193–196): The repetition in two or more nearby words of similar consonant sounds preceeded by different accented vowels. When it occurs at the end of lines, consonance often serves as a substitute for *end rhyme;* see *alliteration.*

Controlling image: The image or metaphor that runs throughout a literary work and determines its structure or nature.

Convention: Any literary device, technique, style, or form, or any aspect of subject matter, characterization, or theme that has become recognized and accepted by both authors and audiences through repeated use.

Couplet (pp. 200–202): A single pair of rhymed lines—when they form a complete thought or statement they are referred to as a *closed couplet.*

Crisis (pp. 16–18; 271–272): That point during the plot when the action reaches its turning point; also called the climax; see *anticlimax.*

Criticism: The description, analysis, interpretation, or evaluation of a literary work of art; see also *historical criticism, new criticism, textual criticism, theoretical criticism, and practical criticism.*

Dactyl (dactylic) (pp. 177–178): A foot of an accented syllable followed by two unaccented ones.

Decorum: The idea, derived from classical theory and thus at times approaching the status of doctrine, that all the elements of a literary work (i.e., setting, character, action, style) must be appropriately related to one another.

Denotation (pp. 112–115; 155–156): The literal, dictionary meaning of a given word or phrase; see *connotation.*

Dénouement: From the French word meaning "unknotting" or "untying." A term sometimes used for the final *resolution* of the conflict or complications of the plot.

Deus ex machina: "God from the machine." Derived from a practice in Greek drama whereby an impersonation of a god was mechanically lowered onto the stage to intervene in and solve the issues of the play. Commonly used today to describe any apparently contrived or improbable device used by an author to resolve the difficulties of plot.

Dialogue (pp. 261–268): The conversation that goes on between or among characters in a literary work.

Diction (pp. 81–82): The author's choice or selection of words (vocabulary). The artistic arrangement of those words constitutes *style*.

Didactic: Literature designed more to teach a lesson or instruct the reader or audience than to present an experience objectively. In a didactic work *theme* is generally the most important element.

Dimeter: A line of poetry consisting of two metrical feet; see *foot*.

Dissonance: See *euphony and cacophony*.

Doggerel: A deprecatory term for inferior poetry.

Domestic tragedy: A type of tragedy (originating in the eighteenth century as a reflection of its growing middle-class society) in which an ordinary middle-class (or lower-class) protagonist suffers ordinary (although by no means insignificant) disasters; also called bourgeoise tragedy.

Double rhyme: See *masculine and feminine rhyme*.

Downstage/ upstage (pp. 248–249): *Downstage* is a stage direction referring to the front half of the stage, the part nearest to the audience; *upstage* refers to the back half of the stage.

Dramatic monologue (p. 198): A type of poem in which a character, at some specific and critical moment, addresses an identifiable but silent audience, thereby unintentionally revealing his or her essential temperament and personality.

Dramatis personae: A play's cast of characters.

Elegy: In its more modern usage, a poem that laments or solemnly meditates on death, loss, or the passing of things of value.

Empathy: The state of entering into and actually participating in the emotional, mental, or physical life of an object, person, or literary character.

End rhyme: Rhyme that occurs at the end of lines of poetry; also called terminal rhyme; see *masculine and feminine rhyme*.

End-stopped line (pp. 173–175): A line of poetry that concludes with a pause.

English sonnet: See *sonnet*.

Enjambment (pp. 173–175): A line of poetry that carries its idea or thought over to the next line without a grammatical pause; also called a *run-on line*.

Epic: A long narrative poem, elevated and dignified in theme, tone, and style, celebrating heroic deeds and historically (at times cosmically) important events; usually focuses on the adventures of a hero who has qualities that are superhuman or divine and on whose fate very often depends the destiny of a tribe, a nation, or even the whole of the human race.

Epigram (p. 202): A short, pointed, and witty statement, either constituting an entire poem (often in the form of a two-line couplet) or "buried" within a larger one.

Epigraph: A quotation prefacing a literary work, often containing a clue to the writer's intention.

Epilogue: The final, concluding section of a literary work, usually a play, offered in summation, to point a lesson or moral, or to thank the audience (reader) for its indulgence; see *prologue.*

Epiphany: Applied to literature by James Joyce to describe a sudden revelation, or "showing forth," of the essential truth about a character, situation, or experience.

Episode (pp. 20; 274): A single unified incident within a narrative that may or may not advance the plot.

Epistolary novel: A type of novel in which the narrative is carried on by means of a series of letters.

Epithalamion/ epithalamium: A song or poem celebrating a wedding, from the Greek meaning "poem upon or at the bridal chamber."

Euphony and Cacophony (pp. 193–196): *Euphony* describes language that is harmonious, smooth, and pleasing to the ear. Harsh, nonharmonious, and discordant language is *cacophony;* cacophony is also referred to as *dissonance.*

Exposition (pp. 16–17; 269–270): The part of a work that provides necessary background information.

Fable: A story with a moral lesson, often employing animals who talk and act like human beings; see *allegory.*

Falling action (pp. 16–17; 272–274): The part of a dramatic plot that follows the *crisis* (or *climax*) and precedes the *resolution* (or *dénouement*).

False rhyme (p. 190): Rhyme pairing the sounds of accented and unaccented syllables.

Fantasy: A work of fiction that deliberately sets aside everyday reality.

Farce: A type of comedy which achieves its effect through ridiculous and exaggerated situations, broad, often crude, verbal humor, and various kinds of buffoonery and physical horseplay.

Feminine rhyme: See *masculine and feminine rhyme.*

Fiction: A prose narrative that is the product of the imagination.

Figurative language (p. 158): Language used imaginatively and nonliterally. Figurative language is composed of such figures of speech (or tropes) as *metaphor, simile, personification, metonymy, synecdoche, apostrophe, hyperbole, symbol, irony,* and *paradox.*

Flashback (p. 21): The interruption of a story's narrative in order to present an earlier scene or episode; a method of *exposition.*

Foil (pp. 54; 275–276): A character who provides a direct contrast to another character.

Foot (pp. 166–171; 176–179): The basic metrical or rhythmical unit within a line of poetry. A foot of poetry generally consists of an accented syllable and one or more unaccented syllables arranged in a variety of patterns; see *scansion.*

Foreshadowing: A device by means of which the author hints at something to follow.

Form: A term used either as a synonym for literary *genre* or type, or to describe the essential organizing structure of a work of art.

Free verse (pp. 105; 184–185): A type of poetry that deliberately seeks to free itself from the restrictions imposed by traditionally fixed conventions of meter, rhyme, and stanza.

Genre: A *form,* class, or type of literary work—e.g., the short story, novel, poem, play, or essay; often used to denote such literary subclassifications as the detective story, the gothic novel, the pastoral elegy, or the revenge tragedy.

Haiku (p. 209): A Japanese form of poetry; three lines of five, seven, and five syllables, respectively, present a single concentrated image or emotion.

Heptameter: A line of poetry consisting of seven metrical feet; see *foot.*

Hero/ heroine (p. 24): The central character in a literary work; also often referred to as the *protagonist.*

Heroic couplet: A pair of rhymed iambic pentameter lines; a stanza composed of two heroic couplets is called a *heroic quatrain.*

High comedy and low comedy: Any type of highly verbal comedy whose appeal is mainly intellectual and sophisticated, often with a basic seriousness of purpose, is *high comedy* (e.g., a *comedy of manners*). *Low comedy* is nonintellectual and lacks serious purpose (e.g., a *farce*).

High style and low style (pp. 96; 267–8): *High style* is a formal and elevated literary style rich in poetic devices. *Low style* is casual and conversational in tone and sometimes ungrammatical and colloquial.

Historical criticism: Seeks to understand and explain a literary work in terms of the author's life and the historical context and circumstances in which it was written.

Hubris: The excessive pride, arrogance, or self-confidence that results in the defeat or downfall of the *hero;* see *tragic flaw.*

Hyperbole (p. 133): A figure of speech that achieves emphasis and heightened effect (either serious or comic) through deliberate exaggeration.

Iamb (iambic) (pp. 169–170): A foot of an unaccented syllable followed by an accented one.

Identical rhyme: Rhyme achieved through the repetition of the same word or two words that have the same sound but are spelled differently and have different meanings.

Imagery (pp. 135–141): Most commonly refers to visual pictures produced verbally through *figurative language,* although it is often defined more broadly to include sensory experiences other than the visual.

Incongruity (p. 131): A word, phrase, or idea that is out of keeping, inconsistent, or inappropriate in its context.

Initiation story: Commonly used to describe a narrative focusing on a young person's movement from innocence toward maturity as a result of experience.

In medias res (pp. 18–19; 269–270): Latin for a narrative that begins "in the middle of things."

Interior monologue: See *monologue.*

Internal rhyme (p. 189): Rhyme within a line of poetry; also called middle rhyme.

Intrigue: A scheme that one character devises to entrap another, thus providing impetus for the plot.

Irony (pp. 89–91; 131–135): Refers to some contrast or discrepancy between appearance and reality.

Italian sonnet: See *sonnet.*

Juxtaposition (pp. 149–150): A form of implied comparison or contrast created by placing two items side by side.

Limerick (pp. 209–210): A light, humorous verse form composed of five anapestic lines, rhyming AABBA; lines one, two, and five contain three feet (trimeter), lines three and four contain two (dimeter).

Literal: Accurate, exact, and concrete language, i.e., nonfigurative language; see *figurative language.*

Locale: See *setting.*

Low comedy: See *high comedy and low comedy.*

Lyric (pp. 198–199): A short, songlike poem, by a single speaker or a single subject, expressing a personal thought, mood, or feeling.

Masculine and feminine rhyme (p. 189): The two most common kinds of end rhyme. *Masculine end rhyme,* predominant in English poetry, consists of accented words of one syllable or polysyllabic words where the final syllable is accented. *Feminine rhyme* (or *double rhyme*) consists of rhyming words of two syllables in which the accent falls on the first syllable. A variation of feminine rhyme, called *triple rhyme,* occurs when there is a correspondence of sound in the final three syllables, an accented syllable followed by two unaccented ones.

Melodrama: In its original Greek sense, a "melodrama" meant a play with music (*melos* means "song"). But by mid-nineteenth century the term had become synonymous with a highly conventionalized type of sensationalistic play pitting stereotypic hero and villain against one another in a series of suspense-ridden, emotion-charged, and violence-filled scenes. The term *melodramatic* is used generally to describe sensational, emotional, and action-oriented writing, e.g., the cowboy western or the gothic novel.

Metaphor (pp. 143–144): A figure of speech in which two unlike objects are implicitly compared without the use of *like* or *as;* see also *conceit* and *simile.*

Metaphysical poetry (pp. 98–101): A kind of realistic, often ironic and witty, verse combining intellectual ingenuity and psychological insight written partly in reaction to the conventions of Elizabethan love poetry by such seventeenth-century poets as John Donne, George Herbert, Richard Crashaw, Thomas Traherne, and Andrew Marvell. One of its hallmarks is the metaphysical *conceit,* a particularly arresting and ingenious type of metaphor.

Meter: See *rhythm and meter.*

Metonymy (pp. 144–145): A figure of speech in which the name for an object or idea is applied to another with which it is closely associated or of which it is a part.

Mixed metaphor (p. 160): Two or more metaphors combined together in such a way as to be incongruous, illogical, or even ludicrous.

Monologue: An extended speech delivered by a single speaker, alone or in the presence of others. In a general sense, *asides, dramatic monologues,* and *soliloquies* are all types of monologues. When the monologue serves to reveal a character's internal thoughts and feelings, it is sometimes referred to as an interior monologue.

Monometer: A line of poetry consisting of a single metrical foot; see *foot.*

Mood: See *atmosphere.*

Motif: An idea, theme, character, situation, or element that recurs in literature or folklore; see *archetype, convention, stock character, stock situation.*

Motive (p. 35): The cause that moves a character to act.

Myth: Broadly, any idea or belief to which a number of people subscribe.

Narrative: A series of unified events; see *plot* and *action.*

Narrative poem (pp. 197–198): A poem that tells a story.

Narrative technique: The author's methods of presenting or telling a story.

Narrator: The character or voice that tells the story; see *point of view* and *persona.*

Naturalism: A post-Darwinian movement of the late nineteenth century that tried to apply the "laws" of scientific determinism to fiction. The naturalist went beyond the realist's insistence on the objective presentation of the details of everyday life to insist that the materials of literature should be arranged to reflect a deterministic universe in which man is a biological creature controlled by his environment and heredity; see *realism.*

New Criticism: The New Criticism refers to a type or "school" of criticism that seeks to analyze and study a literary work as autonomous, without reference to its author's intention, its impact or effect on the reader, the historical or cultural period in which the work was written (see *historical criticism*), or the validity of the ideas that may be extrapolated from it. Its method is based on the close reading and analysis of the verbal elements of the text, although its leading exponents and practioners (academic critics such as John Crowe Ransom, I. A. Richards, Cleanth Brooks, Robert Penn Warren, Allen Tate, R. P. Blackmur, Yvor Winters, and Kenneth Burke) often disagree on just how this analysis is to be undertaken. The term originates from the title of John Crowe Ransom's book *The New Criticism* (1941) and is "new" in the sense that it constituted a deliberate break with the older subjective and impressionistic theories of art that allowed extrinsic rather than solely intrinsic considerations to influence the evaluation of art.

Novel: The name generally applied to any long fictional prose narrative.

Novelette: A longish prose narrative, not long enough to be regarded as a novel but too long to be a short story.

Obligatory scene (p. 271): A scene whose circumstances are so fully anticipated by the audience as the plot develops that the playwright is "obliged" to provide it.

Occasional verse: Poetry written to celebrate or commemorate a particular event or occasion.

Octameter: A line of poetry consisting of eight metrical feet.

Octave: See *sonnet.*

Ode (pp. 208–209): a long lyric poem, serious and dignified in subject, tone, and style, sometimes with an elaborate stanzaic structure, often written to commemorate or celebrate an event or individual.

Onomatopoeia (p. 195): A word (or a group of words) whose sound has the effect of suggesting or reinforcing its denotative meaning.

Ottava rima (p. 206): A stanza of Italian origin consisting of eight iambic pentameter lines rhyming ABABABCC.

Oxymoron: A figure of speech, used for rhetorical effect, which brings together and combines antithetical, paradoxical, or contradictory terms, e.g., "living death," "wise fool," "sweet sorrow."

Parable (p. 151): a story designed to convey or illustrate a moral lesson; see *allegory* and *fable.*

Paradox (pp. 129–131): A self-contradictory and absurd statement that turns out to be, in some sense at least, actually true and valid.

Paraphrase (pp. 158–160): A restatement, using different words, of the essential ideas or argument of a piece or passage of writing. To paraphrase a poem is to restate its ideas in prose.

Parody: See *burlesque.*

Pastoral: A literary work dealing with, and often celebrating, a rural world and a way of life lived close to nature. *Pastoral* denotes subject matter rather than form; hence, the terms *pastoral lyric, pastoral ode, pastoral elegy, pastoral drama, pastoral epic,* and *pastoral novel.*

Pathetic fallacy: A form of personification, which attributes human qualities or feelings to inanimate objects. Although first used disapprovingly by John Ruskin in *Modern Painters* (1856), the phrase today no longer necessarily carries with it Ruskin's negative connotation; see *personification.*

Pathos: The quality in a literary work that evokes a feeling of pity, tenderness, and sympathy from the reader or audience. Overdone or misused pathos becomes mere *sentimentality.*

Pentameter: A line of poetry consisting of five metrical feet; see *foot.*

Perfect and imperfect rhyme (pp. 186; 189–190): In *perfect rhyme* (also called full rhyme or true rhyme) the vowel and any succeeding consonant sounds are identical and the preceding consonant sounds different. Some poets, particularly modern ones, deliberately alternate perfect rhyme with *imperfect rhyme,* in which the correspondence of sound is inexact, approximate, and "imperfect." Imperfectly rhymed words generally contain identical vowels or identical consonants, but not both. Imperfect rhyme is also referred to as approximate rhyme, half-rhyme, near rhyme, oblique rhyme, off-rhyme or slant rhyme. *Alliteration, assonance* and *consonance* are types of imperfect rhyme.

Persona (Pl.: personae): Applied to the voice or mask the author adopts for the purpose of telling the story or "speaking" the words of a lyric poem. The term *persona* is a way of reminding us that the narrator of the work is not to be confused with the author, and should be regarded as another of the author's creations or fictions.

Personification (pp. 145–146): A figure of speech in which an idea or thing is given human attributes or feelings or is spoken of as if it were alive; see also *pathetic fallacy.*

Petrarchan sonnet: See *sonnet.*

Picaresque novel: Derived from the Spanish word *picaro* meaning "rogue" or "rascal," the term *picaresque novel* generally refers to a basically realistic and often satiric work of fiction chronicling the career of an engaging, lower-class rogue-hero, who takes to the road for a series of loose, episodic adventures, sometimes in the company of a sidekick. Well-known examples of the type are Miguel de Cervante's *Don Quixote* (1605), Henry Fielding's *Tom Jones* (1749), and Daniel Defoe's *Moll Flanders* (1722).

Picture poem (pp. 212–213): A poem printed in such a way as to create a visual image of the object or idea described.

Plot (pp. 13–22; 269–275): The patterned arrangement of the events in a narrative or play. See also *exposition, complication, crisis, falling action, anticlimax,* and *resolution.*

Poetic justice: The doctrine (now generally discredited in theory and practice) that good should be rewarded and evil punished—that characters in the end should reap their just rewards.

Poetic license: Used to describe (and justify) literary experimentation: a writer's deliberate departure from conventions of form and language—and at times even the departure from logic and fact.

Point of view (pp. 44–60): The angle or perspective from which a story is told.

Polemic: A work vigorously setting forth the author's point of view, usually on a controversial subject.

Preface: The author's or editor's introduction, in which the writer states his or her purposes and assumptions and makes any acknowledgments.

Prelude: A short poem introducing a longer one.

Prologue: A prefatory statement or speech beginning a literary work, usually a play, preparing the audience for what is to follow; see *epilogue* and *preface.*

Proscenium (p. 243n.): In modern stagecraft the proscenium is the forward part of the stage between the curtain and the orchestra. The arch from which the curtain hangs is the *proscenium arch.* The area in front of the proscenium is sometimes also referred to as the apron.

Prosody: The description and study of the underlying principles of poetry, e.g., its meter, rhyme, and stanzaic form.

Protagonist (pp. 24–25; 275): The chief character of a literary work. Also commonly referred to as the *hero* or *heroine;* see *antagonist.*

Pun (pp. 127–129): A play on words, involving words with similar or identical sounds but with different meanings.

Quantitative meter (p. 183): A metrical system (used originally in Greek and Latin verse) in which units are measured not by stress but by the length of time it takes to pronounce long and short syllables.

Quatrain (pp. 202–205): A four line stanza employing a variety of rhyme schemes.

Quintet (p. 205): A five line stanza employing a variety of rhyme schemes.

Realism: The nineteenth-century literary movement that reacted to romanticism by insisting on a faithful, objective presentation of the details of everyday life; see *naturalism.*

Recognition scene: The moment in a fictional or dramatic work in which one of the characters makes an important (and often decisive) discovery that determines his or her subsequent course of action.

Refrain (pp. 122–124): A line, in whole or in part, or a group of lines that recur, sometimes with slight variation, in a poem or song, at the close of a stanza and help to establish meter, sustain mood, or add emphasis. In a song the refrain is usually called the chorus and listeners are expected to join in.

Resolution (pp. 16–18; 272–274): The final section of the plot in which the major conflict, issue, or problem is resolved; also referred to as the *conclusion* or *dénouement.*

Revenge tragedy: A type of tragedy (popularized in Elizabethan England by the plays of Thomas Kyd and Christopher Marlowe), that turns on the motive of revenge, revels in violence, horror, and other forms of sensationalism, and typically has a bloody ending.

Reversal: The protagonist's change of fortune.

Rhetorical question: A question to which no response or reply is expected, because only one answer is possible.

Rhyme (pp. 186–193): The repetition at regular intervals in a line or lines of poetry of similar or identical sounds based on a correspondence between the vowels and succeeding consonants of accented syllables; see also *end rhyme, false rhyme, identical rhyme, internal rhyme, masculine and feminine rhyme, perfect and imperfect rhyme,* and *visual rhyme;* also *alliteration, assonance* and *consonance.*

Rhyme royal (p. 206): A stanza of seven iambic pentameter lines rhyming ABABBCC.

Rhyme scheme (p. 191): The pattern of end rhymes within a given stanza of poetry.

Rising action: See *complication.*

Rhythm and meter (pp. 164–186): *Rhythm* is the general term given to the measured repetition of accent or beat in units of poetry or prose. In English poetry, rhythm is generally established by manipulating both the pattern of accent and the number of syllables in a given line. *Meter* refers to the predominant rhythmic pattern within any given line (or lines) of poetry.

Rubais (p. 203): An iambic pentameter quatrain in which the first two lines rhyme with the last one, AAXA.

Run-on line: See *enjambment.*

Sarcasm (p. 134): A form of verbal irony delivered in a derisive, caustic, and bitter manner to belittle or ridicule its subject.

Satire (p. 133): A type of writing that holds up persons, ideas, or things to varying degrees of amusement, ridicule, or contempt in order, presumably, to improve, correct, or bring about some desirable change.

Scansion (pp. 167–176): The analysis of a poem's metrical pattern.

Scenario: The brief outline of the plot of a dramatic or literary work, providing the key details of scenes, situations, and characters.

Scene (p. 226): A self-contained segment of a work of fiction or drama; also used as a synonym for *setting;* see *act.*

Sensuous: In literature, *sensuous* refers to writing that appeals to one or more of the reader's five senses.

Sentimentality: The presence of emotion or feeling that seems excessive or unjustified in terms of the circumstances; see *pathos.*

Septet (p. 206): A seven line stanza employing a variety of rhyme schemes.

Sestet: See *Shakespearean sestet and sonnet.*

Setting (pp. 37–44): The time and place in which the action of a story, poem, or play occurs; physical setting alone is often referred to as the *locale.*

Shakespearean sestet (pp. 205–206): A six-line stanza rhyming ABABCC.

Shakespearean sonnet: See *sonnet.*

Short story: A short work of narrative prose fiction. The distinction between the short story and novel is mainly one of length.

Simile (pp. 143–144): A figure of speech in which two essentially dissimilar objects are expressly compared with one another by the use of *like* or *as;* see *metaphor* and *figurative language.*

Soliloquy (p. 248): A dramatic convention in which a character, alone on stage (*solus*), speaks aloud and thus shares his or her thoughts with the audience. See *aside* and *monologue.*

Sonnet (pp. 210–211): A poem of 14 iambic pentameter lines expressing a single thought or idea and utilizing one of several established rhyme schemes. The sonnet in English generally follows one of two basic patterns: The *Italian sonnet* (or *Petrarchan sonnet* named after the Italian Renaissance poet) consists of an eight-line *octave,* rhyming ABBAABBA, followed by a six-line *sestet,* rhyming variously CDECDE, CDCCDC, etc.; and the *English sonnet* (or *Shakespearean sonnet*) consists of three four-line *quatrains* and a concluding couplet, rhyming ABAB CDCD EFEF GG. A variant of the English sonnet, the *Spenserian sonnet* (named after English poet Edmund Spenser), links its quatrains by employing the rhyme scheme ABAB BCBC CDCD EE.

Spenserian sonnet: See *sonnet.*

Spenserian stanza (pp. 206–207): A nine-line stanza consisting of eight lines of iambic pentameter and a concluding line of iambic hexameter, rhyming ABABBCBCC—named after English poet Edmund Spenser.

Spondee (Spondaic) (pp. 179–180): A foot of two accented syllables.

Stanza (pp. 200–209): A group of lines forming a structural unit or division of a poem. Stanzas may be strictly formal units established and patterned (with possible variation) by the similarity of the number and length of their lines, by their meter and rhyme scheme, or as logical units, determined by their thought or content.

Stock situation: A situation or incident that occurs so frequently in literature as to become at once familiar: e.g., the family feud, the missing heir, the love triangle, the case of mistaken identity.

Stream of consciousness (pp. 33n.; 55–56): The narrative method of capturing and representing the inner workings of a character's mind.

Structure: The overall pattern, design, or organization of a literary work.

Style (pp. 80–87): The author's characteristic manner of expression; style includes the author's diction, syntax, sentence patterns, punctuation, and spelling, as well as the use made of such devices as sound, rhythm, imagery, and figurative language.

Subplot (p. 19): The subplot (also called the minor plot or underplot) is a secondary action or complication within a fictional or dramatic work that often serves to reinforce or contrast the main plot.

Suspense: The psychological tension or anxiety resulting from the reader's or audience's uncertainty of just how a situation or conflict is likely to end.

Syllabic meter (pp. 182–183): A metrical system (common to Japanese and Romance verse but rare in English) in which units are measured by the number of syllables in a line.

Symbol (pp. 69–76; 150–152): Literally, something that stands for something else. In literature, any word, object, action, or character that embodies and evokes a range of additional meaning and significance; see *allegory.*

Synechdoche (pp. 144–145): A figure of speech in which the part is used to signify the whole *or,* less frequently, the whole is used to signify the part.

Synopsis: A summary or resume of a piece of writing.

Tercet (p. 202): A stanza of three lines ending in the same rhyme.

Terza rima (p. 202): A verse form composed of interlocking three-line stanzas, or *tercets* rhyming ABA BCB CDC, etc.

Tetrameter: A line of poetry consisting of four metrical feet.

Textual criticism: The kind of scholarship that attempts to establish through reconstruction the "correct" and authoritative text of a literary work as its author originally wrote it.

Theme (pp. 61–69; 162–163): The controlling idea or meaning of a work of art.

Theoretical criticism and practical criticism: *Theoretical criticism* is concerned with identifying and establishing the general, underlying principles of art; *practical criticism* (or *applied criticism*) concerns itself with the study and analysis of specific individual works.

Thesis novel/ play: A novel or play that deals with a specific problem and advocates a "thesis" in the form of a solution; also called a problem novel or problem play.

Tone (pp. 87–89; 161–162): The author's attitude toward the subject or audience.

Tragedy (pp. 283–285): Broadly, any serious literary work in which the protagonist suffers a major reversal of fortune, often leading to his or her downfall, destruction, and/or death; see *classical tragedy, domestic tragedy, revenge tragedy, tragicomedy.*

Tragicomedy: A type of drama (most often associated with Elizabethan and Jacobean drama) that mixes the conventions of tragedy and comedy and in which the protagonist, although subject to a series of crises (often including the threat of death), manages to escape to celebrate a happy (and frequently highly contrived) ending.

Tragic flaw (p. 284): The principal defect in character or judgment that leads to the downfall of the *tragic hero.* In Greek tragedy this flaw is often *hubris,* the hero's excessive pride or self-confidence.

Tragic hero (pp. 283–285): The name given to the protagonist of a tragedy.

Trimeter: A line of poetry consisting of three metrical feet; see *foot.*
Triple rhyme: See *masculine and feminine rhyme.*
Triplet (p. 202): See *tercet.*
Troche (Trochaic) (pp. 176–177): A foot composed of an accented syllable followed by an unaccented one.
Trope: Another name for *figure of speech.*
Unreliable narrator (pp. 50–51; 58–60): A narrator whose knowledge and judgments about characters or events is sufficiently incomplete or flawed to render him an unreliable guide to the author's intentions.
Verisimilitude: The quality of being lifelike or true to actuality.
Versification: An all-inclusive term for the art and practice of writing poetry.
Visual rhyme (p. 190): Words that rhyme to the eye but not to the ear; their spelling is similar, but they are pronounced differently: "plow" and "blow."
Well-made play (pièce bien faite) (p. 275): A type of play, written according to formula, characterized by a tightly structured, suspenseful plot that turns on a secret; quickly rising action; and a series of reversals, inevitably leading to a climactic scene that reveals the secret and allows the hero to triumph.